James W. Silver

Running Scared

Silver in Mississippi

by JAMES W. SILVER

UNIVERSITY PRESS OF MISSISSIPPI
Jackson

Library of Congress Cataloging in Publication Data

Silver, James W. (James Wesley), 1907–
    Running scared.

    Includes index.
    1. Silver, James W. (James Wesley), 1907–   .
2. Mississippi—Social conditions.   3. Mississippi—Race
relations.   4. University of Mississippi—Faculty—
Biography.   5. Historians—United States—Biography.
I. Title.
E175.5.S49A37   1984   976.2′0072024   [B]   83-25921
ISBN 0-87805-209-7

The University Press of Mississippi thanks the following publishers
and copyright holders for permission to reprint material used in this
book:
Alfred A. Knopf, Inc. for the excerpts from *Lanterns on the Levee*
    by William Alexander Percy. Copyright 1941 by Alfred A.
    Knopf, Inc. and renewed 1969 by LeRoy Pratt Percy.
Random House, Inc. for the excerpt from *Light in August* by
    William Faulkner. Copyright 1932 and renewed 1960 by William
    Faulkner.
The New York Times Company for "Mississippi Must Choose,"
    copyright 1964.
Southern Humanities Review for "Faulkner's South" by James W.
    Silver, volume 10, (4) Fall 1976, pp. 301–12. Copyright 1976 by
    Auburn University.
Mrs. Jill Faulkner Summers for the excerpt from *Light in August*
    by William Faulkner.

Photographs courtesy of the following:
Frontis: Martin Dain; pp. 6, 51, 68, 91, 102, and 125: James W.
Silver; p. 37: the Brodsky Collection; p. 79: the Associated Press;
p. 94: Archives and Special Collections, University of Mississippi;
p. 113: the University of Notre Dame.

To
Dutch
for her selfless perseverance,
Joe, Bill, and Dave,
for their inspiration,
and
Mississippi,
for her relentless pursuit
of the good life for all her people

Contents

Preface

Why did I put together this book? Basically, to help straighten me out on the life of Jim Silver in Mississippi. And, I suppose, to rationalize that experience. When I came to the Magnolia State in the midst of the depression, I was eager to be accepted, in earnest about conforming so that I might become one of the boys. Yet from the beginning I began to question the stated convictions of most of my brighter students, and after World War II my views were increasingly at odds with what I perhaps erroneously assumed to be the majority assumptions of Mississippians.

Since the publication of my book *Mississippi: The Closed Society,* I have felt considerable anguish because a few former friends have downgraded my views to the point of challenging my common sense as well as my integrity. I have fretted about a former leader on the Ole Miss campus, for instance, who performed gallantly in the war, who as a member of an old-line legal family in Jackson made it quite clear that he considered me a traitor to our state. Another former student whom I encountered in a friendly way several times in the Pacific during the war was converted into an opponent of mine as chairman of the Board of Trustees. It was a segregationist friend who remarked that inasmuch as I found it impossible to achieve eminence as a historian, I decided to become notorious. There were, of course, some associates who in my time of troubles simply dropped the connection. I believe, too, that numbers of people who were aware of my existence, especially those who thought I was in error in my interpretation of recent history, feel no more antagonism than they did yesterday, and have no quarrel with my right to speak and write as I see fit. The loss of friendship with many allies from my involvement in athletics has bothered me very little. Nor have I been overly concerned about the feelings of the hangers-on in Mississippi society.

Looking back, I see myself as an extremely bright and somewhat pampered child who failed to live up to his potential in secondary school and college. My four years in Chapel Hill must be deemed largely a disaster, particularly as to growth in the social graces and self-assurance. The longer time spent in Tennessee was more pleasant and helpful in that I gained in knowledge of the world though I completed that period lacking the confidence I was to attain quite late in life. Hence I was still fearful of lack of success in the career that had come to me by chance. Admittedly, I moved on to Mississippi with a tendency toward liberalism (to me, support of the underdog), and with the certainty that all problems could be solved by men of good will in search of truth.

After a few years at Ole Miss my wife and I concluded that we hoped to enjoy the good life in Mississippi for the rest of our days. We also made the conscious decision that a healthy participation in campus affairs should take precedence over a dedication to pure scholarship and advancement in the academic world.

In my first high school and college teaching I assumed that the superior instructor laid out the various points of view while maintaining a strict neutrality. But gradually there emerged an understanding that when the evidence logically pointed to correct answers the teacher of wisdom became obligated to declare his convictions. In effect he became a propagandist, perhaps a crusader. The word propaganda lost its evil connotation. The teacher of integrity must disseminate truth (as he saw it) while not penalizing those who disagreed with him. It was also obvious to me that few in my classes cared enough in their quest for ultimate knowledge to do the necessary hard work to achieve that goal. Of course, truth is approached, seldom achieved, which reminds me that Faulkner once concluded that the sound hunter pursues his quarry not for the reward but for the pursuit itself—that is, in the woods the captured game is released so that it can be pursued another day.

Because of my training in the value of primary historical materials, I hoarded every scrap of evidence about my tumultuous years in Mississippi. My intention is to turn this documentary over to the archives in the Ole Miss library. But in writing the present historical sketch, I first put down from memory more than a hundred pages of narrative. Then I examined the documents for verification and expansion. Thus, my confrontation with the Board of Trustees in 1964 required only three pages while I had kept more than twenty times that amount of material and still more has become available. To overcome this inherent dilemma, I have followed a procedure I used in the second section of my previous book, one followed on the advice of my editor, Bill Goodman, who convinced me that I should add "Some Letters from the Closed Society." This means simply that I have included in an appendix the more pertinent documents on which my narrative is based.

I believe this evidence will make clear the meaning of my story. While I came to Mississippi with a sympathy for the underprivileged of the past and among the living, in general it was the unacceptable behavior of the radical conservatives and the exigencies of events in the state that drove me to speak out as I did. I still defy the opposition to point to error in *The Closed Society*.

I have believed for a long time that when he has made himself ready, the good teacher will have something to say beyond his classroom. This is what I have attempted to do in various writings, in speeches, and in my principal book.

I chose the present title because it most aptly describes my state of mind until some moment in the Meredith crisis when I stopped "running scared." When I decided to take a public stand regardless of the personal consequences, I was able to develop a serenity of mind which lessened the apprehension that had held me prisoner for most of my life. This does not mean that I was without fear but that the fear no longer influenced what I felt I had to do.

For some time I have been thinking that I should write down bits and pieces from my story that did not appear in *Mississippi: The Closed Society*. In that volume I was fairly successful in keeping out my personal life, except perhaps in the forewords and the letters added at the suggestion of my editor. I have been retired from teaching (Notre Dame, 1964–1969; University of South Florida, 1969–1979) for several years and am in better health than a decade ago, but I find it difficult to remember details and to read for long stretches. One cannot fish all the time because of weather, marina hours, and lessening interest. Publishing more doesn't appeal to me, for I believe what small reputation I have rests with *The Closed Society*. My other books were soon forgotten, a fate probably deserved, though I think the life of Gaines (*Edmund Pendleton Gaines: Frontier General.* Baton Rouge: Louisiana State University Press, 1949) and two or three articles are noteworthy. I seem to have enough income to meet my meager requirements in spite of inflation and the Republicans, and God knows I'm too lazy to begin anything of a scholarly nature. Perhaps these reflections will be of use to people curious about Mississippi and the South, and I rather suspect that one day my children will enjoy reading this book, as I have been entranced by the diary of my father.

I have not been overwhelmed by my own abilities as a technical historian, nor by most of the books by historians I have forced myself to read. As a matter of further confession, I have carefully read very few articles in the journals I have subscribed to and even fewer history classics. For one foolish enough to start out in the business of teaching history (a splendid and easy-going life), my advice is to spend summers not in the classroom nor in research, but in becoming thoroughly immersed in the great books of the world. Of course, such will keep you in the economic doldrums, but that is the situation you have chosen anyway.

One more point: This is not an autobiography. I have been lucky to have led a reasonably full life, but I have put before the public only the essential story that led to the publication of *The Closed Society* and to my departure from Mississippi.

I am neither a hero nor a scoundrel, though there may be some evidence of both in these pages.

Acknowledgments

In writing *The Closed Society* I appealed to hundreds of people for assistance and testified as to their contributions. With *Running Scared* my call for help went only to a few associates. They are:

Evans Harrington, who read and recommended the manuscript and who performed a multiplicity of chores at Ole Miss;

John Dittmer, whose examination of every sentence led to a large measure of admonition, most of which I accepted;

Seetha Srinivasan, who battered me with some severity on a number of things, on which she was usually right;

Cecile Pulin, a skilled word processor who performed with grace well beyond the call of duty;

Frank Smith, who has kept the faith for nearly half a century;

Carvel Collins, who carefully studied my section on William Faulkner, the great writer on whose career he is the leading authority;

and Margaret (Dutch) Thompson Silver, whose memory of many intimate details of our life together is demonstrably superior to my own.

I hereby absolve these friends of any responsibility for what I have written.

Running Scared

Silver in Mississippi

CHAPTER ONE

Preliminaries to Life in Mississippi
(1865–1936)

I have often speculated about the inevitability of my confrontation with official Mississippi, a tug-of-war that ended with my departure from the state where my three children were born. It couldn't have been my birthplace (Rochester, New York), for at twelve I moved to North Carolina where I attended high school and the state university. Nor do I believe it was a matter of ancestry, for a great-grandfather on my mother's side was named Andrew Jackson Squier, which should have put any descendant of his in tune with a legislature meeting in Mississippi's capital city. It could not have been family political inclination, for I am the only member of my immediate clan who has not unswervingly voted for the Republican ticket in whatever election. There are no reformers in my heritage that I am aware of, just plain hard-working farmers and craftsmen who would not have been out of place in the Magnolia State. My folks were ever on the poor side, so much so that I was the first to have a try at what is called higher education. Yet, it seems to me that the mental baggage I brought with me into Mississippi must have an explanation for what the chairman of the Board of Trustees of Institutions of Higher Learning called my tendency toward "contumacious conduct."

One-Horse Enterpriser
(1865–1930)

In attempting to establish the background for my peculiar

3

way of thinking, I went back to that part of my father's diary I edited for *New York History* exactly thirty years ago. Despite little formal schooling, Henry Dayton Silver, born on a farm near Lake Ontario in the last year of the Civil War, recorded in some thirteen hundred pages of beautiful script his daily musings and experiences. We don't keep diaries anymore, but it was this journal that instilled in me a desire to write something for my own children and, more certainly, helped me to comprehend and love my own father.

Henry Silver was literally a one-horse enterpriser. The panic of 1893 drove his little family back to his folks in the country in upstate New York; the next year he returned to Rochester to start peddling groceries north of the city. He and his wife "slaved away," accumulating nickels and dimes until in ten years they owned three grocery stores. As the family increased to five children, my father looked eagerly to the day when he could retire, travel, and cultivate himself. He realized his own lack of formal education, but insisted that five degrees from Dartmouth College would not have made him a better grocer. Rather typical of those in his status, he loathed labor unions and corporations alike, contending that the National Biscuit Company bought cardboard at 4¢ a pound, turning it into cookies to retail at 14¢. Silver developed his own brands of coffee and baking powder. In his decade of peddling with wagon and sleigh through the slushy winter months of what he called fierce and beastly weather, he developed aches and pains that gave him a desire to "light out" for more favorable climes. Various members of the family journeyed with him to Florida four or five times beginning in 1904.

Silver read voraciously in American fiction and history. He patronized the local library and liked to read to his children from his own sets of Dickens and Mark Twain. Each week he devoured the *Saturday Evening Post* from cover to cover. He was particularly solicitous of the development of his firstborn, at one time sending Earl to an "academy" out in the country. It seems that the youngster had learned to smoke and swear, and his father says at one point of exasperation in the journal that he will be content if Earl never goes to jail, never joins a labor union, and stays out of the clutches of the Democratic party. My father believed firmly in the Puritan ethic, expressed in his conviction that, lacking something better to do, one should dig a ditch in the morning and fill it in the afternoon. Though in his early married years he had been a Methodist deacon, he was later of the opinion that church members were the most likely to beat a grocer out of just obligations. When one winter in St. Augustine he had his pocket picked of $200, that very day he got a job clerking in a store until he had earned back the precise amount. He liked to walk around strange cities and talk with new acquaintances, always striving to improve himself. Fortunately for me, he believed so much in education that he willingly put up the $2000 it cost for me to attend four years at the University of North Carolina. I would like to think now that he considered it a good investment. My father died in 1930, a quiet, tolerant man, willing "to live and let live," who raised his hand against no man and did not, as nearly as I can remember, concern himself with social problems.

Yankee
(1907–1919)

Sometimes I think I can remember what happened in my early years on Lexington Avenue more distinctly than the events of yesterday. I was eternally shy, a rather chubby and clumsy boy (called "Bub" by my older brother Henry) who did well enough in grammar school and learned to swim in the Erie Canal after being first carried across its Western Wide Waters on the shoulders of my father. With nostalgia I now recall the gaudy pleasure of floating along on huge blocks of frozen water to the icehouse on the banks of the canal and in the summer chasing horse-drawn wagons to filch slick pieces of ice, of sailing on skates for miles on the canal's smooth surface, jacket spread wide with the wind behind my back, and in the warmer months, happily naked, clinging to the towrope between tugboat and barges pushing along on the state's chief waterway. One day I remember I fell from the roof through the chimney hole to the first floor of a new house my father was shingling. He was a good carpenter, able to select at a glance the proper piece from a woodpile, important because in those days the craftsman constructed from scratch everything from window frames to wooden stairs. I was at a loss whether to continue an association with my

The Silver family's house, Rochester

closest buddy when I discovered his parent had actually campaigned for Woodrow Wilson. In those days I looked with contempt on the heathen who went to the Catholic school just one block down Lexington Avenue. I probably absorbed some of the local prejudice against the new immigrants, in this case the Italians. There wasn't a single Negro that I can remember. Although I attended Sunday School with regularity, I was unable to sell the religious calendars I sent away for. My mother returned them.

I must have been something of a proper patriot during World War I, receiving a certificate of proficiency as a four-minute speaker in the fourth grade of P.S. No. 34, collecting peach pits for gas masks, and running up the flag early on the morning of the false armistice. A few of us spoiled brats persecuted unmercifully an old couple living on Linnett Street because they were of German origin. In my last year in the North, I became Standard Bearer for having the highest grades in the new Jefferson Junior High School and ran all the way home and back along the canal towpath to escape the shame of appearing on stage in a khaki shirt purchased in a war surplus store. I remember, too, sharing in the laughter at the expense of twin sisters from Louisiana who convulsed our class because of their strange accent. On one trip to Florida, I got a job hawking peanuts at a Johnny Jones circus in Daytona but failed to sell a single bag because I simply could not face potential customers. On my return to Rochester I was so painfully ill-at-ease that I would not ask a secretly cherished girl to accompany me on a school hayride. I don't remember having any special feelings about the decision of my parents to move to North Carolina. My father sold our three-story house (which he had built) for $4500, rented a freight car, packed our furniture tightly into it, and saw it off before directing the family southward by railroad coach, all to escape the dreary winters on the littoral of Lake Ontario.

Young Tarheel
(1919–1923)

Life in the resort town of Southern Pines was pleasant enough. The high school, even with the addition of students from Pinehurst, was so small that I had little competition for second base and occasionally was permitted to pitch on the baseball team. We fielded a basketball team but had no football. In town we took pride in a first-rate Scout program, with our elegant self-built clubhouse and a permanent camp at Thaggard's Pond. At one time our troop contained a dozen Eagle Scouts. But I was keenly aware that we lived on the wrong side of the tracks in an old boarding house my father had transformed into a comfortable home. My younger sister Margaret seemed able to ignore such social subtleties but a few years ago told me she resented my being described as the bright kid in the family. She attended a teachers' college. Our folks assumed that all southerners were a little on the lazy side. Mother watched over her chickens and our father minded his shop where he stored his tools and polished the family shoes after experimenting with Sunday breakfasts. The only dance I remember enjoying came on a night when I picked out his highly blackened shoes instead of my own. His size ten were extremely comfortable because I had been accustomed to wearing shoes a size or two smaller than they should have been.

After he returned from a couple of hitches in the Navy after World War I, my brother Henry became my instant hero and the boxing sensation of the community. In turn he became a short-order cook in Jack's Restaurant, a night policeman with temerity enough to search out alleged criminals in Jimtown, the section for blacks, and a motorcycle cop who developed a profitable speed trap for unwary motorists. Once he arranged a contest between himself on his trusty Harley-Davidson and a local racing buff in a home-built car, to take place on Highway 1 between Southern Pines and Aberdeen. Bets were down and the vehicles revved up when the sheriff came up and stopped the match. Henry was probably fired. But he got married, took up brick laying, and started building houses in town, aided by our father who drew the plans and taught Henry the intricacies of plumbing and electricity.

In my senior year I was chosen salutatorian of my class not because of excellence in scholarship but for the simple reason that we ceremoniously presented a grand total of six graduates. In an outburst of overconfidence I decided to wing my graduation speech in the downtown theater and was saved from utter disaster when a passing Seaboard freight train kept the audience from hearing what I tried to say. At fifteen I was accepted by the University of North Carolina and that summer I learned a few more of the facts of life while working as a bellhop in a New Hampshire hotel.

Student-of-Sorts
(1923–1927)

Four years in Chapel Hill did little to expand my horizons. It appears now that I was prepared for college academically but struck out socially. Maybe I was just an inveterate loner. Unquestionably I was one of the few who might really have benefited from membership in a fraternity, but none requested the pleasure of my company. I cannot remember being given a single bit of counseling—nor did I request any. In my first year I served tables in the campus dining hall and escaped the normal freshman hazing by means of brazen isolation. My social life was nonexistent except for an occasional trip to see a friend from home at the women's college in Greensboro. I'm sure I never attended a college dance. Before long I had written several hundred dollars worth of postdated gambling checks on my father's account, and to recoup my losses I developed a proficiency at poker. After the first quarter I entertained a cynicism toward academic achievement but was stimulated to make all A's the second quarter of my junior year when I discovered this would mean induction into the mysteries of Phi Beta Kappa. Church attendance lasted but a short time as my Baptist fundamentalism underwent severe attack from class lectures and dormitory bull sessions. In my junior year my roommate and I ventured over to the Savoy Hotel in Durham for our first fling at sins of the flesh. Perhaps foolishly I changed my course from business because in the School of Education there were no tuition charges. I think I was unhappy most of my time at the University of North Carolina.

A spectacular development took place in my senior year. *I was expelled.* By this time I was playing poker regularly for rather large stakes when some twenty contestants were brought before the student council for gambling. We were told that the honor system required an admission of guilt, and when we challenged the council to prove it, we were shipped for lying to that honorable body. We appealed, turning to sympathetic members of the Law School faculty. Matters became more complicated when the president of the student body threatened with front-page publicity those who did not accept conviction. Two of us revoked our appeals (I had accumulated enough credits for graduation), and the others were designated in the headlines as criminals. The whole mess came to a climax in a student referendum which did away with the honor system. So my first exercise in contumacious conduct ended in a kind of personal retreat. At the time I felt as though I had been kicked in the face, but the essential harm was the loss of a chance to compete that spring in the two-mile run on the 1927 track team. I wouldn't have made it because that year Carolina had the best distance runners in the country. So I paid my fee at the Registrar's Office and the following June my diploma was sent to my parents. In the meantime I set out to see the world, and years later I was able to determine cause orders had gone out from the sheriff to round up prisoners whom he could feed on one-third of the 75¢ a day he was allotted for their food. My friend was knocked cold when he tried to talk to the judge. Upon release, he and I separated, apprehensive of not being able to catch rides jointly on the desolate highway headed east. Later that day, I felt most forlorn as I trudged along the Union Pacific tracks in a cold rain. A woman in a shack along the right-of-way sent a little boy out to me with a cap to wear. Toward night I caught up with a wanderer on his way to Norway. After a supper of potatoes baked in a warming and drying fire, I was able to catch a fast-moving freight and next day passed my college friend in a Nebraska division town. We waved and never saw each other again. I walked across the Missouri River bridge into Council Bluffs and read in the headlines that Lindbergh had flown the Atlantic. From there to Chicago, I came close to freezing until a friendly engineer took me into his cab. From there I caught rides on the highway to Rochester where brother Earl gave me shelter and a job as an unskilled laborer. In June I hitched rides to North Carolina, covering the eight hundred miles in twenty-seven hours, thanks to an all-night journey through Pennsylvania with a bootlegger. Home never seemed sweeter, and probably for the first time in my life I felt confident enough to regale all listeners with tales of hobo jungles, confrontations with the police, living off the land, the turbulence of travel by freight train across the Great Salt Lake, as well as miscellaneous adventures at sea. To a few people I was not only a college graduate but a minor hero.

Amateur Coach
(1927–1928)

In the summer of 1927 I was allowed to return to Chapel Hill to attend a coaching school in preparation for a job in a consolidated high school at Ellerbe. My self-confidence was enhanced somewhat when I found I had beaten the number-two man on the Carolina tennis team. Still, I was taken completely unawares when Morris Mitchell, my principal, suggested one Friday in September that we would start a football team the following week. That afternoon I wired to Charlotte for a book on that branch of coaching, which I looked at somewhat at recess on Monday before beginning my chores as Coach Silver. My team used the plays in the back of Pop Warner's treatise and won five of ten games. In basketball we started out in half-hearted fashion when it occurred to me that I should let these country boys do it on their own. From that point the team won nineteen straight games, including one for the regional championship played in the old Tin Can at UNC. In that contest we were down at the half 15 to 1 and came out on top by the score of 16 to 15 (the center jump after each goal explains the low score). I also tried my hand at baseball and track, but my greatest threat of annihilation came when my players challenged me to put on the gloves with a visiting Carolina athletic hero home on vacation. He didn't quite kill me. That year I was selected as the champion geography teacher of the county simply because a class of mine had filled its homeroom walls with color maps of the continents, and I was called on to take the lead in a truncated version of *She Stoops to Conquer.* The performance concluded my acting career. The school's annual athletic dinner, cooked by the home economics girls, was a considerable success because the honored guest, the chairman of the school board, apparently was unaware that the chickens came from his flock. My salary that year of $100 a month was augmented by the personal check of the principal for twenty-five big ones. So I listened to his advice when I was offered twice my Ellerbe income to coach the next year at Wadesboro High and followed the frontier across the mountains to Tennessee for advanced educational work at Peabody College.

Dilettante
(1928–1935)

For the next seven years I lived in Nashville, except for a couple of terms teaching in Shelby County at Whitehaven and Germantown and a short spell at Middle Tennessee Teachers College at Murfreesboro. In this period I studied the gentle art of courtship, learned to play tennis by day and poker all night, and to keep financially afloat by occasionally stoking a furnace and dishing out hash in a sleazy cafe. Lest the latter appear to indicate the hardscrabble life of a potential scholar, I must add I have never felt more content or so free from restraint, and in my more prosperous moments I drove a second-hand coupe with balloon tires and a bullhorn and purchased on time my first tuxedo. The bank holiday of 1933 did hinder my entrepreneurial activities as it caught me with several hundred dollars worth of poker checks which remained permanently invalid. By the time the Blue Eagle appeared I had been seduced by the New Deal and the stirrings of southern labor. In fact I had already witnessed textile clashes in my passing through the mountains of east Tennessee and western North Carolina. The farmers' future was implied in the title of that now forgotten but incredible volume, Arthur Raper's *Preface to Peasantry*.

During my first teaching assignment in Whitehaven, I learned one day by letter from my mother that my father had been buried in Southern Pines. When he was taken to the Moore County Hospital for what turned out to be a fatal operation, she had chosen not to interfere with my new job, and the presence of two older brothers obviated the need for my appearance at the funeral. In my silent grieving I cursed the Puritanism back of her decision.

In the meantime I had transferred my graduate history activities across Hillsborough Avenue to Vanderbilt University, but I had been enjoying life too extravagantly to make much progress toward the degree except for the accumulation of some class credits—that is, until I was brought up short when my major professor casually informed me that he doubted the wisdom of my returning in the fall. This blow may have changed my life, because forthwith I settled down, passed the language exams, and the next fall was given a double fellowship (with a stipend of $900) which called for teaching a couple of classes while completing my thesis. That summer I journeyed to Washington where I delved into military documents in the War Department Archives in the daytime and read old newspapers in the Library of Congress at night.

In spite of my high school experience, the chore of teaching elementary political science students twice a week proved traumatic. I met them for discussion after they had been lectured to en masse by that doughty old professional hypocrite, Gus Dyer. His stern repudiation of Franklin Roosevelt and his embracing of the philosophy of the National Manufacturers Association led me to dispute most of his facts and all of his theories, and even to encourage a boycott by our neophytes. I was instrumental in arranging a debate between Dyer and Professor Ernest Eberling on the economics of the New Deal, in which I must confess my champion was devastated by the histrionics of his clever opponent (such effective but crude tactics as opening his knife and scraping barnyard manure off his shoes while Eberling was speaking).

While teaching in Germantown I had used the *Literary Digest* in classes and had given a tentative order for fall. As I did not return, I assumed the letter of intent had been cancelled. Instead, several dozen copies were shipped each week and the local postmaster allowed them to accumulate in his small office. As a student at Vanderbilt I could not have paid for those magazines if I had so chosen; in any case I didn't make the effort. A collection agency failed to impress me so I was hailed into a justice of the peace court in Nashville, or would have been had I not dodged a process server for months. This was a relatively simple matter as my friends maintained the switchboard in the YMCA Graduate School where I had lodgings on the fourth floor. Finally, I gave up the cat-and-mouse game and, advised by a law school professor, appeared in court, still refusing to pay even a small part of my supposed obligation. So the justice of the peace gave up, and I'd like to believe my intransigence had something to do with the demise of that antiquated legal system in Davidson County.

At Vanderbilt in my day the Confederacy was making its last stand and the agrarians were in full flower, publishing during their bloom *I'll Take My Stand*. In fact I inherited the tiny office of Robert Penn Warren in Calhoun Building and failed to comprehend his erudite public lectures. (Years later I was to dine with him in Boston, long after he had switched to defending student racial protest.) I never did take much stock in the mythology of the agrarians, partly because their association with the land was usually limited to possession of camps on the Cumberland River. Of course, I did and still do envy their brilliance in writing. In graduate seminars I kept my mouth shut. But I failed to hear a satisfactory answer to the question as to why, if so much virtue came from working in the soil, some of it did not rub off on the slaves. (It could have been that the agrarians assumed that antebellum farmers were the yeomen espoused by historian Frank Owsley, one of their own group.) This was about as close to a discussion of racial problems as I encountered in my studies in Tennessee. The Vanderbilt academic community of my acquaintance seldom seemed to reach the heart of social questions, except perhaps in courses on antiquity or in the School of Religion. So, while I had absorbed a good deal of factual and theoretical history in North Carolina and Tennessee, I was unaware of the existence of Faulkner, Cash, or Keynes. I was sadly prepared for the twentieth century. That spring of 1935 I fell in love with a freshman from Alabama and received my degree in history. I was ready to face the world of making a living.

Dust Bowler
(1935–1936)

That summer while I waited on the campus for the academic world to recognize my qualifications, I had plenty of time to read all four volumes of Douglas S. Freeman's *R. E. Lee.* In August I was delighted to receive an offer from Southwestern College, a Methodist institution in Winfield, Kansas. I was to be paid $1980 for nine months, though a little later when the contract arrived, it guaranteed only 60 percent of my salary. Perplexed, I called the president, who assured me the document was drawn that way to comply with the rules of the North Central Association and that I would get all my money. I signed, assuming that if you can't trust a former missionary to China, who can you trust? Besides, I had no other offer. In Kansas, when I discovered an otherworldly approach to college finance, I made tentative plans at once to obtain all that was supposed to come to me. One poor recruit to the faculty, through clerical error was guaranteed 60 percent of 60 percent of $1500, and when he protested, the pious president insisted the contract was valid, implying the Lord's will. Unable to keep his head financially above water, this instructor took on a class of young town businessmen who subsequently put pressure on the president to pay his wages—all $900.

I taught five history and political science classes, probably adding to my factual knowledge but little to my wisdom. I was called upon to act as pallbearer in several funerals wherein I had no slightest acquaintance with the deceased. I don't remember attending church services. That fall Southwestern produced a fair football team, but on the verge of the annual game with a rival in Oklahoma, word came that if the Negro halfback made the trip, he might well be killed. He stayed at home. I was called on to chaperone several picnics in which after the building of a fire and some display of congeniality the various couples invariably took their blankets and disappeared into the night, and this in a church school which forbade smoking and the consumption of alcohol. In Kansas that year the wind never stopped blowing and the dust moved only less fiercely than in 1934, so much so that each morning the desk in my office with tightly locked windows was covered with a fine coating of silt.

Before Christmas the college treasury opened slightly so that I might borrow one hundred dollars in order to return to Nashville to get married. (As I guessed, the president was a soft touch when it came to holy matrimony.) Margaret McLean (Dutch) Thompson and I were joined together in the A O Pi sorority house on the Vanderbilt campus and that night left by train for St. Louis and points west. Our honeymoon included a burlesque show and a visit to the Kansas City stockyards, not a place amenable to romance, but an experience I thought would measurably round out our general knowledge. I had already signed up my new wife for a home economics course at Southwestern, and we ate in the college dining hall, the cost of both to be subtracted from that part of my salary not immediately forthcoming. Dutch had grown up in the kitchen at home, but she still insists all the Kansas girls would let her do was to grate cheese. We slept in the large bedroom of a widow's home with a smelly oil rig in the backyard. For fun we followed the college athletic teams including tennis, which I coached, and joined a science expedition to the Arbuckle Mountains in Oklahoma. We and another newly married couple were dragged around town in a rickety oxcart with a noisy German band in its rear and followed by half the student body. After this typically western charivari, we treated our followers to food and soft drinks at a student hangout across from the campus. That summer we walked down the beds of drought-stricken streams with flashlights in hand and, despite occasional snakes, reached out to pick up dozens of bullfrogs. One Sunday morning four of us cooked 130 frog legs caught the night before. Since that day I have never been able to order that succulent dish in a restaurant. Perhaps the nearest thing to catastrophe the farmers faced during the spring of 1936 were swarms of grasshoppers which gobbled up everything edible in sight, including all our grass and flowers. With summer the temperature reached 110 degrees each day for a fortnight or so; in spite of Dutch's timidity, we slept on cots in the backyard with the oil well. Air conditioning had not yet arrived.

My Vanderbilt professors saw to it that I appeared on the program of the Mississippi Valley Historical Association meeting in Austin, Texas, the spring of 1936. We drove down with our landlady, crossing a Red River almost devoid of water. (A month later we read in the papers of a man drowning in a raging flood at that same spot.) During an excursion train ride to San Antonio, Dutch learned of a job opening at the University of Mississippi, and when we returned to Kansas, I wrote a letter of inquiry. She wanted to return to the South. I was later invited to join the faculty at Ole Miss. Our time in the West had been of great value. Learning about life in a dusty, one-crop state in a depression was a pretty fair preparation for moving to penurious Mississippi, at that time engaged mainly in the production of cotton. We were reasonably sure when we departed in August that a few months later the people of Kansas would vote for Franklin Roosevelt instead of their own governor.

Mississippi in Depression and War

(1936–1945)

Embryonic Mississippian
(1936–1941)

After a couple of weeks in the mountains near Chattanooga, we took off for Mississippi, changing trains after a middle-of-the-night wait in Jackson, Tennessee, and then traveling southward to Oxford on one of the last passenger trains on that old line of the Illinois Central. Arriving in time for attendance at the first fall faculty meeting, I was introduced by the new chancellor to a series of local customs (no alcohol, no politics, no spouse to work for the university) which caused me to wonder whether we had really left the plains of Kansas. My checks of $150 a month were to come with regularity in spite of the depression and a previous "Bilbonic" plague. The sales tax had saved the state, but some of my new colleagues still held Mississippi scrip. Dutch and I rented half a duplex, a one-bedroom apartment, from the head of the history department, and bought all the essential second-hand furniture for seventy-five dollars, on time. Joe Mathews, a PhD from Pennsylvania, and I supplanted Charley Sydnor who had moved on to greener pastures at Duke. The next year Dave Potter came in as a part-time instructor, and in 1938 Bell Wiley came up from Mississippi Southern to take the place of our ousted chairman. (Of these men, I am the only one now alive.) In those first years, my wife and I had not the slightest notion that we would be identified with Ole Miss for nearly thirty years.

18

Always in Mississippi we reached the end of each school year in debt, a deficiency to be erased in the summer so that we could begin the fall with economic decks clear. We surmised quite early that it would be impossible for us to save a dime unless somehow in the future our income might be increased to reach the majestic sum collected by the deans—$3000 a year. So a young professor usually looked for other sources of income: correspondence courses, travel at state expense, a working spouse, and, in my case, coaching the tennis team, which brought me not only the occasional use of an athletic department Buick, but balls and a hundred dollars in cash each season. I found a conspicuous place in intramural athletics, playing on teams that won campus basketball and tennis championships. For ten years I took slow-motion pictures of the football games for the coaches, which enabled us to frolic in New Orleans each fall. At that time it was considered somewhat disreputable in the scholarly world for a new professor to write a textbook. Summer grants were so much lagniappe. One spring morning I pulled out of my box in the old post office (where William Faulkner had worked and read other people's mail) a check for $300 to be used as expense money that summer in research. Exhilarated, I bragged about the great event to a friend (later a member of the Board of Trustees) who congratulated me effusively before telling me that during the previous week he had gotten a pardon from the governor for a local felon and had charged a fee of five hundred dollars.

From the beginning I suspected I did not approach brilliance in my teaching so I sought ways beyond the classroom to make myself indispensable. Mainly I took a genuine interest in all aspects of student life, a somewhat difficult task for a nontalented would-be glad-hander. Before long Dutch and I seemed to know all members of the student body of considerably less than a thousand. We chaperoned our share of parties and dances and had many gatherings of students in our various homes. She took classes and soon began to tutor the athletes en masse (at 50¢ an hour) to help them escape the stigma of ineligibility. She also directed a campaign for funds to build a campus home for A O Pi, the Vanderbilt sorority in whose house we had been married. Her reputation at teaching

everything from astronomy to military tactics inadvertently saved
my hide in my first clash with Mississippi authority. I had been
making a series of speeches under the auspices of the state Department of Education, including one at the Clarksdale courthouse on
the 1938 Wages and Hours Act. I am sure I was extremely cautious
in my remarks about federally imposed minimum wages, not popular
in the Delta even though they didn't apply to agricultural labor. At
that time I was unaware that laborers in the peckerwood lumber
mills were being paid as little as ten cents an hour, and that often in
company scrip. In any case the next morning's Clarksdale paper
vigorously condemned my talk as communist. A couple of days later
I opened a letter from Tom Gibson, a gloomy columnist for the local
press, who announced quite simply that I would be fired at the end
of the year. In fact, he affirmed to several members of the Board of
Trustees his belief that I was a Red. When my name was brought up
in the meeting, Chairman Martin Van Buren Miller—who knew only
that my wife had kept eligible Johnny Whittington, an elusive but
unscholarly halfback—stated with no lack of certainty, "Jim Silver
is no more of a Communist than I am. Next order of business." He
was probably right. Such was my first minor confrontation with
conservative Mississippi.

A summer teaching job at Birmingham-Southern led the following
year to several months with the University of Tours, as it turned out
a fly-by-night outfit which conducted school teachers around the
country by bus while they were earning college credits. Living in
circus tents, we hopscotched up the east coast to Quebec, then
catercornered down to Mexico, and came back north to British Co-
lumbia, returning to Kansas City. Together with the satisfaction that
came from traveling the highways and byways of this broad land, I
quickly sensed that railroad lawyers were not so splendid in their
efforts to put this profit-making educational venture out of business.
By spring I defended the touring "college" before the Interstate
Commerce Commission, and after witnessing the exploitation of
powerless teachers in summer action, I helped to organize its demise. Nevertheless, we saw huge stretches of the country no longer
available by way of the interstate highway system.

Comprehension of the plight of blacks in the South came to me slowly. I still remember the awe with which I, as a youth in Southern Pines, viewed the body of a black man on the ground after he had been shot. In spite of a vague certainty that southern Negroes were mistreated, I cannot recall discussion of racial matters at the University of North Carolina in my student days, though I have a slight recollection of the expulsion of the author of a short story in which a young white woman out of hatred of her family deliberately became pregnant by a black lover. Later, I learned that according to the intelligence of the times, Negro athletes could not stand up to their white counterparts in physical competition, that black babies required less milk for healthy nourishment than whites, and that even when hungry and cold, black people grinned because they were happy. And in my graduate years in Nashville racial matters did not intrude on my education.

At Ole Miss from the outset I puzzled over my advanced students who seemed to have little doubt of the Negro's inherent inferiority. Not willing to take opinion as gospel, I began to collect and study books on the problems of race. I still own most of these volumes, and I still read them. The best of the anthropologists seem to have emerged from the brain of the learned Franz Boas. It would be a matter of supererogation to list even a few of them, but I hasten to say that I read *everything* I could find on race, from Charles Darwin and William Graham Sumner even to those fanciful theorists, Theodore Bilbo, Tom Brady, and Carleton Putnam. The volume I ended up recommending to those who would learn came from the pen of the Virginian Tom Pettigrew, whose *Profile of the American Negro* went unheeded by Mississippi politicians. But I went still further in questioning every racial anthropologist I could locate, from Margaret Mead to the brilliant young Egyptian scientist I met at a cocktail party in Cambridge. She looked at me with withering scorn as I made the usual inquiry regarding black inferiority, answering, "We stopped talking about that in 1911." Needless to say, I was convinced that there was little scientific evidence for white supremacy. Of course I also undertook to learn the history of Mississippi, and I˙ continued my concern with liberal causes, especially attempts to organize southern working people. Almost as soon as it came out, I began to use Howard Odum's *Southern Regions* as a main text. By 1939, I attended regular biracial meetings in the Oxford Methodist

Church, but the dozen or so who gathered there rather quickly disbanded on the assumption that Mississippi's monolithic society was too much for us to crack. That same spring James William (Bill) Silver was born and as a two-month-old baby was driven to Canada where his father attended the last of the international law meetings of the Carnegie Endowment for International Peace. As we crossed the St. Lawrence River at Montreal on our way home, the first day of September, we learned that war had been declared in Europe.

I have been convinced for years that southern Negroes were actually of lesser stature simply because all the factors (education, economics, politics, social custom) controlling their personal development were consciously framed to bring that result. Thera Jones was a fine example of the programming of black people for cultural inferiority in Mississippi society. Our family was extremely lucky to secure for a quarter century her services as maid, nurse, housekeeper, and general factotum. When she started with us she was living with her husband Will, a sharecropper who did fairly well in off-seasons as a well digger. Apparently, Will (I remember him with a couple of front teeth missing) was quite a ladies' man.

Thera developed a goiter which John Culley (owner of the Oxford Hospital and physician to William Faulkner) said would cost her her life unless surgically removed. She agreed to an operation, and I made arrangements with the hospital and surgeon, as well as the local black undertaker who would use his hearse ambulance to carry her from her home on the Hathorn farm and back. (Making arrangements meant guaranteeing payment.) A day after the scheduled operation I went to the hospital to see how Thera was getting along, only to find that she had refused to get into the ambulance when it pulled up to her cabin. So I drove out to see her, learning how terrified she was of entering any hospital. She felt that she would never emerge alive. She would die at home in her own bed if she were going to die. So we discussed for a couple of hours the ramifications of hospital care and dying. She remained adamant. Finally, with both hesitation and irritation, I picked up the 90-pound woman, placed her in the back seat of my Plymouth, and drove her to the hospital. She did not resist. The next day the operation, which probably saved her life, was performed. The ambulance took her home. I don't recall that we ever talked about it afterward.

I remember I once rode over to Batesville to pick up at the Illinois Central station a speaker from Ecuador. On the return 25-mile trip, the two of us talked at length about the general treatment of blacks in the American South. As our conversation reached the problem of medical treatment, we came upon a wrecked car in the back seat of which lay a moaning, bleeding black woman. We got her into my car and openly wondered what sort of reception she would get at the Oxford Hospital. Would they admit her without financial guarantees? I suggested that this would be a good test of small-hospital practice; I did not know the answer. The woman was taken in, was treated successfully, and dismissed a day or so later. Whether this was because I (a regular, paying white patron) brought her in, I never did know.

One Sunday afternoon Thera rushed into Faculty 6, obviously frightened. She and Will had quarreled; he had chased her out into the fields and had fired numerous shotgun blasts at her as she dodged between the cotton rows. She had escaped and had run all the way to the campus and begged protection from the fiend. She never wanted to see Will again. We inquired as to whether she would like to live in our basement, and she was overjoyed. She stayed with us that night, and in the morning I made arrangements with university authorities for the construction of a small apartment downstairs. In the afternoon she returned, and I told her how successfully our plans had been worked out. She replied, "Oh, Will and I are back together." Later they were divorced.

We were not particularly enamored of a good many southern customs, but we quickly learned that Thera had succumbed to most of them. On a trip to North Carolina she did eat with the family on several occasions, with much obvious discomfort. But she always displayed the utmost in tact and sometimes humor. She and I were once discussing the prospects of heaven. Though a fundamentalist, she knew reality from experience. When I suggested that in the promised land we would all be sitting around eating ambrosia, Thera replied, "Maybe so, but more likely, I'd be out in the kitchen grating the coconut."

Her only child we all called "Son." As a teenager he got a job as
delivery boy at Avent's Drugstore. "Son" soon discovered that his
meager wage could be mightily augmented by his selling at discount
prices penicillin he picked off the store's shelves. Later he drove a
stolen car into Tennessee. Inevitably he was caught and placed in
the local jail. The only real help I could give was to induce the
authorities to have him tried in the federal rather than the state
court. So "Son" went to the federal penitentiary in El Reno, Oklahoma, where he learned a trade. When Uncle Sam dismissed him,
he moved to a relative's home in Indianapolis. I think he has prospered. At least Thera went up to see him annually because "Son"
dared not return to the scene of his crime, even for a friendly visit.
The state still threatened to put him behind bars for his local
transgression.

The place of Thera in the family might be suggested by an incident
on our return from a long football weekend in New Orleans. Our
daughter Betty, then about three or four, rushed out to the car to tell
us joyfully that she had slept all three nights with Thera. The miserable wages we were able to pay Thera (my income was less than
$200 a month) never came close to the value of our affection and
love. Like so many blacks in the closed society, however, Thera
could and did turn to us when difficulties arose that she couldn't
cope with. For instance, in the middle of one night deputies had
broken down the front and back doors to her home when looking for
a purported criminal. She reported the terror of the five or six
women (including her bedridden mother, to whom she gave loving
care during the last ten years of the old lady's life) who had been
sleeping without male protection. Dutch immediately drove to the
county office building where she not only complained, but raised
hell with Boyce Bratton, a former employee of the university
cafeteria. The upshot was that Sheriff Bratton swore that Thera's
home would not be disturbed again by the county's law officers, and
my wife knew that he would keep his word.

After her divorce from Will, Thera lived two or three miles from
the campus on sixty acres of worthless land she had somehow inherited. After we departed from Mississippi, Bill reported that
Thera told him she had been offered by a developer a thousand
dollars an acre for her land. For a long time I had considered myself

as Thera's ultimate social security; now maybe she would be able to take care of me. As it turned out, she died before she had the chance.

For twenty-five years I was forbidden to have any meaningful intellectual relationship with a Mississippi Negro. It was always a case of master and servant, the black obviously inferior because God or Nature had so ordained. The doctrine of white supremacy had not really changed since slavery times despite the Civil War, the depression, and World War II. Hence, my memory brings back circumstances and incidents that seem bizarre in retrospect.

In Oxford's principal barber emporium, a black man had operated one of the chairs as late as the early 1930s—for whites only, of course. Also, a Negro doctor had practiced in town, but not in my time. A colored lawyer would have starved to death. The various professional offices in Oxford had their white and colored entrances and waiting rooms, and at least the dentist our family patronized had racially separated chairs. My closest acquaintance with "separate and equal" came in my association with the Oxford Industrial School made up of grades from one through eleven. I developed a considerable but limited friendship with Professor Gooden, principal of the Negro school. Often we sat in his office to ponder the problems of the day, but only once did I visit his home in Freedman's Town, the black section of Oxford. As I remember the occasion, I remained standing the whole time for fear of white reprisals against him if it were learned that we were socializing in private. There was no way, of course, that we could have had a cup of coffee or a drink together in a public place.

My many visits in the school began shortly after I launched an extensive speaking program at Ole Miss. With little money, we were forced to capitalize on the curiosity VIPs outside the South manifested toward Mississippi, generally regarded as the country's most primitive state. Gooden and I worked out a routine by which British prime ministers, U.S. senators, newspaper editors, and scholars visited his school and made courtesy speeches to the entire student body crowded into the auditorium. This arrangement satisfied our needs and supplied the Industrial School with a speaking program unmatched elsewhere in the state.

Emil Ludwig, the popular historian, lectured at Ole Miss, and subsequently appeared in the Negro school. After meager black response to his heavy German accent, Ludwig attempted to arouse interest by asking questions. He inquired as to whether any student felt humiliated by the conduct of local whites. At first there was no response, but when the question sank in, here and there hands began to go up, rather furtively. A boy had had rocks thrown at him on his way to school. A young girl was being waited on in a grocery store when the clerk abandoned her to attend to the needs of a newly arrived white customer. And so it went, much to the edification of Jim Silver, as well as Emil Ludwig.

I'll never forget the scene when a do-gooder friend of mine and her small daughter from Minnesota were attending class in the third grade. The mother was highly critical in examining papers, that is, until her daughter called to her from the back of the room, "Mama, these are the same books we use in St. Paul." The two Yankees soon departed from the black school.

At its name would indicate, the institution specialized in trades, such as brick laying, carpentry, and home economics. Each year the Oxford Rotary Club convened there, with the food prepared and served by the home economics girls. And once a year Gooden spoke to the club in town, always very diplomatically arriving just after the meal had been consumed. Everyone understood the protocol, and I don't remember that anyone was particularly concerned about it. We all shook hands after the speech. In the first instance, the prominent businessmen got to see their Negro school and, in the second, the professor was able to put his needs before the community.

So it went throughout the state. Once when in Jackson I attended the weekly luncheon of the Lions Club. Speaking was the principal from the Piney Woods School, another black professor who arrived at the appropriate moment. As his institution depended largely on donations, he made a most obsequious, Uncle Tom speech. When it was all over a collection was taken, to the tune of nearly four hundred dollars. I wondered who had been taken in.

Local black churches looked to their members for financial support and, therefore, were largely autonomous. This was to be highly significant during the civil rights crises. Some of us were in the habit

of parking our cars on a summer evening near the open windows of
the Second Baptist Church so that we could listen to the singing. (It
was so called because the first building had burned.) Upon my return
from Scotland I presented a slide lecture there which I recall, for one
of the elders hastened me along so that the congregation could move
quickly to the service and the singing.

We took our shoes to Bob Boles's shop for repair. Black and
white customers were treated equally. The Boles family had over
the years driven out several white competitors through sheer
efficiency. And everyone in town seemed to know that these descendants óf plantation slaves possessed some of the superior genes
in the county.

I remember, probably back in the 1930s, a brand of canned sea-
food called Nigger Head. On the label wrapped around the entire
can appeared a widely grinning black man with a flat nose and huge
lips. Some time later the same pictured label designated the brand as
Negro Head. Still later it disappeared from the shelves of the Oxford
groceries. As the product came from Biloxi, it would seem that even
Mississippi enterprisers slowly learned more agreeable salesman-
ship. Or maybe black purchasing power was growing.

The only apparent racial equality turned up on Sardis Lake.
Blacks were generally better fishermen, perhaps because they were
angling for supper. I don't remember ever seeing a Negro with a
casting rod, but most of us fished anyway from old rowboats with
shiners as bait to trap the wily crappie. Usually we moved from bush
to bush in the muddy lake. Many a time have I seen a black man
pulling in the fish while his white competitor sat empty handed, but
never once did I see a white man usurp a black's productive trough
or bush. Once, though, I took a star Ole Miss pitcher frog hunting at
night; most of the time we spent in the icy water after our borrowed
boat sank. Back on land we came upon a Negro cabin we knew was
occupied because of a curling wisp of smoke coming from the chimney. When there was no response to our knocking, we shouted the
direst of threats and were finally admitted and allowed to dry out
before the fireplace in an elderly couple's bedroom. I'm still a bit
ashamed of our forced intrusion.

On the Ole Miss campus worked an elite black crew. My chief

acquaintances and, I believe, friends were specialists in the cafeteria: Uncle Will the butcher, Bondy Webb the pastry cook, and the Buford brothers who sweated amidst the hot stoves. My allergy problems required special diets. Maybe these blacks, along with Joe Sudduth, the general overseer, were old-time servants with an in-born delicacy of manner, but I chose to remember them as highly skilled artisans who had long since learned that good manners did not necessarily spell obeisance.

It is my long considered judgment that William Faulkner believed that while no true Mississippi aristocracy ever existed, there were individual aristocrats (Jefferson Davis, his own great-grandfather and the model for John Sartoris) and a considerable number of leaders who possessed certain aristocratic qualities, such as courage and loyalty (Thomas Sutpen, General Compson). The part of his state he knew best had been incorporated for only twenty-five years at the time of Mississippi's secession. In such a frontier society many who thought themselves gentlemen had actually indulged in Snopesism on the way to great material wealth.

When I went to Mississippi exactly a century after the formation of "Yoknapatawpha" (Lafayette County), I had the privilege of meeting and knowing as colleagues my own candidates for aristocracy, less than a dozen faculty members whose tenure at Ole Miss went back at least to 1910. One or two had served since the early 1890s. As I knew (and revered) them, these professors were gentlemen, hard-working scholars, perhaps the most remarkable group I have ever been closely associated with. The only criticism I ever heard of Alfred Hume (who came to Ole Miss in 1890) was that his dedication to the public good led him, as chancellor, to think that younger members of the faculty would be like-minded. I doubt if Mississippi can duplicate the lives of Alexander Bondurant (1893), David Horace Bishop (1904), Alfred W. Milden (1910), Calvin S. Brown (1901), William L. Kennon (1909), Christopher Longest (1908), or crusty old James Warsaw Bell (1903).

These men were, I think, great teachers who were so smothered in class loads and extracurricular duties that they did little publishing. Yet Wild Bill Kennon wrote the astronomy text most used in the United States, and Calvin Brown published the authoritative volume on Mississippi archaeology while teaching modern languages. His wife Maud Morrow Brown taught Greek and Latin before 1900, and I have heard that the family took turns by the week in speaking only French and German.

Of course I also ran into others, time-serving self-detractors who made their living calling attention to their own deficiencies and asking for sympathy. A friend of mine who coached an athletic team and mainly entertained visiting alumni was alarmed when Head Coach Harry Mehre was fired at the end of World War II. In all sincerity I advised him to establish himself with tenure as a physical education instructor on the premise that he had sense enough to flex his muscles in front of compulsory exercisers. But he stuck it out and emerged as director of athletics, later having a public building named in his honor. The man I learned to despise (who at first convinced me that I was his favorite professor, as he did most new instructors on a routine basis) was the college financial bureaucrat who spent most of his time with feet on his desk, reading the *Commercial Appeal*. (His assistant did his work.) Habitually he made small loans to students who had influential relatives. He lived in one of the fine old homes on the campus and hired a rapid succession of black maids from the cafeteria staff. He tried to get me, as a former Red Cross official, to use my supposed influence to get his son out of the military service. Many times he acknowledged that the New Deal had saved his Delta plantation, yet he decried all help to tenants as he turned bitterly against Roosevelt. Not surprisingly, after retirement he spent his last years raising money for the Citizens Council.

It would seem, looking back, that the state engaged in some rather inept economic dealings, such as building a dormitory for $300,000 and turning it over to a janitor paid $5 a week. As I recall, I performed similar financial marvels: There was little money for collecting speakers in Memphis (brought down by volunteers), so after consulting with Dean Malcolm Guess, I followed the practice of making out travel vouchers and spending the money on illegal whiskey for entertaining, imported from Memphis through the cordon of law officers in Holly Springs. I'm afraid, too, that I encouraged students to take correspondence courses simply because it added to

my meager income. But I was never guilty of such opportunism as
practiced by an assistant in the financial office who regularly bought
up required $12-cafeteria meal books for as little as $5 and resold
them for substantially more. All students were compelled to buy so
many of the books before they could graduate and some just didn't
like to eat in the cafeteria.

This is not to suggest that young professors coming to Ole Miss in
the middle of the depression felt themselves particularly put upon.
We were lucky to find jobs at all, were in the same boat, and probably didn't know any better. Perhaps the greatest financial excitement for Dutch and me came after three years of marriage in the
purchase of a new Plymouth for $800—on time, of course. I'm sure
the walking had done us no harm.

Staid Professor
(1939–1945)

About the time I went to Mississippi, the state launched a
desperate program to secure outside capital investment by granting
factory owners all sorts of economic inducements, including cheap
labor. Factory employees, coming off submarginal farms, were fundamentalist, nonradical Anglo-Saxons, apparently well satisfied
with and even grateful for subsistence wages. Willing to give a full-
day's work for a day's pay, they were likely to stay that way unless
stirred up by outside agitators, the Communist Party or northern
labor leaders, generally thought to be the same. So stated official
pronouncements.

In the 1940s, Ed Blair and I became friends. He was an organizer
for the Amalgamated Clothing Workers of America who, by the end
of the decade, had some five thousand members in Mississippi. Ed
was often beaten up, shot at, and once almost hanged. I visited him
in a Columbus hospital where he lay near death after having been
gunned down. His wife was in the next room under heavy sedation
for migraine headaches, seemingly an occupational hazard in those
days for women married to labor organizers. In time I became an
arbitrator, a function written into contracts between management
and the union, with rather nominal duties. The last time I was called
in a dispute, after the passage of the 1964 Civil Rights Act, I went to

a plant in Adams, Tennessee, just across the Mississippi line, and was amazed to find black women as a large part of the labor force.

Five or six years after World War II, the Amalgamated organized a new Rice-Stix plant in Water Valley, seventeen miles below Oxford. Collective bargaining had failed to produce a contract and the plant was struck. State militia were brought in, ostensibly to prevent violence. The union had spies in the office, and management had spies in the union. Union pickets were carted off to court in Senatobia where the judge assured them of a fair trial before he sentenced them. This scene was part of an educational process because women workers learned for the first time that they were eligible to vote for state judges.

Several times Blair brought workers he was training as union officials to my classes in the library at Ole Miss. His plan, of course, was to turn the union over to local leaders as soon as they were ready. The woman president adamantly presented the union position until she was asked by a prelaw student about the policy of the local on Negro membership. She went into a rage, shouting that there wouldn't be any "damned niggers" in her union. But the Amalgamated won the strike, largely because the Teamsters in St. Louis, in sympathy, threatened to refuse to move the Christmas goods from Rice-Stix warehouses. Several Ole Miss professors attended the union victory celebration in Water Valley.

In the period between World War II and the desegregation decision, it did seem possible that Mississippi could be brought into the modern world of itself. Labor leaders appeared regularly on the University of Mississippi campus, among them Clinton Golden and Jacob Potofsky. The Amalgamated president was received rather coldly by the faculty until it was pointed out that he was president of a bank with several hundred million dollars in assets. By and large the campus atmosphere remained antiunion, as evidenced by an incident in a labor relations seminar. After listening to a probusiness lecture I asked the director when labor's point of view would be presented. He responded by asking those present who planned to work for labor unions to raise their hands. No one did.

In 1948, one of my best students wrote a master's thesis on the history of the CIO in Mississippi, quite a feat as the union at the time was only two years old in the state. But Gene Roper did establish that every conceivable force, ethical and unethical—including the persuasive powers of businessmen, bankers, church leaders, school officials, the press, and town officers—was laid on the workers in such towns as Grenada to get them to vote down the red-tainted organization.

My most bizarre labor experience came in a call from Amalgamated in New York City requesting that I be on the lookout for a garment plant then thought to be traveling in north Mississippi. I did look around, even going to my friend who was executive secretary of the Oxford Chamber of Commerce. It seemed to make as much sense as hunting for an unidentified flying object. But it was no joke. After payment of workers in New York City at noon on a Saturday, the plant had been dismantled, put on trailer trucks, and moved to Coffeeville, Mississippi. Subsequently, a court order resulted in the machinery being trucked back to the Big Apple.

My next-door neighbor was a first-class economist, in sympathy with the state program of balancing agriculture with industry, even at the expense of workers just off the farm. It would not take long, MacDonald Horne maintained, before the docile, native laborers would learn to organize and take care of themselves. In the long run he was right.

In Washington for some historical research in the summer of 1942, I was first caught up in the feverish excitement of military activity. I wanted to participate. But I was called back to Oxford by our family physician who anticipated that my wife would have a miscarriage. Somewhat later I turned down a chance to join the ranks of historians in the service, in part because by then the Ole Miss campus was swarming with bright young men in uniform studying in the Army Student Training Program. The last time I felt the urge to "join up," a naval officer friend of mine recommended me highly to the admiral in charge of the U.S. Navy station in Algiers, across from New Orleans. The admiral told me that if I could pass the physical, he would assign me to the command of a gun crew on a freighter crossing the North Atlantic. I didn't make it. In the letdown which ensued, I signed up with the Red Cross, then advertising for volunteers, practically ignorant of what my duties would be. After indoctrination in Washington and Fort Benning, I was sent to the Pacific as an assistant field director. I was in the Marshall Islands when my planned tour was cut short by the explosion over Hiroshima. Still an assistant field director, I returned to Mississippi.

There were no blacks in the ASTP program at Ole Miss, though one Negro did participate in the naval V12 program. He later transferred to Morehouse College, with Mississippi authority either ignoring his existence or being unaware of his presence. It was my observation that at least in the Pacific blacks in uniform were still second-class citizens. In that racial paradise, the Hawaiian Islands, they were likely to be assigned to the heavy labor details. It also seemed to me that once black soldiers started visiting the USO centers, the whites stopped coming. The Red Cross was apparently as willing to assist blacks as whites; in fact a very large percentage of my clients were of the darker race. One black major I met in the Fifth Replacement Depot on the northern side of Oahu had been there for months playing the slot machines because no outfit wanted a Negro officer. Several nights on Engebe I witnessed Negro soldiers firing 90-millimeter cannon furiously at drone planes streaking across the sky. They had been told, they maintained, that when their ammunition was exhausted, they could go home. I suggested to a couple of Mississippi blacks that they should have saved much of their army pay (there being no place to spend it); the reply was in the negative because each week they gambled it away. Apparently they didn't consider the possibility of winning. I witnessed a decided color bias in the armed forces of World War II. I don't know how much or whether this affected me.

I have never been at ease with administrators, but a series of minor grievances brought me into a perpetual state of animosity toward Chancellor Benny Butts. I still think of him as a short man with great self-esteem. At the beginning of my second year I was forced to take a leave of absence without pay for hospitalization in St. Louis (my wife returned to her family in Montgomery), and when I returned I thought the chancellor had subtracted more than was due from my salary. Before he saw my point of view, I had to threaten to go over his head to the Board of Trustees. A year or so later the WPA houses on the campus were completed, and the administration was committed to renting them to faculty. At that time we were living in an old house on University Avenue next to the Catholic church. The chancellor called me to his office to explain that he had already decided to raise my salary $10 a month, which would almost make up the difference between my $25 rent and the higher fees for the government housing. So we moved to Faculty 6. Later the chancellor informed me that my raise would put my income slightly above that of an English professor whom he considered on a par with me, and therefore he would be forced to reduce my pay by $5 a month. It did not occur to him to allow both of us the $10 increments. Somewhat later as a gesture in the direction of bureaucratic patriotism I dreamed up the plan for High School Day, which became an annual affair under my chairmanship. Commendation for this establishment was later given to a vice-president—which I accepted as normal administrative procedure. During the war I relinquished the job, suggesting to the chancellor that from the beginning I had doubts as to the advisability of a state university enticing students to matriculate, especially as gasoline ration stamps were being consumed in considerable numbers. His reaction: "If you didn't believe in it, why did you do it in the first place?" He was bitterly opposed to my accepting $100 per tennis season from the Athletic Association, mumbling something about academic integrity, but I think it was mere convenience when he removed me from the Athletic Committee. In the spring of 1944 the chancellor and I came out of an exciting forum meeting in the Graduate Auditorium together. He had that day received a letter from his son at Yale who wrote favorably of hearing Norman Thomas. The chancellor wanted to know why we didn't invite Thomas to speak at Ole Miss. "Because you wouldn't let him come," I replied. Upon his disavowal, I succeeded in getting Thomas to agree to give up a Little Rock engagement so that he could make it to Oxford. Grateful, I went at once to the chancellor's office to announce my coup. Butts agreed that the socialist candidate could appear on the campus—provided, in the interest of fair play, I could also secure campaign dates for Franklin Roosevelt and Tom Dewey!

A source of enormous satisfaction to me was the Omicron Delta

Kappa (ODK)—Mortar Board forums which I helped to get started in 1940 and which are still flourishing more than forty years later. Initially, these were the best chance for a student from one of the smaller towns in Mississippi to become acquainted with world-famous statesmen. We were able to bring to the campus outstanding writers, politicians, laborites, business magnates, editors, and scholars, including Emil Ludwig, Edward Weeks, Alexander Kerensky, Virginius Dabney, Clement Atlee, Jacob Potofsky, Eric Sevareid, Gus Dyer, and Sir Oliver Franks. In the beginning, when we were strapped for cash, our student committee would write dozens of people in the hope of getting five or six each year. We were surprised to find how many leaders were curious about the state of Mississippi, and most of those who came from outside the South desired to see a Negro school, a cotton gin, and William Faulkner (or at least his home). Native Mississippians (Mark Ethridge, David Cohn) were enormously helpful, and we learned to depend on the British Embassy for one speaker each year. The stimulation for students who participated in the program was basically inestimable.

A year before its announcement at Harvard, Secretary of State Dean Acheson foreshadowed the Marshall Plan in a speech at the Delta Council spring meeting. Acheson's words in Mississippi were generally ignored by the national press in this country, until their significance was pointed out by Johnny Miller, U.S. correspondent for the London *Times,* home on vacation. Later that summer Dutch and I met John and Madeleine Miller, who happened to live next to friends of ours in Washington. As I did with other knowledgeable people, I invited Miller to come to Ole Miss to address an OKD–Mortar Board forum, and in the same trip he also spoke to the Delta Council. We drove the Millers over much of Mississippi, and we became good friends. It was through Johnny that I made the aquaintance of Nancy Balfour of the London *Economist.*

From 1951 to 1963 I published seven articles in *The Economist,* one of England's primary journals. I was delighted to get these assignments because they were headed "From a Correspondent in Mississippi." Therefore I could write as my conscience dictated, for the Mississippian who might read the *Economist* would hardly be the type involved in persecuting me. Except for an essay on American colleges, all of my articles dealt with the South, and most were specifically about events in Mississippi. Titles (assigned by the editorial staff) may give some idea of their content: "Legacies of the Civil War," "Little White Schoolhouse," "Mississippi Still Says 'Never,'" and "Where White Is Black." I leaned over backward in trying to tell a factual story, in part because I thought of myself as pro-British as well as pro-Mississippian.

After the war, the History Department created its own honors group, the Claiborne Society (later destroyed by a department chairman I had hired in 1946), which recognized achievement and sponsored a series of lectures by first-rate practitioners. Included among the historians who came to Ole Miss were Vann Woodward (Johns Hopkins), Arthur Link (Princeton), Frank Freidel (Harvard), William Hessetine (Wisconsin), Frank Owsley (Vanderbilt), Harry Williams (LSU), James Randall (Illinois), and Walter Webb (Texas), the very best that the academic world had to offer. Over the years the department was able to assist its own graduates to advanced work in the most important institutions because of these contacts.

Though Estelle Faulkner's daughter Victoria (Cho Cho) Franklin was in the first class I taught at Ole Miss in 1936, it was her friendship with Dutch that gave us access to William Faulkner's home, Rowan Oak. In those days Faulkner was an amorphous and to me an awesome figure, jealously protected by his family, and out of town most of the time. Little love was lost between the community and the Faulkner household whose members the community considered eccentric. Oxford's adulation of Faulkner was to come with the Nobel Prize.

I remember Bill Faulkner on the town square in a tattered shirt and torn khaki trousers, sometimes even barefoot. At home, however, he was the country squire, with elegant manners, particularly in the presence of family friends. He dressed in coat and tie for dinner, meticulously presented by Estelle, an aging belle but an agreeable and remarkable hostess because she liked people, I think. After the meal, at least when we were there, Bill usually retired to the library for pipe and brandy and small talk with Dutch, while his wife remained at the table, with me to keep her company. Faulkner

For Professor Silver

William Faulkner
2 April 1962

William Faulkner

had an obsession with Ole Miss baseball, and several times came by Faculty 6 for refreshment before or after football games. Dutch and I drove Cho Cho to the Oxford Hospital for the birth of her only child.

Weeks later Cho Cho was divorced. In China later with her father, she married again, this time to Bill Fielden, an able New Yorker who had gone to the Far East to make his fortune, subsequently setting up cigarette factories throughout the Third World. As war clouds gathered, Cho Cho and her young daughter returned to Oxford. The week before Pearl Harbor, Cho Cho and Dutch drove to California to meet Fielden, who was scheduled to arrive on the *Gripsholm*. During the war the Fieldens stayed in Oxford, and they became our close friends. One night the four of us were noisily consuming juleps concocted from brother Malcolm's grain alcohol, when Faulkner put an end to our loud talk by telling the only off-color story I ever heard from him. It concerned Tallulah Bankhead and was a beauty.

During the war there was a softball game on many a Sunday in the pasture to the west of Rowan Oak. There were few adept players around, so all ambulatory contestants were allowed to play, regardless of sex or age. Faulkner adored the kids, especially his daughter Jill's playmates. I suppose we kept score, but I really remember only that the two Bills (Faulkner and Fielden) pitched for opposing sides, with Dutch and me holding down first base. After the games Faulkner compensated the Fieldens and Silvers for weeding his "liberty" garden by telling them WPA stories. Though the country was fighting for its life, I now recall this period as the nostalgic good old days.

Malcolm (Buddy) Franklin (Estelle's son) joined the army, fought in Europe, and mailed to me a couple of books "liberated" in Germany. After the war he dropped into our campus home at all hours of the day and night, often with horror stories about his military experience and the happenings at Rowan Oak. One tableau had Faulkner lying on his bed drunk and naked, listening to a love letter haltingly read to him by a Negro servant, with Estelle coming into the room, taking the letter, and sitting on the bed's edge, dramatically rendering it for her husband. At the time we assumed that Malcom was telling the truth.

I think it was in 1947 that Maude Brown let me read her copy of

The Wishing Tree, which Faulkner had returned to her by mail. He had borrowed what she assumed was the original so that he could retype it for the young son of Phil and Emily Stone. I saw no reason to doubt her story that "Billy" in February 1929 had appeared at the Brown home on the campus, saying that he had written the fairy tale for her bedridden daughter, Margaret, who died shortly thereafter. With the approval of Mrs. Brown but without knowledge of legal ownership rights, I tried to sell the story to *McCall's,* but quickly ran into complications. Random House's Bennet Cerf corresponded with me and then with Faulkner. At the time I was shocked to hear of Bill's apparent disgust with an old friend because of her attempt to commercialize a gift to a child. Years later I learned that Faulkner had given the same story to Cho Cho in 1927 when he was courting her mother. My conclusion is that he simply did not want the three, or possibly four, recipients of *The Wishing Tree* to know that he had given it to others.

I was no more than an acquaintance of Faulkner until the local filming of *Intruder in the Dust* in the spring of 1949. He was often on the set as a technical adviser. In May there was a dinner party for the cast (Clarence Brown, Will Geer, Elizabeth Patterson, Porter Hall, Claude Jarman, among others) at the home of a retired army officer. I had gone to a history meeting in Jackson, and Dutch had agreed to leave and pick me up at 10 P.M. forty miles south of Oxford in Grenada, where the Illinois Central stopped. As the party warmed up, she told Bill that she was about to depart, and he immediately asked the local Trailways manager for a bus to transport the somewhat inebriated company "to meet Jim." The bus arrived, a bar was set up in its rear, and Faulkner declared he would ride in the front doorwell, blowing his foxhorn. With the bus partially loaded, the hostess Mary Evans suddenly begged the guests to come in for dinner; they did, and I missed my chance at early fame.

In the 1950s Malcolm and Cho Cho confided to us that they had intercepted a love letter to Faulkner from his mistress. They were concerned that their stepfather perhaps had plans to run off with her to Mexico, to desert their mother. Using a pane of glass with a light underneath, they had traced the letter to protect Estelle in case their fears materialized. The copy was to be used as evidence in court, but apparently the necessity for its being made public did not ensue. I never did see the letter.

As *Intruder* was being filmed, Faulkner and I began an extensive conversation about the civil rights crisis then warming up. Soon he was to receive the Nobel Prize, which resulted almost at once in invitations from the State Department to journey to the far corners of the globe as cultural representative of the United States. Though he despised the inroads of the federal government, Bill was a real patriot who accepted the ennui of visits to Japan, Greece, the Philippines, and South America as an obligation to his country. There is enormous controversy regarding his basic racial views, and much contrary evidence. I have believed for years that his being a superb observer of life around him in Mississippi enabled Faulkner in his great fiction to display an enormous sensitivity to the plight of blacks. But I also believe that in his international wanderings, Faulkner learned of an increasingly enlightened world opinion which he accepted and reflected. He was never a crusading activist and when he had spoken from what he must have seen as a bully pulpit, he kept relatively quiet. This may be the reason that his segregationist brother John could erroneously report, in *My Brother Bill,* that in his last years he had returned to the family's fundamentalist racial faith.

Dutch and I were invited to dinner at Rowan Oak when Dorothy Commins (widow of Saxe, Faulkner's editor at Random House) was the guest of honor. The night before she had given a piano concert at Fulton Chapel. At the dinner, she offered to try to secure a graduate scholarship for Malcom to study at Princeton. As talk became serious, I went out into the pantry to telephone an executive in the medical school in Jackson where Malcolm was then employed. I relayed to the diners the message that indeed Malcolm was not qualified for graduate work anywhere, that he was merely assisting professors in their research. A little later, Faulkner, at one end of the table, with Mrs. Commins to his right, began to reminisce about the early days of the family's occupancy of Rowan Oak. Bill stated unequivocally that Malcolm had been terrorized by his grandparents about life at the Faulkners', because the grandparents needed the money sent by Cornell Franklin for the upkeep of the two children. I was sitting next to Estelle and so was able to watch closely her response. She hung her head in silence, as if to agree with Bill's recital. It seemed to me that she was ashamed. This may have been a mistaken impression, however, because much later when writing me about another matter she acknowledged that she was a confirmed coward and simply could not respond to any aggressor. Whether his early years in Oxford had a direct influence on Malcolm's instability, I just don't know. Certainly, his sister, who was with her mother at Rowan Oak while Malcolm lived with the Oldhams, showed no evidence of abnormal development.

On occasion Bill Faulkner exercised demonstrably bad judgment in family complexities. As the patriarch he refused to give his blessing to the divorce of Malcolm and Gloria, perhaps thinking that this marriage could be saved, as had been his own with Estelle. (In their last years together he and Estelle were at least polite to each other.) Bill's decision only postponed the divorce of the young couple from a May session of court until that fall, causing Malcolm to lose half the investment in their home. He had already moved to Jackson to work in the medical school with Dr. Henry Tracy. Gloria married again only two days after the divorce was final. Malcolm was understandably upset when his mother and her sister, Dorothy Oldham, directed him, as a southern gentleman, to proceed to New Orleans and kill the new husband. Mrs. Tracy wrote Faulkner protesting the action of the two sisters. He replied that while he did not necessarily condone their letter writing, he was not a blood relative of Malcolm and therefore declined to interfere.

Some people believe that Faulkner inherited his artistic talent from his mother. At least she achieved in her later years a considerable reputation as a painter of landscapes and portraits. Because Miss Maud hoped to sell her canvases to a wider audience, she encouraged Dutch to do a piece about her, which *McCall's* would publish in October 1956. Faulkner was dead set against what he considered the exploitation of any member of his family. Thus it was with some haste and anxiety that my wife and Bill's cousin, with Miss Maud's prodding, rushed down to Rowan Oak to secure from over the mantel in the library her portrait of her famous son. It was to be used as an illustration in the magazine article. Fortunately, the painting was returned by the conspirators barely a half hour before Bill and Estelle drove in from Virginia.

I'm sure that in his last years, Faulkner made definite plans to move permanently to Virginia. He told me proudly at his home on Rugby Road in Charlottesville, "You know, Jim, I'm on the faculty here." He was impressed by the horse country, and at least secretly he was flattered by the attention that came to him as a local celebrity. He was not an accomplished horseman, but he surely excelled at judging and at handing out the cups and ribbons.

In the summer of 1961 I taught at the University of Virginia. That June my son and daughter left by plane from Boston, and in the same week, I caught the slow train at Michigan City, Tennessee, to ride the coach all night and most of the next day. To my amazement Bill and Estelle met me at the station in Charlottesville. At once he took my bag, about as big as he was, and carried it a few yards before I was able to take it away. After classes most days I walked out to the Faulkner home to have a drink with them. Their rather plain house was always open; I saw no sign of a library. Faulkner a time or two spoke disparagingly of his future biographer who always seemed to be present. One afternoon I was driven by the Faulkners out to the country place of Paul and Jill Summers for some barbecue; Bill and Estelle cherished them and their children. On the way back Bill mused sadly, "You know I've never seen Paul pick up a book."

My next memory concerns Malcolm Franklin, in combination with his mother. Malcolm entered my office in the Graduate Building shortly after Meredith's arrival at Ole Miss, and greeted me with "Jim, I hear you've made a damned fool of yourself." Already under considerable tension, I ordered him to leave. Later in the day, I drove down to Rowan Oak where I was sitting with Estelle on the east patio when Malcolm broke in again. He was still in an accusatory frame of mind, and I exploded once more. As usual, Estelle tried to ease a volatile situation, and in doing so, came up with this gem of an observation: "I just don't understand why *Mr.* Meredith wants to come in where he isn't wanted. It's just a question of good manners." (Shades of William Alexander Percy!) Surely very little of Faulkner's understanding had worn off on his wife of many years.

A year or so before on a mild autumnal day about Thanksgiving time, Dutch and I were having drinks on the same porch with Bill, Estelle, and Cho Cho when we heard a car pull into the west porte cochere and then a screen door slam. Quickly Malcolm emerged from the house. He was covered from head to foot with mud, but had a pleased grin on his face as he faced Bill. For some reason Faulkner stood up. Malcolm was obviously happy as he addressed his stepfather, "Pappy, I brought you a present." It was a turkey feather, a trophy of his hunting in the Delta. Faulkner smiled, reached out his arm and Malcolm, assuming Bill had taken the feather, let go of it. But Faulkner at that moment drew back his hand, and the feather fluttered to the floor. Malcolm was suddenly in a state of shock, and his mother and sister became tearful and flushed as they rushed into the house. Bill's demeanor turned grim, and in a few minutes Dutch and I left Rowan Oak. Never did I witness a crueler performance by Faulkner.

In the civil rights movement he spoke and wrote as a moderate who knew intimately his state and region, one who hoped to help Mississippi make its agonizing transition into the modern world. His special contribution included *Intruder in the Dust* (1948), its movie (1949), and many "letters to the editor" of local and national papers. In Memphis he spoke at a spectacular session of the Southern Historical Association (1955) and consented to have his words made a part of the pamphlet, *Three Views of the Segregation Decisions* (1956). Several meetings were held at Rowan Oak for the purpose of challenging the Citizens Council, and there the *Southern Reposure* was conceived (1956). Faulkner encouraged me throughout the 1950s, as he unquestionably did others, particularaly P. D. East. Often Bill traveled for his country, and occasionally he made what he thought of as the supreme sacrifice: he put up at Rowan Oak strangers recommended by Washington. Though essentially conservative, he plumped for a middle course in articles in *Ebony, Life,* and *Harper's*. I saw him one day throw into his waste basket a telegraphic communication from W. E. B. Du Bois, challenging him to a debate, another evidence that he considered himself neither activist nor extremist. At times he used bad judgment, as when he equated the Citizens Council and the NAACP. Faulkner saw Governor Coleman's political efforts as stemming the tide of reaction. All in all he was—perhaps justly—attacked by the radicals on either side. His chief desire was to have his state avoid the violence that later erupted with Meredith at Ole Miss. At the same time he understood that blacks would in time become completely integrated into American society.

While in Mississippi I continued to believe in my ability as a consummate poker player. I helped to organize a largely faculty group that met weekly for twenty years. One night when we were playing in George Carbone's upstairs flat, Faulkner joined us. His actions indicated that he thought of himself as an expert, especially as he snapped each card with professional zeal as he dealt the rounds of stud. He lost about thirty dollars. Later I ran into him in the Mansion Restaurant, where he suggested he'd like to get his money back. I agreed that he should have the opportunity and a game was arranged at Rowan Oak the following evening. The players all seemed eager, for most of them were unfamiliar with the Faulkner home. Next afternoon I called to see if the necessities of the game had been taken care of. Estelle answered the phone and called to Bill. He had forgotten our plans, was busily engaged, and begged off. I think that night we convened in Faculty 6.

Many of the anecdotes attributed to the famous are apocryphal. But I can vouch for the following about William Faulkner. In Charlottesville Estelle confirmed that Bill had said—when he learned of his invitation to the Kennedy White House for dinner with the Nobel laureates—that this was too far to go for a meal. I was at the table in Oxford when Bill was summoned to the phone by a call from Ed Murrow (ostensibly to arrange for an appearance on the "Person to Person" program). Somewhat disgruntled, he quietly folded his napkin, went to the pantry telephone, and said, "This is William Faulkner. I am at dinner. Good night." When Estelle fell by the wayside, Dutch pitched in to help carry out the plans for Jill's wedding. A year or so later she happened on the funeral of Estelle's mother, Mrs. Oldham. When she expressed sorrow about not knowing earlier of Mrs. Oldham's death, Faulkner remarked, "Don't worry, Miss Dutch, we just save you for weddings." Once when some of us were discussing the movie *The Bad Seed,* just seen in Oxford,

Faulkner opined, "It would make a great plot for 'Car 54, Where are you?' "

Martin Dain appeared in the Oxford area at all seasons over a period of three years, taking some 3500 pictures which he culled for use in *Faulkner's County: Yoknapatawpha.* He usually stayed with us at Faculty 6. In the beginning I doubted his capacity for public relations because he looked the part of an alien in Mississippi. Yet he obtained releases from all of his subjects. He and I were sitting in the Rowan Oak kitchen one afternoon, drinking coffee with Estelle, when we both noticed Bill meandering about outside. Martin looked at me and I looked at Estelle, who quickly signaled her consent to Dain's photographing her husband. He hurried outdoors where he snapped dozens of pictures, thus antagonizing Faulkner who asked him to stop. Dain returned to the kitchen, slightly depressed, and soon we took our leave. As we drove out through the cedars, Faulkner came up on one of his horses. I remember how imposing and majestic he looked, a slight man astride a huge animal. Bill apparently had second thoughts of his brusque treatment of my friend, for he asked us back to the house for drinks. Still a little miffed, we drove on to the campus. Two or three days later, I received a letter from Faulkner requesting that I make "Mr. Dane" aware that he did not have permission to use pictures he had taken of Faulkner, his family, his home and grounds, his animals, and his servants. I thought this a little much and so did not inform Dain of the letter until after the publication of his book.

On June 5, 1962, Dutch, Gail, and I left Oxford for Oregon, with an offer from Bill Fielden to rent Rowan Oak for ten years at $35 a month, heat included. Bill and Cho Cho had made arrangements with Pappy to buy the Faulkner home by paying some $22,000 to Jill. Fielden planned to retire in a decade, by which time he would have a small fortune. I was far from certain that I wanted to accept this generous offer, partly because of my love-hate relationship with Cho Cho. In any case, events determined otherwise. In early July Faulkner was dead, and all arrangements were off. Later, when I mentioned all this in my introduction to *The Closed Society,* the publisher wanted more proof than I chose to offer, and the statement was removed. I believe that Bill Faulkner was seldom motivated by economics alone, but in the late fifties, when we were sitting on the veranda of Rowan Oak, he confided that his estate would save $100,000 in inheritance taxes if he were to move his residence to Virginia. He probably would have been there by the time of Meredith's arrival at Ole Miss had he lived only a few more months.

There is no accounting for the genius of William Faulkner. I consider it a great privilege to have known him for a quarter century and, on the basis of a mutual pursuit of harmony for our state, intimately for a decade. I make no claim to an understanding of the man or the craft at which he was so skilled. He was able to transcend the heritage he had accepted. I am able to go along with the notion that aside from his production of some of the world's superior literature, he was not an extraordinary person. It seems to me, also, that his passionate pursuit of privacy may well have been the result of his nonacceptance by the reading public until his capture by the academics and by the exigencies of economic privation complicated by the pressures of household and community.

CHAPTER THREE

Controversy
(1945–1959)

Optimistic Moderate
(1945–1954)

In many ways my most satisfactory period at Ole Miss was between the years 1945 and 1954. As a thunderbolt from the blue, I was shifted from being a lonely professor in quest of another job to the chairmanship of a department, responsible for the hiring of all its members. After the war Bell Wiley and Joe Mathews had moved over to Emory and not only the head coach but also the chancellor had been dismissed. I was able to expand the history department gradually until when I voluntarily gave up the chairmanship a decade or so later, there were eleven members, nine of them full professors. They had earned their doctorates at top universities throughout the nation, no two from the same institution. The recently appointed chancellor was attractive, aggressive, seemingly liberal for Mississippi, with prospects of becoming an educational statesman. Perhaps most pleasing of all, a good many of us believed the state would continue to expand in wealth and wisdom, and would be able to reform itself to the point of making all its citizens first class. The new dean of the Law School recommended to the Board of Trustees that he be allowed to bring in a pair of cooperative Negroes to avoid the cost of setting up a court-imposed separate school for blacks. The editor of the *Mississippian* called for the admission of nonwhites to the student body, and for a day or so it seemed that the chancellor would agree to the forum committee's request that the head of the NAACP, a Negro dentist from Meridian, be allowed to state his case in Fulton Chapel. Faulkner's *Intruder in the Dust* was made into a movie, and Frank Smith was elected to Congress. I was given two leaves of absence, first as a Fulbright scholar to the University of Aberdeen in Scotland in 1949–1950, and two years later to be a Ford fellow at Harvard.

Due to my absence from the state, I did escape several of the traumatic racial incidents that plagued Mississippi. But I was intimately associated with the shocking treatment of Nathan Cohran, a black friend and fellow employee of the university. When *Intruder in the Dust* was being filmed in Oxford in 1949, Nathan was in the old city jail awaiting trial for attempted rape. MGM's public relations people were fearful that the movie mob scene might be transposed into a real-life lynching.

Nathan was truly one of the remarkable Mississippians I have met. The Silver family got acquainted with him when we moved into a dilapidated house on University Avenue at the edge of the campus. The rent was $25 a month, paid to Ole Miss. A magnificent specimen of a man, Nathan stood a few inches over six feet and weighed around two hundred pounds. When we took possession of Faculty 6, Willie Reynolds was the head electrician, plumber, and general handyman for university holdings, but we quickly learned to call Nathan when things went wrong with the furnace, the lights, the kitchen appliances, or the bathroom facilities. He was available (24 hours a day), competent, and something of a philosopher. Born at the right time and in the right place, Nathan would have been, I believed, an all-American football player and/or a Phi Beta Kappa.

By himself, Nathan moved a jungle gym out to our campus home. It was a singular physical feat. Later, for $25 he constructed a patio behind our house, along with a barbecue pit. The cost was small because all the materials were university owned. It must be understood that during the depression, when income barely covered survival needs, there developed a community spirit of live and let live, and almost a feeling that state property belonged to us all. (Back in 1912, the legislature had investigated a dean of one of the colleges for feeding dining-room slop to his own pigs.) When, for instance, I built at the beginning of World War II the strongest chicken house in America out of stadium lumber, I was merely transferring state property from one place to another. And when we left Mississippi, the patio, the barbecue pit, and the chicken house remained.

Meanwhile, Nathan Cohran had built up a thriving private plumbing business partnership with a white entrepreneur. They did well, in part, because a substantial proportion of their materials originated on the campus at no cost. The white artisan lived with his wife in a huge ramshackle building west of town, actually not far from Nathan's home. Some evenings after work Nathan drank beer with the couple in their kitchen. Jobs became scarce, forcing Nathan's partner to spend weeks at a time in Birmingham where he found work. With rather poor taste and certainly flouting the severest caste imperative, Nathan did not entirely stop his evening beer drinking in the white kitchen.

One Monday afternoon the woman, niece of a former sheriff, reported to her lawyer boss in Oxford that Nathan had tried to rape her the previous Saturday night. The black was arrested and soon lodged in the Holly Springs jail for safekeeping. His trial was scheduled early in 1949 in the Lafayette ("Yoknapatawpha") County courthouse.

Judge Taylor McElroy assigned a local lawyer to defend Nathan, but his effective counsel consisted of the volunteer services of two able faculty members of the Ole Miss law school. Bob Farley and Glenn Fant were of distinguished old-line Mississippi families, for whom *noblesse oblige* was part of their way of life. I collected money for Nathan's family and gathered character witnesses from among the community's soundest citizens, but both Farley and Fant affirmed that they would have to withdraw from the case if we brought in either the NAACP or the ACLU.

The scene was set for the trial; the courtroom was filling up when a conference was called in one of the chambers. Nathan's lawyers and the prosecuting attorneys were there. I was permitted to attend. The gist of the problem as presented to the accused was that if the emotional white woman were called to the stand to testify about the intimate details of the alleged crime, the community would be aroused to such a state of hysteria that Nathan's family would be endangered. They could not be protected from certain wrath and potential violence. The judge, not present, had agreed that if Nathan would plead guilty, he would be sentenced to three years in Parchman, and as soon as the furore ceased, he would receive a governor's pardon. Nathan continued to protest his innocence and, believing him, I hoped he would stand steadfast. But I could not encourage him to risk the lives of his wife and three children. Nathan finally did plead guilty, was sentenced to three years in prison, served every minute of his term, and after his release moved from the state. I never saw him again.

At the time I believed that Nathan had been terribly indiscreet, but innocent. I still do. It seemed to me that Nathan and the woman had indeed been drinking beer in her kitchen, and that when he departed around midnight she suspected (and agonized about it over the weekend) that her neighbors had witnessed the late departure of a black man from her home, with her husband away. I have not speculated further as to what did occur on that Saturday night, but I myself have agonized many times in the last thirty years over the horrible dilemma faced by Nathan Cohran in the spring of 1949.

Nineteen forty-nine turned out to be a vintage year for the Silver family because we not only watched the filming of *Intruder in the Dust,* but late that summer took off for our year in Britain. I knew, of course, that most Mississippi whites claimed Scottish ancestry, but I was not prepared for the wild beauty of the land nor for the poverty of her people. I'll never forget the luxurious green landscape on the train ride up to London nor the thrill I felt just to be in England and then in Scotland. Before leaving Mississippi I had made dozens of 35-millimeter slides of depression-era, unpainted farm houses with their dogtrots, but I was shocked at what the Scottish audiences saw in these pictures. Practically every sharecropper's cabin had beside it a shiny, old, stationary carcass of an automobile that brought howls of delight that people from Scotland had done so well. It is true that British cars were smaller, but the ones I saw at least were mobile. I remember an incident when I answered a question that in my opinion there remained as many Indians in America as when Columbus arrived. This brought a frown to the face of an

Dutch and Jim Silver in Aberdeen

eager young listener and later, when I inquired as to her
discomfiture, she exploded: "You are supposed to say the 'cooboys'
killed them all." Indian and cowboy pictures were popular all the
days of the week, but on Saturdays exclusively so. At the University
of Aberdeen I taught only one class and had to compete with the
British notion that nothing much had happened in America before
the Revolution and after the Civil War.

We lived on the former estate of Lord Aberdeen, still an elegant
residence which had become a second-rate boarding house. The
children adapted to the Scottish schools as soon as they put on their
uniforms, Bill (10) in the grammar school once attended by Lord
Byron, and Betty (6) in Girls High where she quickly fell into an
Aberdonian accent. All of us learned that national medicine was not
the scourge it had been depicted in Mississippi, and I was able to
make the acquaintance of a live Communist. I never did learn the
intricacies of long division in pounds, shillings, and pence, while Bill
and Betty discovered that their companions were likely to go all day
without once thinking of the USA. They began to comprehend that
some of the world's great thinkers were non-Anglo-Saxon, especially when they visited the homes of Marconi and Volta in Italy.

To force myself to do and see as much as possible, I wrote an
article each week about my new experiences, from going down into
a coal mine under the North Sea to touring factories in Italy with
George Carbone as my guide. Some forty of these were published in
various southern papers—from Richmond to New Orleans. In one of
these columns I remarked on the joy of listening to noncommercial
radio programs and called attention to the reading of Faulkner's "A
Rose for Emily" on the third program. The Ole Miss graduate who
edited the *Times-Picayune* responded belligerently, "When the
American public demands that 'A Rose for Emily' be read over the
air, you can be assured that the American advertisers will give it to
them." It seemed to me then as it does now that people in the old
country were more civilized than their blood relatives in the new—
and much less fearful of the Russians.

Many of my investigations in Britain were aimed at problems
unsolved in Mississippi. For instance, the propaganda mills at home
were filled with the notion that the British Empire had gone through

the ringer because of the socialization of its resources. So I decided to take a hard look at nationalized medicine and industry, the Labor government, the threat of Communism. I think I found out what, if anything, had forced the empire down the drain, why British coal productivity was considerably less than that in the United States, and why the people in Britain remained such good allies of my countrymen. I wrote about the functioning of Parliament and the views of medical practitioners; I added a few columns meant to be amusing: on travel in Europe, on distinctions between American and English language, and on the inroads of such U. S. institutions as Coca-Cola.

I think my favorite places in Scotland were the Aberdeen fish market, the Dee river with its jumping salmon, and the lovely port of Stonehaven and nearby Dunnator Castle. During the summer of 1950 we lived in Oxford with excursions into the English country-side and to Wales and Ireland. I'm not sure whether the year was more beneficial to me or my children in its expansion of southern horizons.

A year back in Mississippi and then the family took off for Cambridge; I had gotten a Ford fellowship to study economics at Harvard. About all I learned about the dismal science was that one could believe whatever he wished and find a leading authority for that point of view on the Harvard faculty. I was able to empathize with the feeling of William Alexander Percy that Boston is indeed the cultural center of the country. That thought must have become an integral part of our children's thinking because all three (even Gail, who was not yet born) chose that region for their college education. We were a little surprised to discover much New England prejudice against various ethnic groups, though while we were there one New Hampshire city chose a black man as town moderator. In my mind a year in Britain and another in New England were tremendous liberalizing influences on the thinking of the Silver family.

For a long time I have assumed that it is sheerest folly to return to the scenes of your childhood. The old places never look the same, friends have died or departed, imagination over the years has distorted one's perspective, and the net result is likely to be painful.

But on the trip home to Mississippi from Boston, we planned to cut through the White, Green, and Adirondack mountains to visit my sister in Watertown, New York. I suspected that her frugal Yankee husband would harass us on our way in a few days (as he did) and then the question arose as to whether we should take the children by the old home where I had lived the first dozen years of my life, the home which my father had built in 1908 at 527 Lexington Avenue, in the city of Rochester.

It never had been a great house nor an expensive one but a child does not remember or care about that sort of thing. When I visited it in the late thirties, it had looked incredibly small, run-down, and had definitely lacked one or more coats of paint. The old iron fence had been taken away, and the hedge had looked as though it had not been cared for in twenty years. Altogether it had been a depressing experience.

In any case it was decided that Billy and Betty should take a look at the house their grandfather had built and that their father had lived in for so long. On the way to Rochester we inspected casually Savannah, North Rose, Sodus Point, Clyde, and Cato, upstate towns my mother and father had grown up in. The nearer we got to Rochester, the less sure I was of the wisdom of visiting the old homestead. It must be in terrible shape by this time, I thought, and surely we didn't want our children to think that the grandfather they had never seen had constructed a sharecropper's cabin.

All this time, of course, I was thinking of the old home as I had known it. The well-kept yard with the clipped hedge, the lilac bushes in the side and back yards, and the summer house, the parlor seldom used except on Sundays or when company came, No. 34 school across the street. I could remember pulling on the gas lights and my dad in the dead of winter thawing out the pipes with newspaper torches, the front attic windows out of which my older brother Henry had jumped when Earl was chasing him, the Bell telephone which was useless when we wanted to call friends tied in with the Home system, the shop where I had once fallen on my head from a rickety trapeze, the cellar well stocked with preserves and jellies, and the Erie Canal three blocks away where I had learned to swim and to skate on ice—the normal sort of memories almost everyone has.

We crossed the Genesee River, drove through Maplewood Park, and now we were coming up Lexington Avenue, past the Catholic church and school—and then the house. I must have given a gasp of surprise and relief. For number 527 was as spic and span as it ever had been under the care of my mother—freshly painted (even with a touch of red and blue, but mostly white), the yard, hedge, and trees well mowed and clipped, brightly colored flowers and green bushes everywhere.

We got out of the car and were welcomed into the house by an elderly lady who immediately brought out milk and cokes and beer and all sorts of pastries she had made herself. She introduced her daughter and son-in-law and how many children I can't remember. In obvious pride she showed us through the house and in obvious pride I told my own children little things that had happened here and there.The house had changed hands several times in the thirty-two years since the Silvers had moved away. Fannie Storti, the present owner, came with her husband to this country from near Florence, Italy, a generation or so ago. The climax in the lives of these new Americans had been reached in the purchase of the house, something they had worked and saved for year after year. Now Mrs. Storti was carrying on and putting every dime she could earn working in the public schools of Rochester into her home. Evidently this was a kind of memorial to her husband (who died years ago) and an evidence of what industrious people in this country can achieve.

This may sound too nostalgic and sentimental, but you may see why I left Lexington Avenue that afternoon with the feeling that my own father would have been highly pleased if he had known that the home he had built so carefully and painstakingly was destined to fall into such capable and worthy hands.

The mark of a highly successful faculty is its publications and by this standard the Ole Miss history department must rate at the very summit. Its scholarly articles were legion and its books numbered in the dozens, some of them classics. The University of Mississippi has always been a stepping stone to more prestigious places in academe, for both students and professors. The Mississippi Historical Society and its magazine, *The Journal of Mississippi History,* were largely sustained by the Ole Miss department. In 1948 the Southern Historical Association met for the first and only time in Jackson, memorializing the one-hundredth anniversary of the opening of the state's university. In the period after World War II there were numerous educational innovations in our department, from team teaching (three professors joined to instruct in world events, and the entire faculty took over the class in historical criticism) to week-long excursions by graduate students for assignments in the state archives. The department also published an eleven-page bulletin governing regulations for requirements for the master's degree. Excellence was the standard and morale was high for students and professors, at least until the gathering crisis began to drive the latter away, usually to much higher salaries and to institutions of repute.

Call it nostalgia if you will, but I do believe both professors and students of the thirties, forties, and fifties possessed a purpose and discipline unmatched in the hysterical sixties and restless seventies. Let me tell you why. Starting out in the depression, we were hungry and eager. Class loads were heavy (one quarter I taught twenty-two hours) and there were all kinds of campus chores instructors were supposed to perform. There was little pressure to publish or perish, yet those who were or had been on the Ole Miss history faculty between 1935 and 1960 published close to one hundred hardbound books. It was a matter of self-discipline.

Three of these professors were elected to the presidency of the Southern Historical Association. Dave Potter presided over both the Organization for American Historians and the American Historical Association. Refugees from Ole Miss chaired history departments at Emory, West Virginia, Florida State, Georgia State, and Miami, edited the *Yale Review* and the *Journal of Southern History,* headed the Graduate School at Duke, and won innumerable fellowships (Fulbright, Ford, Guggenheim) and prizes (Anisfield-Wolfe award).

Though most Ole Miss teachers of history placed scholarship above indoctrination, like university professors everywhere they leaned in their philosophic convictions toward liberalism and enthusiastically supported programs of change. In Mississippi they were inclined to favor the New Deal, organized labor, and the elimination of racial injustice. Particularly in the period between the end of World War II and the desegregation decision of the Supreme Court, these men of goodwill were convinced that Mississippi could reform itself from within. They worked to that end. But after *Brown* v. *Board of Education,* with the increasing tension in the state, there was general speculation that massive resistance would lead to violent confrontation with the federal government. The department itself began to break up as its more prominent members departed for better jobs. Left behind were those few conservatives who were well adjusted to the intellectual climate, including one who designated himself as a "sentimental segregationist." As I look back, though, it seems to me that in the period from 1935 to 1960 the Ole Miss history department did help the people of Mississippi prepare for that inevitable social change that has since taken place.

Indigenous Negro leadership in Mississippi during the 1950s shocked most whites (when they found out about it) brought up to believe in inherent black inferiority. For instance, in 1954, a hundred blacks withstood the enticements of Governor Hugh White and House Speaker Walter Sillers. Negroes I came to know best—Aaron Henry, Medgar and Charles Evers, and James Meredith—had two things in common: economic independence and service in the U.S. armed forces. Brought up on a family-owned farm near Kosciusko, Meredith was unaware until he was fourteen that he was supposed to be inferior. A high school education (completed in St. Petersburg) and seven years in the Air Force, mostly in Japan, convinced him not only of his rights, but of his duty to do what he could toward freeing fellow blacks in his native state. Unquestionably, the outstanding Negro in Mississippi from World War II until the present, Aaron Henry has always been able to fall back on the security of his Fourth Street drugstore in Clarksdale.

An occasional Negro speaker, usually from Rust College in Holly Springs, came into Ole Miss social science classes during the war. Greenville opinion had already spoken in the case of a huge memorial commemorating those from Washington County killed in the war. Names of Negroes who had died in defense of their country were denied a place, and the subsequent brouhaha resulted in the memorial remaining blank. Oxford solved the problem in slightly better fashion. When the town fathers announced that a marker would go up on the courthouse lawn commemorating only the white dead, there were letters of protest to the *Oxford Eagle,* including one from William Faulkner. Today the heavy metal plaque is there on the courthouse grounds, listing the white dead at the top and those OF THE NEGRO RACE at the bottom. Separate and almost equal.

As might be expected, the student editor of the college paper leaned somewhat to the left, and editorially espoused the admission of blacks to Ole Miss. Despite almost universal denunciation, at least he was not expelled. His flaunting of the social mores brought a flood of protest letters, including a barely legible but lengthy one (now still in my possession) from an elderly Birmingham zealot who declared he had proof that once a white woman felt the glories of sexual association with a Negro, she would never return to her pale consort.

Sometime in the late fifties, I drove to Jackson with Episcopal priest Duncan Gray to attend a meeting at Tougaloo College. I was somewhat embarrassed when Aaron Henry hugged me in the presence of photographers, and still more so when Duncan called on me in the back of the auditorium where I was trying to be inconspicuous. Neither event escaped reporters from the *Clarion-Ledger.*

Quiet Reformer
(1954–1959)

Within two weeks of the 1954 Supreme Court desegration decision, I delivered the commencement speech at the Oxford Industrial School. Except for a handful of white patrons on the front row, the audience was all black. My main proposition that night was that *Brown* v. *Board of Education* constituted by far the most powerful event in the lives of those in the auditorium, but that none present would see drastic change. On the second count I was entirely wrong. After a few months of indecision, that summer the Citizens Council was born in the Delta and started the massive resistance that was supposed to prevent the implementation of the Supreme Court decision. Less than a dozen local citizens met several times in William Faulkner's home to forestall the violence that was soon to become the hallmark of Mississippi. We were right in believing that in our part of the state the council would develop neither leadership nor respectability but mistaken regarding the course politics would eventually take. In 1955 the people had the good sense to elect James P. Coleman, a governor who followed a moderate course in keeping the Citizens Council in check, but four years later turned the state over to Ross Barnett who inaugurated a confrontation of force with the federal government.

Among the high school graduates that soft night in 1954 was an enormous mechanic named Wade Ward who might well have been the prototype for Lucas Beauchamp in *Intruder in the Dust*. For years he had taken care of Faulkner's ancient Ford and my Plymouth, but it was only after we came to be close friends that I discovered what a marvelous rebel he was. In fact he was my introduction to a considerable number of blacks who were admirable in their willingness to risk all so that they and their children might have the joy of striving on an equal basis for the rewards of a competitive society. For example, Wade Ward had already begun writing letters to the President of the United States (protesting the conditions of black people in Mississippi) but with discretion enough to send them by way of a sister in St. Louis. Wade supplied much of my information about housing conditions among the poor blacks; once he pointed out a shack with the toilet in the kitchen, a spectacle I didn't have the fortitude to investigate myself. I bought a worn-out white Cadillac off a Memphis lot for $600 with Wade's assurance that he could fix it up and keep it running. He did just that and the auto kept to the highways until Indiana mechanics stopped it cold. Rumor had it that my elegant car was the gift of the NAACP. If this had been true, I surely would have been placed in the very lowest echelon of the civil rights hierarchy. When I was collecting information on Faulkner's life before I arrived in Mississippi, it was Wade Ward who gathered a half dozen or so of his black friends for an afternoon discussion of their association with the Nobel Prize winner. Wade was my eyes and ears into the black community. He was to be one of my mainstays until I left the state.

For the 1955 meeting of the Southern Historical Association at the Peabody Hotel in Memphis, I was in charge of the program. On my committee was John Hope Franklin, the leading black historian in

the country, chairman of the department at the University of
Chicago. Some years before I had attended (with some misgivings) a
social gathering of historians at Franklin's home in Washington,
where he taught at Howard University. Franklin worked hard on the
committee, but at the last minute decided not to come to Memphis,
stating that while he was pleased we had arranged for blacks to
attend the luncheons and dinners, they could not stay overnight at
the Peabody. His letter affected me greatly, for it poignantly stated
the possibility of a racial incident whenever he left the security of his
white friends. He was simply tired of running into brick walls. Years
later I was to travel from Tampa to Dallas to see John Hope Franklin
inaugurated as president of the Southern Historical Association.

Some of us agreed at breakfast the morning after Faulkner spoke
at the Peabody that his speech and those of Cecil Sims and Benjamin
Mays should be published. The following year the pamphlet, *Three
Views of the Desegregation Decision,* was released by the Southern
Regional Council. This was a moderate reply to those who had
become exhilarated at the acquittal on murder charges of the two
Mississippians who had acknowledged kidnapping Emmett Till. In
Mississippi I was accused of presiding at the "Faulkner meeting,"
which I could truthfully deny, as two ex-Mississippians—one the
head of the History Department at the University of Kentucky, the
other the president of the University of Louisville—were actually in
charge. Even the *Clarion-Ledger* did not say I was guilty of treason
simply because I attended the session.

The one practical result of the three or four meetings held at
Faulkner's home Rowan Oak was the publication of the only issue of
the *Southern Reposure.* This was an attempt to ridicule the forces of
reaction represented by the Citizens Council. The divisive influence
in the state became not the Negro (who was never mentioned) but
the Scotch-Irish (which implied most whites). The paper was to have
been printed at least quarterly, but because of the enormous
difficulty and expense, the amateurs who composed it fell back in
disarray after the first issue. Indeed, the *Southern Reposure* would
not have appeared at all had it not been for the indefatigable efforts
of P. D. East, publisher of the *Petal Paper* and author later of *The
Magnolia Jungle.* He wrote most of the copy, saw it through the

editorial process and printing, and was largely instrumental in the distribution of several thousand copies.

P. D. East has an important place in Mississippi journalism history because of his editing of the *Petal Paper* and the publication of *The Magnolia Jungle.* A man filled with anguish and uncertainty, East had taken over the ownership of the small newspaper in a suburb of Hattiesburg and within a year or so performed a remarkable feat by reducing the local subscription list to zero. In the middle fifties East was among the first to campaign boisterously against such right-wing organizations as the Klan and the burgeoning Citizens Council. Before long he became an irritant to most of official Mississippi. His increasingly sardonic front-page editorials became famous among those displeased with the state's bureaucratic rhetoric, especially the one of April 21, 1955, in which he made the case for changing Mississippi's symbol from the magnolia to the crawfish, and the full-page "Yes, You Too, Can Be SUPERIOR" attack of March 1956 on the Forrest County Citizens Council. Much of P. D.'s crusade was repetitious and amateurish but admirably adapted to the Mississippi climate. Shortly after the Supreme Court's decisions he began making regular trips to Oxford, mainly, I think, because he needed to get away from the tribulations of south Mississippi and because of his inordinate admiration for William Faulkner. He always stayed overnight at Faculty 6. As I mentioned before, he played the leading role by far in the publication of the *Southern Reposure,* that one-time document conceived in Faulkner's Rowan Oak to combat the rapid spread of racism in the state. East saw to the collection of materials for this castigation of the Citizens Council, wrote pieces to flesh out its six pages, and saw the paper through to printing with the help of Easton King of the *Pascagoula Chronicle.* Hundreds of copies he addressed to important people in the state, and the papers were trucked from Hattiesburg to Jackson early one morning for clandestine mailing. P. D. must not have been normally an early riser because he dropped them into a laundry collection receptacle and had to wait until the driver appeared hours later so that he could retrieve them and deposit them in a proper mailbox. I distributed a few hundred copies in the Ole Miss area and kept a couple of mailbags full hidden under our basement coal pile until we left the county. The venture cost us great effort and about $500 in cash, and the fact that no second issue ever saw the light of day convinced me that amateurs cannot sustain even the best of campaigns for long. In his autobiography, East wrote frankly about his own illegitimacy, using names of purported relatives which I assume were apocryphal. One amusing sidelight developed from his book, *The Magnolia Jungle*. East wrote of me as Josh Brass, which may have saved my neck, for when the book was published, I was in trouble with the authorities. Afterward, the principal biographer of Faulkner, dedicated researcher that he was, noted this reference and remarked that Faulkner, East, Josh Brass, *and* Jim Silver went sailing in the *Ring Dove* on Sardis Lake. At least it is true that East and Silver crewed for Faulkner, who after an interminable silence, asked, "Well, Mr. East, anybody put any dead cats on your front porch lately?" In his *Brother to a Dragonfly*, Will Campbell writes lovingly of P. D. East in his last days in south Alabama.

For years I believed in the academic leadership of Chancellor Williams. Perhaps I should have been forewarned regarding his conduct in crisis situations. In gratitude for the financial contributions to the university of Robert M. Carrier, who had made his fortune in Mississippi timber, Williams decided to have his biography written and asked me to do it. After deciding that Carrier had performed constructively in the organization of the lumber industry, I accepted. For the better part of a year I worked night and day on the project and had achieved a considerable rapport with him. But he was terminally ill, and in his last days became obsessed with the erroneous notion that I intended to "expose" his rumored complicity in a Sardis murder in his younger days. Without consulting me, he requested Williams to stop the enterprise, assuming that as head of the chain of command, the chancellor could give the order which would be obeyed. Williams called off the writing, at that time 90 percent complete. As I had been foolish enough to proceed without a formal contract, I felt I had no recourse except to comply. I published a couple of articles* from the material I had assembled, it is

---

*"Paul Bunyan Comes to Mississippi," *Journal of Mississippi History* (April 1957); "The Hardwood Producers Come of Age," *Journal of Southern History* (November 1957).

true, but the incident undoubtedly diminished my respect for the judgment of academic administration and may have influenced my later behavior.

Of the governors of Mississippi during my time at Ole Miss, I felt closest to James P. Coleman, a graduate of the university before my time. I was instrumental in bringing about a meeting of Coleman and Faulkner at Aubrey Seay's Mansion Restaurant because I knew of their mutual regard for each other. But the foundation for our friendship probably was my assembling materials for a speech entitled "The Origins of the Constitution of 1890" which Coleman made to the Mississippi Historical Society in February 1957 at the Eola Hotel in Natchez. I introduced him when he spoke. But it was in the fall of 1955 that I sent to governor-elect Coleman a clipping of an article advocating interposition by segregationist James J. Kilpatrick on the editorial page of a Richmond paper. As I remember it, he later asked me to gather documents on the historical folly of state interposition so that he could deliver a "special message" to the legislature shortly after his inaugural. He failed to do so and signed the law creating the Sovereignty Commission. While he was governor he kept his promise that he would hold the Citizens Council as well as the integrationists at bay. I had high hopes for Mississippi while Coleman was in the forefront of politics because I understood his great interest in history and his enthusiasm for the nationalism of Andrew Jackson. And I listened with sympathy to his son Tom who told me one Sunday night over coffee in the Student Grill that on the previous day Coleman had instructed Ross Barnett in the intricacies of the governor's office and had returned to his family at supper to lament over the governor-elect's lack of knowledge. My enthusiasm for J. P. Coleman cooled somewhat during the early sixties, perhaps because my views had changed. I noticed that after 1961 the ex-governor signed his letters to me "J. P. Coleman" instead of the more friendly "J. P." He was the judge assigned to head the federal panel in Greenville where I planned to testify in 1969. Then he greeted me most cordially. Ten years before, in 1959, when I was being attacked by alumni Hooker and White, Governor Coleman requested that he be informed if the Board of Trustees decided to

take action against me. I felt at the time that I had a friend in high
places.

In his compelling *Brother to a Dragonfly,* Will Campbell writes
vividly of the two years he served as university chaplain at Ole Miss
when, as he says, he took on the college administration, the state
legislature, and the mores of the South. I have since learned more
details of Will's confrontations, while recalling with gratitude that
the Campbells left the Silver children their homemade, steel-pipe
jungle gym when they moved away. But I see Will's single-
paragraph description of Carl Rowan's visit to our campus from a
perspective considerably different from his.

As I recall it, one morning in 1956, I got a call from Jackson saying
that a couple of reporters from the *Minneapolis Tribune* wanted to
stop at Ole Miss for some conversation on their way to Memphis. I
was delighted; I invited them to attend my night class in the library
and suggested that they stay overnight in the Alumni House. After
some hesitation, the fellow on the other end of the line said his
colleague was Carl Rowan, which was supposed to put me on guard
but told me nothing. I was then informed that Rowan was a Negro. I
stuttered that they should come on up anyway, thinking I could
work out something while they drove the 165 miles to Oxford. They
arrived at Faculty House 6 on the campus as Dutch's bridge party
was breaking up. The ladies were as astonished to meet a well-
dressed black man moving down the sidewalk as would have been
my next-door neighbor, Hugh Clegg, former assistant to J. Edgar
Hoover and then university Director of Development. It was one of
the campus jokes that Clegg had been housed in Faculty 5 so that he
could keep an eye on the radical Silver whom Campbell designated,
somewhat to my surprise, as the most liberal man on campus. In any
case, the situation seemed to require something more than just good
southern manners.

The problem was solved. The white reporter ate with my family
and went with me to the history class. *I did not dare to have Rowan
at our table or in the class.* Will and Brenda Campbell, who lived out
in town, provided the stranger with bed and board, as befitted their
uncomplicated Christian logic. After my class adjourned that night,

about half of the students went out to the Campbell home for discussion with the black man from the North. Such was the delicacy of communication between blacks and whites in the middle of the 1950s on the campus of Mississippi's leading university.

As we moved deeper into the fifties a considerable unease developed in the history department and among the faculty generally. Still, most campus leaders seemed to sit back to contemplate the brutality and futility of Mississippi's treatment of its minority population. The chancellor withdrew an invitation to an Ohio clergyman to speak at Religious Emphasis Week upon the discovery that he had donated prize money to the NAACP. The Board of Trustees required the listing of all organizations to which faculty members belonged. I was in the clear on this because I had never been much of a joiner, but a law professor was pilloried for being a member of the ACLU. But in the middle of February 1955, the board adopted a regulation that did affect me directly. All speakers invited to any state campus first had to be investigated and cleared by the head of the institution and their names filed with the executive secretary of the board. As I was involved with both the ODK forums and the Claiborne lectures, I was deeply troubled by this encroachment on free speech. At first I backed a resolution by the local AAUP denouncing the board action then out of caution phoned the chairman of that body, Oliver Emmerich of McComb. He strongly felt that his board had acted to forestall more serious controls imposed by the state's governing body. He had been informed by the governor of a crisis situation among those dedicated to the defense of the status quo in Mississippi and was instructed that if the board failed to take drastic steps to prevent subversive speakers from coming into the state, that he, Governor White, would himself "stir up" the legislature. As I recall it, Emmerich told me rather shamefacedly that the board had no plans to screen speakers beyond the vagaries of its resolution, that, indeed, the mandate would become a mere formality. Convinced that the university and other institutions were in good hands and probably overwhelmed with my own political wisdom, I took it upon myself to explain the situation to members of the AAUP, who proceeded to recall their resolution of censure. Later I was not at all sure I had done the right thing. Morton King, chairman of the Sociology Department, resigned, as did an instructor at Mississippi State. Faculty meetings were quite exciting in those days, with the chancellor always importuning us to wait for a later crisis before we determined "the ditch to die in." By the time I wrote my book in 1963, I was convinced that for Chancellor Williams that time would never come.

In 1957 Harris Warren left the history department to assume a chairmanship at Miami University in Ohio. During the first semester of the following year while convalescing from a severe bout with pneumonia, I became convinced that it was downright silly to spend so much time on paper work in the department. So I quit the chairmanship, perhaps just in time, because the controversy already was swirling over our heads. For massive resistance in Mississippi had by this time led to the murder of at least a dozen blacks, whose only crime consisted of attempting to change the voting patterns of their fellow beings. It was unquestionably this indecent treatment of 40 percent of the state's people that caused my own slow radicalization.

It must have been inevitable that sooner or later there would be differences between my changing beliefs and those of some of the state's citizenry, especially as we moved into the period of emotional controversy. My feelings about the New Deal, for instance, had once brought the accusation before the Board of Trustees that I was following the Communist line, and again in 1949–1950 when I was sending back commentaries from Britain somewhat favorable to nationalized medicine and industry, the same charge was pressed in the state legislature.

The most absurd and therefore the most easily refuted charges emanated from two super patriots, politicians who were graduates of Ole Miss, one a member of the Mississippi House and the other an ex-representative. These accusations were finally put into writing, at the request of the board, in November 1958. I must say at the outset that the board acted with equanimity and justice all through the controversy. It did not violate its own rules. Through the educational hierarchy I was apprised of the charges and in March and April 1959, I answered them in memoranda to Dean A. B. Lewis.

Finally that August when I was away from the state in a summer teaching assignment, the trustees expressed confidence in the administration of Chancellor Williams and found that the accusations were "without foundation in fact." The matter would have ended there had not the accusers decided to take their charges to the press. The editor of one Jackson paper demanded that I be fired while another expressed satisfaction with the board's position. United Press International requested a statement from me, but when I referred the manager to the board the whole affair faded into dormancy.

In view of my later history, the substance of the charges may be of interest. First came a list of "keystone principles" of Mississippi civilization: (1) a belief in God, the accuracy of the Bible, and the possession of immortal souls, (2) the sovereignty of the state and its reserved powers, (3) "the inalienable right to preserve the identity of the white race," and (4) the right to "profitably engage in private enterprise." My accusers probably did not see their last point as a state guaranty against failure in business. Subversion was deduced from certain statements attributed to me—I was a Socialist and didn't care who knew it; I was an integrationist; I had acted in collusion with Faulkner when he condemned the South for segregation; Mississippi was a backward state and should "rejoin the Union"; Clennon King, a Negro, should be allowed to register for doctorate work—not given—at Ole Miss; Confederate generals were "numbskulls" (some were in reality very low people); and that Dr. Silver "loves labor unions and curses the South for the War of Independence." Added too was my education at Vanderbilt, "well known for its integration sentiments." Somewhat later another allegation states that a master's thesis written under my direction "defames the internal government of the people of Mississippi during the period of the Civil War. This thesis could well be the fruit of Dr. Silver's lecture." Sure enough.

The board may have been impressed by the truth that while attending the state university from 1931 to 1934 (before I arrived), one of my accusers had received four A's in physical education and in the social sciences two grades of C, five of D, and one F. My main point here however is that the board had followed its rules, had

required the charges in writing, had gone through channels to the
university administration which also acted with integrity in securing
my written responses; without a great deal of publicity the whole
matter was disposed of. When the politicians tried to make further
capital from these accusations, there was little response. The board
and the administration had acted responsibly.

One result of the increasing tension in Mississippi was that I made
a conscious effort to get away each June. I was fortunate in being
offered summer jobs at Emory, Harvard, Missouri, Virginia, Port-
land State, Emory again, and finally Rutgers. So, during many of the
more dramatic moments, I wasn't even in the state. These academic
excursions probably reinforced my basic beliefs. During this period
I was working steadily on what I considered my own major historical study of the formation of southern public opinion. At Ole Miss I
had long since added a course called The Rise of Southern Nationalism (pre–Civil War) to my Recent American History. The various
chairmen who invited me for summer instruction seemed to assume
that any Mississippi history teacher would be primarily concerned
with his state and region, and thus I was always asked to give
courses in southern history. It is not difficult to imagine my anguish
in the summer of 1961 (I was teaching at the University of Virginia)
when I learned that the editor of the recently published *The Southerner as American* (containing articles by friends of mine) had been
jailed as a freedom rider in Jackson, Mississippi.

Betty, Dutch, Bill, and Jim Silver, 1950

CHAPTER FOUR

Paper Radical

(1959–1965)

Now come my most strenuous, exciting—and last—years in Mississippi.* My academic career reached its peak as the civil rights crusade shifted into high gear. I edited one volume of *Mississippi in the Confederacy*. In charge of the Fifth Annual Conference on the Civil War at Gettysburg College, I wrote for the introductory session a paper, "The Tragedy of Southern Leadership, 1820–1860." I worked for Frank Smith in his unsuccessful bid for reelection to Congress. I befriended James Meredith as a student at Ole Miss.* I was elected vice-president of the Southern Historical Association and succeeded to the presidency in 1962. For my presidential address a year later I wrote "Mississippi: The Closed Society" and developed it into a book of the same name. Thus my contest with the political leadership of Mississippi and my confrontation with the Board of Trustees of the Institutions of Higher Learning came to a climax. Last, I transferred to the faculty of the University of Notre Dame.

For two years I contributed all my spare time to the collection of materials for a project sponsored by the Department of Archives and History. In 1961 the Louisiana State University Press published

---

*I had originally planned to write about the dramatic events of Meredith's arrival at Ole Miss and what happened while he was there. But this important history has been well covered in Meredith's own *Three Years in Mississippi*, in Russell Barrett's *Integration at Ole Miss*, and in Walter Lord's *The Past that Would Not Die*. Moreover, there are contemporary accounts in the letters published in *The Closed Society*. Also, countless other books and articles have touched on the racial revolution in Mississippi in the sixties. So this account is limited to some of my own history and rather personal thoughts.

Mississippi in the Confederacy: As Seen in Retrospect, which comprised what I thought were the very best pieces written since 1865 about the state during the Civil War. The book was a magnificent publication containing lavish illustrations but with one colossal defect. There was little in it about the black man and nothing written by him. It was as though the majority of people in Mississippi throughout history had never existed. Certainly no one reading the volume would understand the causes of the war nor realize the roles played by Negroes in it. And so it is all the more difficult to understand the inquiry of the chairman of the Senate Finance Committee, Russell Fox. He asked the state archivist, "Why did you let Jim Silver do it?" Obviously, ignorance played a large part in this centennial memorial to Mississippi in the Confederacy. I have since wondered what excuses the forty-four white historians have to offer for their two-volume *History of Mississippi* published by the University and College Press long after the civil rights revolution supposedly had been won. Perhaps in time blacks will pay enough taxes to get their share of the glory.

There are usually preliminaries to any main bout. Among the chores of the Mississippi Sovereignty Commission was the dispatching of articulate natives to convince outlanders of the sanity of the state's culture. Judge Sebe Dale once suggested, for instance, "There is no ill feeling between the races in Mississippi." The Commission also brought into the state such speakers as Myers Lowman, executive secretary of the Circuit Riders of Cincinnati and a person widely known for his attacks on leftists. The Board of Christian Social Concerns of the North Mississippi Conference of the Methodist Church complained to the Sovereignty Commission about its sponsorship of a Lowman speaking tour, calling it a violation of the separation of church and state. In any case, Lowman spoke in Fulton Chapel on the Ole Miss campus late in February 1961, awarding the university a clean bill of health but listing Hodding Carter, Jr. and other Mississippians as Communists. I said nothing that night, but Lowman was given a hard time by students in the question period, and a few days later he included me among his Reds. On March 3, I was scheduled to speak to the Mississippi Historical Society and used about half my time to attack Lowman

Gail Silver

and inferentially his sponsor, the Sovereignty Commission. I finished thus: "Mississippi has been a minority group in a nation largely controlled by liberal officials. I would suggest that for one hundred and thirty years logically minded Mississippians have been asking for protection of their minority rights, but through people like Myers Lowman we have at the same time denied the rights of minorities and minority opinions." I also suggested that there were cycles in writing history, and that Mississippi was virtually closed in 1961 to unorthodox ideas concerning the Civil War: "If historians [Bettersworth, McCain, for example] were to write today what they wrote twenty years ago, they would be in trouble." Mississippi's society was closed. Certainly, a series of minor incidents over the years must have convinced some people that indeed I was a Communist. It was not the first time I had been called one and it would not be the last.

Toward the end of the spring semester of 1961 I was invited by Will Campbell to go with a small group to Washington to talk with Burke Marshall and John Doar in the Justice Department. We were questioned about the future in Mississippi when James Meredith surely would win his way through the courts and be admitted to Ole Miss. As I remember it, we met for most of one day, agreeing that a show of force would be sufficient to get Meredith registered. Little did any of us suspect the violence that would erupt when he finally made it nor did we anticipate the intransigence of the Barnett regime. It is possible, even probable, that if Meredith had not been forced to make his long run through the courts, we might have avoided that last-ditch resistance.

At the University of Virginia in the summer of 1961 I was handed a copy of Carleton Putnam's *Race and Reason*. I studied the book quite seriously, only to conclude that it made a false case for existing racism. So I was not surprised that fall when Putnam was brought to Jackson as the principal speaker at a "Race and Reason" rally sponsored by Governor Barnett and the Citizens Council. Putnam questioned Mississippi's emphasis on states' rights as a defense of her customs and suggested she turn instead to his assurance that blacks were biologically inferior. I could see little evidence that the people of the state accepted his message or that they had even read his book. They simply recommended that others study the volume before passing it on. Thus the Putnam craze proved to be only a transitory phenomenon.

On the ninety-eighth anniversary of Lincoln's most famous address, I read a long paper to the Fifth Annual Civil War Conference at Gettysburg College. My subject was "The Tragedy of Southern Leadership, 1820–1860." It was later suggested to me (by Bell Wiley, once chairman of the department at Ole Miss, who had also spoken at Gettysburg) that I use this paper as my presidential address to the Southern Historical Association. At the time of delivery, I did not have enough confidence in its contents to have it published. Still, the *Jackson Daily News* quoted an Associated Press excerpt from the talk: "In the thirty years before the Civil War the South was victimized by its own authoritarian special pleading. Most tragic of all, the southern creed became fixed, static, an article of faith to be accepted, not examined." A *Washington Star* headline, "South's Secession Laid to Thought Control," brought a phone call from I. F. Stone. On the way back to Mississippi I had lunch with him in the nation's capital, and he requested permission to print my speech in his popular weekly. Duly cautious, I answered that it was already in the public domain, that he could do as he wished, but that if it were published, I would encounter strong opposition in Mississippi which might well result in my being fired. Stone agreed that this was reason enough for him to put aside his idea. Years later I had my only other meeting with him, at another luncheon in Washington, in which we congratulated each other on his earlier forbearance, which may well have helped the writing of *The Closed Society* in the first place. At least the Gettysburg speech brought to my mind the fact that in a hundred years Mississippi leaders had not learned to avoid tragedy for their people.

Between April 1961 and September 1963, I published twenty-two pieces on the Civil War in the monthly *New Mexico Electric News*, edited by Carl Turner, a friend of mine and graduate of the Ole Miss Law School. Two decades later, I still approve of them. (I am reminded that it was Chancellor Alfred Hume who came to my rescue in the days when the Mississippi Historical Commission was erecting markers throughout the state. He insisted that we call it the *Civil War* instead of the *War between the States* because that is what it was. Also, the shorter name used up less of the limited space on the markers.)

I wrote these articles because I had been reading about the Civil War since high school days and considered myself something of an expert on the Southern Confederacy. Also, I was delighted in this period to have a steady extra income of twenty-five dollars each month. As the essays came from the class notes as well as from off the top of my head, they imposed no great intrusion on my time and were fun to do.

During the heyday of Mississippi controversy, a Jackson columnist ventured the prophecy that anyone who challenged the community's values would come to no good end. On occasion I felt that various tensions were driving me to fulfillment of this gentleman's hopes and expectations. As I became more and more angry at my state's response to the blacks' demand for greater participation in the electoral process, the pressures became increasingly frightening. Officially the Mississippi bureaucracy insisted that potential dissidents go along with the prevailing wisdom, or at least keep their mouths shut. This became more and more difficult to do as Mississippi ferociously resisted change. I had studied enough history to know that exactly a century before, those people on the verge of becoming exceedingly well off developed a passion for unanimity of thinking and that this had contributed to the secession of Mississippi. Likewise, in the 1950s, there was a tendency among those busily accumulating riches to turn the problems of government over to such as the Citizens Council or perhaps the Klan. In both instances there came an overpowering demand for conformity within the white ranks. As time went on, it became more difficult for me to go along even with the University administration, whose main purpose seemed to be to avoid trouble. Partly to ease the chancellor's problems, I secured a leave of absence to teach at Notre Dame in 1964, and after a stint in the Ole Miss summer school in 1965 became a permanent member of the Notre Dame faculty.

Mississippi lost a seat in the House of Representatives as a result of the census of 1960, and there is little doubt that the legislature under the leadership of Speaker Walter Sillers decided to use this occasion to drive Frank Smith from Congress. Lafayette County was placed in the new First District, resulting in the only downright political activity of my life. I was warned informally of a threat by Sillers that the university would lose a million dollars in state appropriations if faculty members held an organization meeting for Smith on the campus. So we held it in the Oxford City Hall instead. At least I learned from this campaign about the manipulation of poll-tax payments by various county commissioners. I was told, too, that Jamie Whitten, Smith's opponent, had been spreading the rumor in the Delta that Smith had appointed the "son of that Communist, Jim Silver" to be a page in the House when, as a matter of fact, the appointment had come from Whitten himself and had been extended by a month in the Senate by John Stennis. Despite our amateurish campaign, Whitten won overwhelmingly, as directed by the political powers in Jackson.

On June 5, 1962, Dutch and I voted for Frank Smith, drank coffee in the Mansion Restaurant with Bill and Estelle Faulkner, and left about noon to drive (with Gail) to Oregon where I was to teach that summer. When we left plans were still up in the air about the purchase of Rowan Oak by William and Victoria (Estelle's daughter) Fielden. The couple had approached us about renting the place. Then all negotiations were ended with the startling news over the radio one morning early in July that William Faulkner had died. I wired Estelle that I would return to Oxford at once if I could be of help, not realizing that his funeral would be turned into a circus by a curious world. The businessmen on the square in Oxford even closed their doors for fifteen minutes as the funeral cortege was passing by on the way to St. Peters Cemetery. I am just as pleased that I was not there to witness such a display.

While in Cambridge in the spring of 1952, I had a lengthy conversation with John F. Kennedy about his possible visit to Mississippi to speak at an Ole Miss forum. I had even written him a long letter suggesting he would be foolhardy to challenge Henry Cabot Lodge for his seat in the U.S. Senate. (Lodge was an admirable senator and no one could beat him in Massachusetts anyway.) Still, when the time came I had so little faith in President Kennedy that I really believed that Meredith might well be registered by force in the university one day and transferred to another college, perhaps Harvard, in a matter of hours. Such was my disillusion regarding the promises of politicians that I looked for sinister motivation behind the public facade of principle. From the standpoint of a more-or-less idealistic college professor, however, I must admit that by and large the Kennedys did no wrong in the Meredith crisis.

I had been concerned for a long time with the formation of public opinion in the Confederacy, and so I requested a leave of absence for 1962–1963; I wanted to expand my talk, "The Tragedy of Southern Leadership," into a book. That year the Social Science Research Council paid my salary. The chancellor seemed a little miffed when it became evident that I intended to spend my leave on the campus. In the fall, of course, James Meredith presented himself at Ole Miss. And instead of a volume on the Confederate States of America, I wrote the speech on Mississippi as a closed society.

I have been asked at times how I happened to write and publish *Mississippi: The Closed Society*. Even though I have never solicited a job (except the first one in Kansas) and have not campaigned in any way for office, I was elected vice-president of the Southern Historical Association and succeeded to the presidency; the only real duty I had was to make a speech in Asheville in the fall of 1963. At that time I was immersed in details of the formation of public opinion in the South and contemplated using my Gettysburg talk. Then I considered drawing a comparison between two Mississippi governors, John Pettus and Ross Barnett, elected exactly a century apart, each dealing with state and civil rights, and rather badly. They brought violence, death, and failure. But with the Meredith crisis, I was shocked to hear undergraduate hoodlums equate themselves to Hungarian freedom fighters and to watch practically all state agencies—and some brought into existence for this express purpose—undertake studied campaigns to distort the truth about the entrance of Meredith into Ole Miss. Their purpose was to convince state and country that the Kennedys were responsible for a preconceived attack on Mississippi and that the marshalls caused the insurrection at Ole Miss when in fact they were victims of that violence. The case against the marshalls was analogous to that of a woman blamed for rape because she had asked for it by wearing flimsy apparel. It almost seemed that the people of Mississippi were in desperate need of being assured of the innocence of their leaders and that the federal government would be whipped if they were so convinced. I had already been amazed when friends of mine in the university administration had sworn to false testimony in federal court about the existence of segregation at Ole Miss.

Thus I undertook to relate the facts as I knew them in my speech to the association. First I went to Miami Beach a month after the riot to tell the historians in an impromptu session what had happened. Then I spent a year gathering information and made an agreement with Ira Harkey, owner of the *Pascagoula Chronicle,* to publish the speech in his paper and in pamphlet form. In the summer of 1963 while teaching at Emory University in Atlanta, I began assembling my information and learned that Harkey had sold his business. That summer I visited the office of the Southern Regional Council (SRC), whose executive director, Leslie Dunbar, agreed to print and distribute my paper. Later, after he had seen a copy of the first draft, he made a self-denying suggestion that a pamphlet would have little effect as compared with the impact that the speech—expanded into a book—might have. The gathered material came to about a hundred long pages which the SRC duplicated and which I sent to some twenty-five experts in and out of Mississippi for correction and suggestion. I realized at the time that one false statement would be pounced upon to discredit the whole work. Bill Goodman, an editor from Harcourt, Brace and World, signed me to a book contract in Asheville. After I had given the speech, Les Dunbar came to Oxford for three days of consultation on dividing the manuscript into appropriate chapters, and I worked feverishly the next four months to expand it into the book. Goodman was of inestimable help, particularly in convincing me that someone not acquainted with Mississippi, say in Peoria or Council Bluffs, would read the volume and therefore its contents must be made simple and understandable. *Mississippi: The Closed Society* was completed in February and published the third week in June 1964, the day after the disappearance of the three civil rights workers in Neshoba County.

In the fall of 1962, Bill was home in Faculty 6, between his graduation from college and induction into the army. He had done some local radio work while still in high school, and thus it was natural for him to join Richard Valeriani of NBC during the Ole Miss crisis. That first night he requisitioned all my dimes, to be used in calling the radio post Valeriani had set up in an Oxford motel. As with most reportage by national news services, the story was told with great objectivity. Still, Bill's connection with the reporting may have been the origin of rumors that he was in the employment of the FBI or army intelligence, that indeed he was a spy. One afternoon in November he could not be found, and none of the usual agencies in the local network could locate him. His mother was frantic. After several hours we discovered him in the most protected place in Mississippi, in Meredith's Baxter Hall room. After the television crew pulled out of town, Bill worked as a stringer for NBC. He would observe events on campus, return home, write his story, and call it in to the network in New York City. Depending on the urgency of news at the time, his reports would be heard on radio "from our correspondent in Mississippi." One night he and I witnessed the slashing of tires on an army jeep in front of the cafeteria. We noticed that the chancellor was also an observer and that he did nothing to stop the violence. Bill went home to send in his report which we heard on the 9 P.M. news. We both expected that next morning I would be called on the carpet for his temerity in reporting what we had both seen. There was no repercussion. The only real precaution Bill took that I can recall was his decision not to attend a football game in Jackson when he was warned against it by army intelligence.

One evening six of us crowded into my ancient Oldsmobile to drive over to Clarksdale to visit with Aaron Henry. We saw both of his Fourth Street Drugstore windows smashed with the bricks still inside—with their displays of the Declaration of Independence and the Emancipation Proclamation. We repaired to the Henry home where, as it turned out, all the visitors made an effort to stay out of range of the living-room picture windows. I know that I consciously visualized the possibility of a missile coming my way. Every hour or so we could see and hear what Henry described as the customary rounds of the local police. About ten that night we were served a late supper, perhaps the first time I had ever eaten in a black man's home in Mississippi. We called Oxford just before leaving, and really expected to be stopped on our way home. When we were almost there, Bill said, "You know, I've been told over and over that 'they' are out to get us. I'm not sure that 'they' even exist." Several weeks later I sent to Bill, by that time safely training under live ammunition at Fort Benning, a clipping from the front page of the *Commercial Appeal,* headed by a picture of the living-room window of the room where we had sat, smashed in. The Henry home had been firebombed, and severely damaged, by night riders. Across the top of the news story, I wrote, "They don't exist—but . . . ." At least at the time I felt that Bill was safe in the good hands of the United States Army.

One profound experience during the Meredith crisis I subsequently used in my classes to explain the nature of historical evidence. On the night of the riot I frequently returned to my home at Faculty 6, and I happened to be there to receive a call from Eric Sevareid just before 9 P.M. On returning to the scene of disturbance,

James Silver (far left) and two other Ole Miss faculty members join James Meredith in the cafeteria.

I noticed a small group listening attentively to a stranger perched on the hood of a small car which proved to be a Nash. He had on a sweat shirt with the name BRUCE printed over the chest and wore a built-up shoe as befitted a person with a club foot. In his harangue to the onlookers he declared he was from Georgia where he had been involved in every "right, right wing movement" since the days of Roosevelt (whom he excoriated) and that he had driven from his home in Decatur to help Old Ross in his fight with the feds. Still, I was shocked to see him hand what he identified as a 30.06 rifle to an apparent colleague who had emerged from the darkness behind the Y building. The man had requested a weapon to be used against the marshalls. At this I urged a friend of mine to make mental notes of everything from the license number to a description of agitator and car. Only then did I recall having seen the same peculiar vehicle going toward Oxford some two hours earlier and its return later. As I remembered it, the auto had been parked between the Y and the (old) Library; the driver emerged, opened the trunk, lifted out a heavy five-gallon can, and lugged it awkwardly toward the crowd in front of the Lyceum Building. Some time later several cars were set on fire in the Circle Road, aided, I assumed, by the gasoline from the can. The next morning I took my story to federal agents in the Lyceum, who had already picked up Melvin Bruce.

The following summer the "agitator from Decatur" was tried in federal court in Oxford for aiding and abetting an insurrection. I was called from Atlanta to testify under oath in the trial. First, I went over my evidence carefully with the U.S. attorney handling the prosecution. On the stand I recalled my story in the most straightforward way possible. Defending Bruce was J. B. Stoner, founder of the National States' Rights Party and publisher of its paper called the *Thunderbolt*. He led me through my testimony without apparent animosity, with considerable emphasis on my seeing Bruce return to the campus with what I assumed to be gasoline. After my appearance on the stand I was dismissed but allowed to return to the courtroom when the lawyers summarized the evidence. Stoner calmly stated that I could not possibly have seen Bruce stop his car, open the trunk, and remove the gasoline, as the automobile, a 1957 Nash, *had no trunk*. I was dumbfounded but searched out Bruce's car, parked outside the federal building, and Stoner's description was correct.

I tried then and afterward to discover the cause of my substantial error. As Stoner claimed, I had lied. This is my explanation: I had reconstructed the event after the fact, to the best of my ability. Bruce had parked his car near a streetlight, but my vision was obscured by clouds of tear-gas smoke from the Circle in front of the Lyceum. He had gotten out of his car on the left side, had gone around its rear where a spare tire gave me the illusion of an open trunk, and had come to the right side whence he took out the heavy can. The facts, I still believe, were essentially correct, but as the *Thunderbolt* later proclaimed in headlines, the professor had lied in federal court under oath. So much for the reliability of sworn testimony. Bruce was acquitted, as he would have been in any case by a jury looking for excuses to set him free.

College teachers seem naturally to be less aggressive and domineering than, let us say, their counterparts in business or politics. The very fact that able men and women on the Ole Miss faculty opted for quiet and scholarly lives did not mean that they lacked intensive feelings about the treatment of blacks in Mississippi and particularly the official acts of the state concerning the admission of Meredith. I was privy to some of their beliefs and actions, and now I feel I can list the names of some who have left Mississippi. Robert Rands, Washington native and Harvard PhD, professor of anthropology for ten years at Ole Miss, was one such man. In the fall of 1962 he came into my office to talk about what he might do to counteract some of the mythology dispensed as truth in Mississippi. From our conversation came six articles scientifically destroying Carleton Putnam's *Race and Reason;* I arranged for their publication in Ira Harkey's *Pascagoula Chronicle* in January 1963.

Statements by my graduate students and my association with him convinced me that William Willis was the very best teacher at Ole Miss. Native of Mississippi, graduate of Mississippi College with a PhD in classics from Yale, Willis was unquestionably the faculty leader of committees that often held the chancellor's feet to the fire. His wife, also from Meridian and an activist in cultural activities, was as determined as he to dedicate their lives to the advancement of knowledge in Mississippi. When they and their daughters moved to Duke University, Ole Miss lost its first academic family.

Frank Howard was an instructor in economics who took to eating in public with Meredith and who wrote brilliant letters to the editor, one of which appeared anonymously in *The Closed Society*. William P. Murphy, a native of Memphis with a law degree from Virginia and a doctorate from Yale, was hounded through most of the 1950s because he would not tailor his classes in constitutional law to meet the desires of extremists in the legal profession and in the legislature. After several forced leaves of absence, he became professor of law at the University of North Carolina, and in 1967 published his authoritative study of state sovereignty, the Founding Fathers, and the making of the Constitution, entitled *Triumph of Nationalism*. He wrote a seven-page paper for me, "On Reading the Constitution in the Closed Society," which appeared without his name in my book.

I had intended to request essays on the influence of race in ancient history and specifically in the Bible by well-known Mississippi authorities (Bill Willis and Duncan Gray) to counteract the propaganda put out by the likes of Brady and Eastland, but these projects fell by the wayside in the rush of writing and publishing my book. Many incidents of harassment came to my attention in Mississippi; one such occurred after a professor of science who at least partly because of his fundamentalist faith had invited Meredith to dinner. Somewhat later his small daughter received her Christmas present at a school drawing; it was a black doll with "nigger lover" emblazoned on it. The most courageous of the academics who risked their professional careers were the native Mississippians who decided to stay on at Ole Miss, many of whom protested the lack of civility in their state in daring ways. I have no intention of presenting names, although I would like to tell the world about these fine people who have continued in their quest to make Mississippi safe for all its citizens.

After nine months of excitement on the campus with Meredith, I took off for Atlanta and the repose of summer teaching at Emory. It didn't turn out quite that way. My first encounter—literally—was with a mass rally of the Citizens Council honoring Mississippi's Governor Barnett. I had never before or since witnessed such bedlam as when he marched down the aisle. He was cheered to the rafters with every step and every racist exhortation. The platform in that overcrowded auditorium was occupied by a dozen extremists, the least of whom sat there apologetically, barely tolerated as a kind of recording secretary. Lester Maddox was already basking in local sunshine coming from his Pickrick Restaurant advertisements that featured fried chicken for white patrons and ax handles for blacks audacious enough to contemplate eating there. A Chinese student from my class was driven away by cigar smoke constantly blown into his face by spirited defenders of Caucasian supremacy. Altogether I kept a subdued profile while comprehending that the Mississippi mania had spread abroad.

The summer session was hardly under way when I was asked to speak to an all-university group on the year's turmoil in Mississippi. I did my best to lay out before a large and responsive audience a calm and judicious picture. Some heckling came from a small band gathered around my "agitator from Decatur," then under indictment for his participation in the Ole Miss insurrection. (It was later that summer that I returned to Oxford to testify against him.) The most articulate of my detractors proved to be a local anesthesiologist, who subsequently attended several of my classes, motivated by curiosity as to what kind of radical I was. He soon quit coming, possibly out of boredom. The prime results, at least of my performance, were a few uncomplimentary telephone calls and the apprehension that filled my mind the following week when I drove up to a Ku Klux Klan rally in the country outside Athens.

At the time it seemed wise to fill my 1957 white Cadillac with six strapping men for the venture into Klan territory. My son Bill went along, as well as Karl Fleming, then southern reporter for *Newsweek*. Outside of Athens, we were misdirected from one place to another, until we finally came upon a kind of armed camp miles into the woods at a rural white frame church, surrounded in spotlights and milling people. As we parked, my vehicle was at once closed in by old cars and pick-ups with their gun racks so that escape would have been unlikely. But the palace guards, taking notice of my

Lafayette license tag, assumed we were emissaries from and defenders of the Mississippi faith. Luckily they were not newspaper buffs, as the Atlanta papers had carried my speech at Emory. So we were accepted as brethren in the cause of white supremacy. The area was aglow with light and the remnants of dinner were on the grounds and the air was filled with bitter language pouring out of loudspeakers. I particularly remember conversing with a grandmotherly woman with a small sleeping boy on her lap, both dressed in extravagant satin costumes, topped with pointed hoods. While still outside the church we heard an appeal "to smash pushy but chicken-hearted niggers," but the minute we entered, the language became restrained. The entire ceremony reminded me of a fraternity recruitment, directed by the head Klansman from Atlanta trying to set up a new chapter. Recognizing Fleming, he stopped mid-sentence to ask, "Karl, did you bring your equipment?" It was obvious from the reference to recording devices that the speaker was fully aware of modern media relations, that the Klan was, as Fleming later pointed out, emulating the public procedures of Martin Luther King. Volunteers were called—who would the next day fill the restaurants of Athens, order glasses of water only, and out-sit the anticipated black "sit-inners." Their listless response helped me to understand the miserable plight of Klan organizers, already defeated by the summer of 1963. After a rather friendly discussion with the leaders, we returned unscathed to Atlanta.

All that summer there was daily activity. One afternoon I went out to see first-hand an integrated playground. The swimming area was closed, but black and white children were obviously having a happy time pushing themselves into exhaustion on a wooden merry-go-round. Couples swinging together seemed to have little notion of racial animosity, at least until an ancient Chevrolet screeched to a stop, and an irate, voluble mother emerged to snatch up her young blonde child from such camaraderie.

My twenty-year-old daughter went through Atlanta en route from Washington to Jackson where she worked in the state archives uncovering data for John Doar's Justice Department. As Betty stayed by herself in a Mississippi motel, we were somewhat apprehensive for her safety. Later we learned that her only irritation came from being interrupted in her task by a man who tapped her on the shoul-

der and said, "I hear you're going to marry a nigger." Would that all
harassment had been so gentle.

In August came an invitation to address a training group of SNCC
partisans on the campus of Atlanta University. By then I had written
exactly sixteen pages of my prospective speech to the Southern
Historical Association and I figured this would be an auspicious
occasion to try them out. So I drove out to the campus after supper,
finding my mixed audience still playing softball in the evening glow.
Finally, shirtless men and women in shorts came in from the warm
athletic field, I presumed to listen to my words of wisdom. But each
time I girded myself for oratory as I thought my introduction immi-
nent, someone in the back of the room would start up another
chorus of "We Shall Overcome." When I did get up to speak, I had
long since despaired of reading even the Gospel to such a wildly
demonstrative audience, and so I made a few remarks regarding
what I thought I had learned in Mississippi. A question period
brought pertinent inquiries, including one about whether there was
any way "they" (Bill's "enemy") could get to me. Without much
thought, I answered that I certainly was vulnerable through my nine-
year-old daughter. Immediately, a large black shouted at me the
impossible question: "Ya mean ya wouldn't sacrifice your daughter
for the cause?" My reaction was somewhat emotional, to the effect
that I wouldn't sacrifice Gail for all the Negroes in America, and I
may have added Africa to boot. The room temperature dropped to
the point of refrigeration, and I was later told that occasionally
thereafter I was referred to as "Uncle Tom Silver." When I had
calmed down, I realized that Negroes had sacrificed, unwillingly,
their daughters for two centuries, but I'm afraid the episode only
added to my perplexity as to how to get along with blacks.

The most pleasant experience of the summer came when Bill and I
spoke for a couple of hours with Benjamin Mays in his office at
Morehouse College, and later were treated to an extended lunch by
Ralph McGill. On our way back to the Emory campus, Bill remarked, musing over the elegant manners of our hosts, "I feel I've
been in the presence of two southern gentlemen."

For the first years at Ole Miss I had allergy problems that one
February took me to St. Louis for treatment. Thenceforth I had to

go to the university cafeteria to pick up nonallergy foods, and in the basement kitchens I met some magnificent blacks, the chief cooks and butchers. Aubrey Seay, the manager, and I became fast friends. Later he was dismissed from his job (a common occurrence in Mississippi) so he bought a hamburger emporium in Oxford, which eventually he turned into the Mansion Restaurant. He and his new wife Martha worked exceedingly hard, with Mrs. Seay toiling half of many nights to produce home-made pies, but their success came mainly from the influx of soldiers to the campus during World War II. In any case the Seays prospered, so that he was able to purchase a superior fishing boat. For years Aubrey and I pursued the crappie in Sardis Lake. In the 1950s George Carbone and I drove over to the Mansion for our 10 P.M. coffee two or three times a week. A member of the history faculty, George was a flamboyant extrovert who primed our bull sessions. One night, after the racial controversy had heated up, Aubrey told me with considerable trepidation that he had been warned that my presence was hurting business. I laughed. A week later he repeated the admonition and I stalked out of the restaurant, never again to return or speak to the proprietor. Our long friendship had become a casualty of the internal strife in Mississippi. Later I was told by a mutual friend that Aubrey was grieving over our loss of contact. I agreed to make a gesture of reconciliation, but I regret to say that I never did get around to it. After I left Oxford, the Mansion burned, and still later Aubrey died. I shall always believe that I allowed a minor altercation to develop into a real personal tragedy.

But see p. 75

My entire life had unquestionably been a preparation for my "Mississippi: The Closed Society" speech in 1963. I devoted almost an entire year to the collection of materials for my most ambitious undertaking. I wrote to knowledgeable people for their ideas on what made Mississippi unique, and now, some twenty years later, I have just reread thirty-eight responses received in July and August 1963. Twenty-four correspondents were natives of Mississippi, sixteen were then living in the state, and twenty had resided there at one time. I had turned to the higher ranks of the academic world, sixteen historians, four professors of English, one of economics, and seven college administrators responding. An even dozen lawyers, half born in Mississippi and half practicing in the state, and only three professors of law, were among my contributors. There were three Mississippi businessmen and three editors. One professor in the Ole Miss medical school wrote me. Sixteen of my correspondents had written books, a few of national distinction. All of these people seemed to take my inquiry most seriously, and only four were antagonistic toward what they considered my approach to the subject. As in the case of letters addressed to me after the speech and subsequent to the publication of the book of the same title, an astonishing proportion of those who had been born or had lived in Mississippi professed an abiding love and feeling of responsibility for the state, although none who had left Mississippi indicated a willingness to return. A breakdown of the responses as to the causes of Mississippi's uniqueness may serve no purpose though more than half mentioned the state's history and lack of leadership in politics, education, and the press. Next came the poverty and ruralness of Mississippi, as well as the large percentage of blacks (more than half of the state's people were Negro for a century after 1830). Fear, isolation, and religious fundamentalism completed the list. The earnestness of my respondents was evident. Perhaps the most thorough statement came from a Millsaps historian who had moved on to become a dean of the graduate school in a North Carolina university. Each person was inclined to emphasize his own specialty and very few questioned my views which had resulted in large part from thirty years of study, observation, and historical orientation.

For months which slowly turned into years I was fearful of reprisals which would surely follow my taking a public stand on the racial issues in Mississippi (I was accused of biting the hand that fed me, of selling out to the Communists, of general stupidity, of being a "nigger lover," of betraying my white heritage, and so on). Though I put in some very uneasy moments, nothing of physical violence occurred and as I look back, I sometimes wonder whether my apprehensions were justified. Probably so; maybe my caution paid off. On my daily walks, usually out toward Sardis Lake, I was accompanied by Gail's German shepherd named Rex who looked much fiercer than he acted. At least on the early morning of the riot when the rioters were being driven between our house and that of Evelyn Way, there is no evidence that Rex woke up. He was with me another time when I was crossing on foot the bridge over the Hilgard Cut through which Illinois Central freight trains ran, when a car came to a screeching halt, and the driver screamed at me, "You nigger-loving son of a bitch," and as rapidly drove off. My family quickly adjusted to obscene and threatening telephone calls, especially in the early morning hours, soon learning that the phone volume could be turned down so that the ringing in the kitchen could not be heard in the bedrooms. Once, about supper-time, I received a nasty call from a husky-voiced man who claimed he wanted to destroy me. I arranged for a meeting in the Student Union Building, where I knew there would be numerous witnesses who might not take mayhem lightly, but my caller failed to show up.

I was accustomed to playing the old campus golf course by myself, usually hitting three balls in the round. On the long third hole one day, after driving the balls, I noticed a truck sticking out of the woods on the left, some two hundred yards from the tee. I knew there was no road in the area and quickly surmised that the occupants of the vehicle were out to harm me. Still, I could not bring myself to retreat to the clubhouse (and lose my balls), so with considerable unease I grasped my nine iron and pulled my cart up even with the truck. Then I used my brassie to blast each of the balls, with my back to the intruders. Nothing happened, except that I sweated a bit. I concluded that my assumed attackers were a couple of college students out drinking a little beer.

One noon my wife rushed into my office in the Graduate Building to say that in the Dean of Women's office (where she worked) there had come information from spies in the state capital that three carloads of men had left Jackson earlier with the blessing of the governor who was heard to say that he would close the university "after the bloodshed." I realized that part of that blood might well be mine. Dutch wanted me to get out of town. Instead, I bought an enormous flashlight and a dozen shells for the shotgun we kept in Faculty 6. We invited friends in for an evening party. Professor Fortenberry brought a rifle but forgot the cartridges, while Karl Fleming of *Newsweek* thought he recognized the sound of open mufflers from the cars of the invaders. Altogether we had a hilarious time, with a little tension running through it. After midnight when our guests departed, I could not sleep. Our house was on a dead-end circle, with the rear unapproachable because of a deep drop-off (and Rex in the basement). So I arranged, in case of a commotion, to stand with my shotgun in the front bathtub—where I would be protected by the wall up to my shoulders—while my wife was to shine the light on potential intruders from the living room. It's just as well there was no invasion as Dutch might have been sacrificed behind the torch.

I saw to it that whenever I traveled by car, there was usually another passenger and always a loaded gun. Often I worked in my office on the ground floor, where anyone could have approached the screened windows on either side of my typewriter, until one or two in the morning. Then I walked home through the silent campus, but I cannot remember even once being accosted except by one of the night police. On a Saturday evening when six or seven of us were playing our weekly poker in Bob Farley's home on the campus, he got a call about midnight ostensibly from Clarksdale made by a fellow who claimed he was on his way over to shoot the law dean. Farley answered in his usual unflappable manner that he hoped the caller would get there in time for the refreshments. We were unconcerned that evening probably because of numbers, and perhaps I should have been at ease all through this trying period, but I considered discretion the better part of valor. Gail never really understood why we wouldn't let her ride her bike to grammar school in Oxford. One night, after the admission of Meredith, I was assigned as part of a faculty patrol to keep peace in the area of the men's dormitories. In the dark I was soon surrounded by a group of menacing "students" who kept prodding me with nasty questions as they tightened their ring around me. I felt rather certain that evening that I was saved from violence by the presence of a friend standing a little distance away, dressed with a coat and tie which most assuredly pointed him out as a member of the secret service. At least that was the beginning and end of my participation in policing the campus.

I received many critical letters while Meredith was a student at

Ole Miss. Women who wrote were likely to be more gentle in their denunciation than angry and frustrated men, less apt to use foul language and obscenities. The wife of a high state official in the early days of the conflict stated with controlled fury: "Our state has been invaded, our rights violated, and our honor tread upon all for a DECREE of the courts forced on us by illegal action. I would suggest that you go to one of the other states you are so much in sympathy with and where you will be appreciated. I am sure there would be no weeping and wailing at your departure." An occasional letter came addressed to "Fort Meredith." The envelopes of some were decorated with such slogans as AMERICA AWAKE, BROTHERHOOD BY BAYONET and MAILED IN OCCUPIED MISSISSIPPI, and a few included HONORARY NIGGER cards. Letters from blacks were few but occasionally noteworthy as one from Jackson shortly after the admission of Meredith: "If more white people like you could be heard with the expressive attitude of truth giving justice and righteousness regardless of old custom but obeying law and order, this good earth would be the place where the Lord's Prayer is referred to when it says 'Thy Kingdom Come.' Thank you again, and we are praying for you." (These letters may be found in my correspondence filed in the Ole Miss Archives.)

On the morning after the assassination of Medgar Evers (June 12, 1963), I came across a statement an emotional Meredith had released to the press. I found him in a class at the University High School and got him to delete the following words in time for them to be omitted from the wire reports: "If I were charged with the responsibility of finding Medgar Evers' killer, I would look first and last among the ranks of law officers of this state. The chances are at least 100 to 1 that there is where the killer is to be found."

On November 6, 1963, Gail rode with her mother and me to Asheville where I was to speak at the meeting of the Southern Historical Association. The other two children came from Washington and Boston. Before the speech was delivered I had gone over it with Claude Sitton, the southern reporter for the *New York Times,* to select what I considered the most important paragraphs, thus assuring a front-page story the next day. At the head table I refused to begin the address until a television camera was removed, because I

"Verse" in men's restroom, Lafayette County Courthouse

simply could not risk its effect on my presentation. At one point I
came up with a blank page in the talk, but this caused no interruption
as a mimeographed one was quickly supplied by my wife who was
silently reading along with me. Afterward I did talk with reporters
for a few minutes, but the next day I escaped by taking a tour of the
Vanderbilt Biltmore estate. At the end of the address there was a
standing ovation for a few minutes by all in the dining hall except
those at one table from Mississippi Southern. The dinner session of
the association I had arranged in Memphis when William Faulkner
and Benjamin Mays had spoken had elicited a similar response.
When we drove back to Oxford a few days later, I made sure there
was not a bottle of liquor in my car for I anticipated our being
stopped by the state highway patrol shortly after we entered Mississippi. Nothing happened. Accounts of the talk were minimal in the
state and local press. At a meeting of the executive committee of the
Mississippi Historical Society, I was told, William D. McCain recommended a vote of censure, which failed passage when it was
found that no one present had read the speech. A year before he had
requested approval by the same group for my election to the presidency of the Southern Historical Association.

Betty Silver and Chris Little were married in the Oxford Episcopal Church during the Christmas week of 1963. The graceful antebellum church which appeared in the opening scenes of MGM's
Intruder in the Dust has long seemed to my fantasy mind as the
proper setting for the 1838 wedding of Thomas Sutpen and Ellen
Coldfield. I realize this would have been impossible historically for a
number of reasons, but I can easily visualize Sutpen and his bride
emerging from that church to the unsavory barrage of decayed fruit
and vegetables thrown by local hoodlums. Perhaps I rewrite *Absalom, Absalom!* because at the 1963 wedding I fully expected pick-
eting, if not mudslinging. The newlyweds had embraced the civil
rights movement, and the presiding priest had long championed
equality for blacks. But there was no demonstration as the folks
moved to the campus for the reception.

In the crowded days after World War II, Jane Herring had lived in
Faculty 6 while an Ole Miss student. Here she was courted by a

handsome medical practitioner named McLarty. Even after their marriage, Chester often came to the Silver home for surcease from his heavy labors. One day when I was bound for my office he cautioned me, probably in jest, about returning with James Meredith. I answered with some venom. Whatever the circumstances, this incident seemed to drive a chilly wedge into our previously close relationship, except when we spoke rather formally in our accidental meetings for coffee at Leslie's Drugstore.

But with the approaching wedding, Jane (who never let the tense Mississippi climate interfere with her love for the Silver family) asked that the McLartys be allowed to host the rehearsal dinner. On that occasion, dozens of friends with whom relations had grown cold indeed forgot their sociological hostility, and we all made merry in the camaraderie of a southern small town. This joyous Christmas (Christian?) fellowship lasted almost till the New Year.

Fifteen years after the wedding Betty and Chris came back to Mississippi for the first time, along with Tim (10) and Meg (7). The Little entourage followed by a month or so a similar nostalgic pilgrimage by Bill and his wife Terry, traveling from their home in the Virgin Islands. Brother and sister made certain their sentimental journeys to the community of their birth included lengthy reunions with Thera Jones, Chester and Jane McLarty, and Bob and Alice Farley.

Bob Farley had sustained me—as did Bill Faulkner—in my slow change of attitude regarding Mississippi's leadership in the 1950s. When I felt isolated and somewhat fearful of antagonizing those who ran the state, Bob convinced me that he knew people in every town who thought as I did. And Bill made it known to me in a multitude of ways that he agreed pretty much with my convictions. Both pointed to a moderate course that would have avoided the later excesses of the Barnett regime.

Bob was an exuberant fellow, the only person I've ever known who might be patted on the back by a victim he had just called a "son-of-a-bitch." He earned the intense allegiance of the faculty of the Ole Miss law school because of his own loyalty to his professors. He was the life of every party, and often I observed the anticipation of those who had arrived early as they waited patiently for Bob and

Bob Farley, dean of the Ole Miss law school from 1946 to 1963

Alice. As far as I know, he was not a scholar, yet he was often in demand as a speaker to legal associations throughout the country. In the Mississippi tradition, Bob was a fine story teller, not technically but, as observed by David Cohn, simply because he seemed to enjoy himself extravagantly. In those days we relaxed on many a fish fry, usually at Sardis Lake, where Bob was high priest in the boiling of coffee, in the singing, and in marvelous friendship.

Bob and Alice moved into university housing across the gully from Faculty 6. Shortly thereafter, Bob's hunting dog killed one of my chickens. Feeling abused, I phoned him and at once he asked that I meet him between the two houses. He appeared with his dog and a baseball bat. Handing it to me he said, "Here, take this and kill the damned dog." Of course I couldn't do it, and Farley and Silver became fast friends.

We did a lot of fishing together. It has always seemed reasonable to me that two rods would result in twice as many crappie on the stringer as one. One day, with Bob in the other end of the boat displaying a single pole, I tried three. As anyone might guess, all four baits were struck at once, and in the resulting confusion, the boat nearly swamped. Totally exasperated, Bob sat with an unusual calmness and finally observed, "Jim, do you realize how lucky you are?" Innocently, I queried, "Why, Bob?" "Because you are the only bastard in the world who will never have to go fishing with Jim Silver."

Bob was as selfless a man as I have ever known. We had been trying to find a fish one winter day when the lake was down and the Tallahatchie no more than a trickle. Toward evening we came into the landing where our car was parked, and heard voices back up the stump-infested river. Bob insisted that we wait and finally a couple of bedraggled carpenters from Tennessee made it to our fire in the dark. They were lost, having left their vehicle on the north side of what was left of the lake. Farley brought them to Oxford, got Alice to feed them supper, and then called me to see if I would accompany them back to their car. A little ashamed, I went along as Bob drove the aliens fifteen miles more by way of Abbeville to their convey-ance. Farley knew no strangers.

Another time on the swirling Tallahatchie, we stopped for an hour

while Bob untangled a black man's fishing line caught on a bush in
the stream. This incident reminded me that I had heard long before
that when Bob served as Oxford's youngest mayor, he worked hard
as a laborer in the construction of the local Rosenwald black school.

Because Bob Farley had earned his doctorate in law at Yale, he
must have had a serious side, but my memory brings back only
whimsical actions. Though the law faculty was the envy of all of us
regular professors because of their higher salaries, Bob had a considerable talent for the distribution of his excess cash at poker sessions and other charities. But he was in earnest on the race question,
as his distinguished ancestors must have been, realizing that blacks
had always gotten a raw deal in this country. When he became sixty-
five, instead of following the normal course of stepping down as
dean of the law school and continuing to teach, Bob Farley went
quietly by simple resignation. Chancellor Williams let him go. But
for several years into retirement, he taught classes in law at the
University of Florida. He said he needed the money to purchase a
tractor for his little farm outside Oxford.

There was never any ill feeling on the part of the Farleys. I must
admit that what really impressed me about him was the fact that his
two grandfathers were killed in the Civil War. As dean of the Ole
Miss law school, he had been one of the two or three state lawyers
who had constantly warned that sooner or later even Mississippians
would have to obey the decisions of the Supreme Court. Thus, he
lost many friends (whom the Farleys had in abundance). I saw one
letter from the wife of a Delta couple who declared their longtime
relationship was then and there severed. If she or her husband were
ever to run into Bob on the streets, they would cut him dead. After
this classic denunciation of their formal mutual regard, the letter
writer signed her name and added a postscript, "Please give our love
to Alice."

Having completed the manscript for my book, I agreed to speak
on the situation in Mississippi at Southwestern College in Memphis
in the spring of 1964. A week or so before I drove to Tennessee, a
request had come from the secretary of the Board of Trustees for my
appearance before a special committee of the board the morning

after my Memphis date. My decision was to keep both engagements. Before my speech that evening I attended a faculty party and afterward a reception for the audience. In the question period I was asked about Aaron Henry, head of the Mississippi NAACP, and without any real thought, I answered that he might well be the greatest man in the state. That night I reached Oxford between one and two in the morning, and a few hours later I began the long drive to Jackson. At 9 A.M. I was ready for the subcommittee meeting at the Woolfolk State Building. M. M. Roberts of Hattiesburg was its chairman, and after some flattering words, he said, "Professor Silver, we have decided to drop the charges against you if you will agree to stop speaking about Mississippi outside the state." This was my first awareness of what turned out to be the accusation of "contumacious conduct." I was flabbergasted. After a half hour or so of more talk, mainly by the chairman, I quietly told Roberts that I disagreed with his assumptions and would make no promises. His manner immediately changed to one of hostility. The board member (H. E. Carpenter) sitting to my left excused himself and when he returned he carried the early green edition of the *Jackson Daily News*. At once he called my attention to the front-page quote from my previous night's interrogation, the statement about Aaron Henry. "Did you say that?" he asked not unkindly. I started to tell him the circumstances of the remark but quickly said simply, "Yes." At once his demeanor let me know that for all time I had lost his vote in the committee. About noon the meeting came to an end, with Roberts stating that I would hear in writing the consensus of the committee. So I drove back to Oxford, tired but sure that what I would learn boded little good for me at the University of Mississippi.

The communication promised by Roberts proved to be the most pretentious I have ever received. A four-page letter signed by E. R. Jobe, secretary of the board, was posted on April 27, 1964. It requested that I appear before a subcommittee (M. M. Roberts, H. E. Carpenter, and Tally D. Riddell) to state under oath "such comments or responses" as I cared to make regarding fifteen specific questions. The first five were apparently quotations from my Asheville address, and the next five were said to be from other speeches I had made in Atlanta, Memphis, and Denver (where I had never spoken). The remaining inquiries constituted an even greater fishing expedition, especially the fifteenth, which starkly requested information on "such other matters as your comments or responses would warrant further information or inquiry." It was clear that Roberts et al. intended me to answer under oath very general questions over a period of hours or perhaps days, so that a clever person could go through my sworn testimony with a fine-tooth comb to look for instances of perjury. This would, of course, lay the basis for charges of "contumacious conduct." It was entrapment at its best.

I was able to delay my answer for several weeks. For seven or eight days I was in traction at the Lafayette County Hospital, and then I moved to the Baptist Hospital in Memphis for a serious back operation by Raphael Semmes, an eminent surgeon and a descendant of the famous commander of the Confederate raider, *Alabama*. I have never felt so alone in my life, as I saw it then, without friends, money, or legal advice. I was completely isolated and I easily could envision a grinning M. M. Roberts just over the horizon. Fortunately I had agreed to speak at Brandeis University, and upon my return to New York City I dropped by the national offices of the ACLU. That afternoon the prestigious law firm of Paul, Weiss, Rifkind, Wharton, and Garrison heard my sad story and almost at once urged me to agree to be taken into federal court for a possible injunction against the board. My son Bill encouraged me to accept the offer, but I finally decided that as I intended to remain at Ole Miss the rest of my life, I did not think it wise to become this particular federal case.

Upon leaving New York, I stopped over in Washington to meet with the chief officers of the AAUP. After a lengthy discussion it was laughingly suggested, as a last alternative, that if I could get a Mississippi law firm to defend me, the AAUP would take care of the tab. I had little hope, but when I returned to Oxford, I called George Rogers in Vicksburg. (I had participated in his marriage to Muriel Oulpé whom he had met in England when a Rhodes scholar; later she obtained a grant in history at Ole Miss when George came back to enter law school.) Rogers was the junior member of a fine law firm (Teller, Beidenharn, and Rogers), which agreed to take my case. After lengthy study and interrogation of many people including

Chancellor Williams, Landman Teller answered the board's letter of April 27 to say that henceforth all communication would be through the Vicksburg firm. As far as I know, that ended the correspondence. The board's effort at intimidation had come to a dramatic close, except that on September 16, 1965, the board unanimously voted to approve a legal fee of $960.03 "for services rendered in the case of Dr. James Silver."

Paul Johnson served as governor of Mississippi during my confrontation with the Board of Trustees, but he made no effort to have me fired. He did state in an interview (deposited in the Lyndon Baines Johnson Library) more than two years after he left the mansion in Jackson, that in its infighting the board had been "encouraged to some extent by members of the legislature." In the revised edition of my book (1966), I had indicated some hope for the Johnson administration, suggesting "Revolution Begins in the Closed Society." By 1970 Johnson must have mellowed considerably as he spoke of friendship between us in his student days at Ole Miss and saw me then as "a pretty good history professor."

During his first year as governor (1964), he had gone to New York City to confer with the big names in television (Cronkite, Huntley, Brinkley) and the publishers of the *Wall Street Journal, Newsweek,* and *Time,* to correct the image of Mississippi depicted in *The Closed Society.* He claimed that in that volume I had "stated many things that were not true," though he failed to specify a single error. He considered his trip fruitful, "the best thing I did while I was governor."

But in relating the events of the Meredith crisis (when he was second in command to Barnett), he must have been still in a state of shock over what he saw as the federal invasion of a sovereign state. He stated categorically that Meredith would not have been admitted to the university even if he had been white, implied that he knew of two or three Negroes (one in the law school) who had attended Ole Miss before Meredith, and saw Tom Hederman as a moderate adviser to Barnett. He attributed violence on the campus at Oxford to the Kennedys, made Robert responsible for setting up 155-millimeter cannon in Abbeville "to shoot that place [Ole Miss]

apart," had the marshalls driving the coeds from their dormitories
with tear gas, and saw "tremendous numbers of colored troops" at
Ole Miss. In fact, his account eight years after the event made no
provision for revision in the interest of historical accuracy.

Paul Johnson was the first governor of Mississippi to have attended Ole Miss while I taught there. I was gone from the state
during most of his tenure as governor and make no judgment of him
as a political leader.

In the spring of 1964 rumors and lack of communication between
the contending parties led to excessive fears and actions by all concerned (including the legislature) with the coming invasion of Mississippi by an avalanche of civil rights crusaders. One such incident is
documented by stories on the front page of the *Oxford Eagle* of May
7, 1964. Headlined " 'Peace marchers' detained in city and pay
$19.50 fine," the account told of Sheriff Boyce Bratton having
stopped at 2 A.M. a small car containing three black men and three
white men pulling a trailer filled with 3500 to 4000 books destined for
Rust College in Holly Springs. One picture at the top of the page
showed Bratton examining several cartons of books while another
10″ × 4″ photo was headed "Sheriff Bratton Poses 'Line Up' by
Lafayette County Jail" where the arrested men were incarcerated.
They were let go the next afternoon after paying the fine for having
no tail light on the trailer but not before the books were displayed on
the lawn of the jail. Books listed in the article were *The Marxist* by
C. Wright Mills, *Negro Slave Revolts* by Herbert Aptheker, and
Negroes with Guns by Robert Williams, but also *The Bobbsey Twins
Keeping House, The Prince of Graustark,* and *The Girl from Scotland.* Included in the load were enrollment applications for freedom
schools and a large number of two-page mimeographed appeals for
money, teachers, workers, and materials. Most of the boxes had
been addressed from out-of-state to Greenwood, Mississippi, and
the return address on the forms was Council of Federated Organizations (COFO) in Jackson. Interrogation revealed that some of the
men had been involved in race riots in Florida while others had been
expelled from high school and had been arrested several times. After

paying the fine, the men drove toward Holly Springs where they "were stopped for wreckless [*sic*] driving. They were fined and placed in jail awaiting further disposition." Bratton said that one admitted "that he did not believe in working for a living" while another subscribed to "marriage between whites and Negroes." Aside from the obvious harassing tactics of the law and the press in Lafayette and Marshall counties, I remember clearly that shortly after the incident, a deputy came out to the Ole Miss campus to tell me that he had resigned from his job because he had seen a colleague pull the wires loose from the trailer's tail light, thereby extinguishing it and setting up the excuse for the arrest and the fine.

Mississippi: The Closed Society made a kind of publishing history because it came out on Monday, June 22, 1964, the day after three civil rights workers (Chaney, Goodman, Schwerner) disappeared near Philadelphia, Mississippi. For some six weeks the entire nation was aroused and intrigued, before their bodies were found in an earthen dam in Neshoba County. President Johnson had a considerable part of the Navy threshing through the bayous in Mississippi searching for them, and the FBI had set up its second largest office in Jackson. During that time and for some weeks later the book appeared on the *New York Times* and *Time* best-seller lists because of the widespread anxiety, even rising a notch higher than Faulkner's last work, *The Reivers*. When in New York City for a series of TV, radio, and press interviews arranged by Harcourt, Brace, I remember distinctly visiting the publisher's store on Third Avenue, with dozens of copies of my book in the display windows, to see if anyone had actually bought one of them. The manager kept a penciled list of all books sold, and I was somewhat relieved to find that *one* of mine had been bought that first day. Dutch, Gail, and I were put up at the Algonquin Hotel where one noon there was a luncheon arranged by Bill Goodman for New York City historians. I soon became tired of answering the same questions propounded by reporters though one interview on radio was memorable: Frank McGee, the Alabama-born newsman from NBC, put me at such ease that neither of us missed a beat during our conversation on the air.

While attending "Blues for Mr. Charlie" with my family, I missed the entire second act as I was called out for an interview on live television.

That first year some thirty thousand hardback copies of the book were purchased. The second year an enlarged edition, including the story of Mississippi's notorious summer of 1964, was published both in hard and soft covers. It still sold well though the Mississippi columnists who had declared I was doing it for the money would have been amazed at my small return from the book. In any case the attractive volumes put out by Harcout, Brace and World pleased me very much. It is true, though, that my income from teaching and lecturing when I left Mississippi did make my adventure financially profitable, especially when measured against my Ole Miss salary of somewhat less than $10,000 annually after twenty-eight years on the faculty. It would have been difficult not to have done better than that.

James Silver in his Ole Miss office

CHAPTER FIVE

Proper Hoosier
(1964–1969)

Sometime in February 1964 Vincent De Santis called to inquire whether I would be interested in a teaching job at Notre Dame. There had been a few—very few—offers of employment, mostly from friends who knew I was in trouble with authorities in Mississippi and maybe with myself. I was not enamored of made work nor of the idea of leaving Ole Miss before retirement. The call from South Bend came as I was completing *Mississippi: The Closed Society,* and I put Notre Dame's history chairman on hold. Besides, it would not do to have the book announced when I lived outside of Mississippi. It had been known early in 1963 that at least a third of the regular faculty would be gone by fall, though the administration had played down that fact. In 1964 I was somewhat hesitant about switching to a Catholic institution even on a temporary basis. In the late spring I did take off for a couple of days to visit South Bend, and while walking around the campus, I happened to hear a down-to-earth discussion of birth control through the open windows of a classroom filled with nuns and seminarians. I felt that an institution where such a conversation took place could not be all bad. Later I was to conclude that there was little difference between being a Baptist in Mississippi and a Catholic in Indiana. It was all a matter of how the church affected the individual. Certainly I needed to get away from Mississippi, so soon after my South Bend visit I applied for and received a leave of absence from the Ole Miss administration and accepted what I presumed was a temporary position at Notre Dame. In the late summer of 1964, Dutch, Gail, and I pulled a U-

HAUL trailer to South Bend. At the time I had no doubts about returning to Mississippi in the fall of 1965.

I can compare my years at Notre Dame to the excitement and optimism of the period after World War II; they were almost spectacular. In South Bend I was more in tune with my environment, and partly because of the publication of *The Closed Society* I moved about on something of a plane of equality with leaders in the community. This included relationships of varying closeness with such celebrants of the revolution in human rights as Roy Wilkins, John Sigenthaler, Louis Lomax, Theodore Hesburgh, and Ralph Ellison, as well as dozens of local and lesser figures. I listened as Lomax (whom I introduced to a college audience) declared that Lyndon Johnson was the premier civil rights leader in the nation. I drove Ellison out to the western section of town to show him the nightly violence (which did not materialize), and I remember being ordered from a choice seat in an auditorium because Leroi Jones had reserved several rows for "his friends," in violation of federal law.

One of my close associates was an elderly black who had moved to South Bend in the early 1940s after he had performed locally as a member of a Kansas choral group. Personable, Jesse Dickinson was soon elected to the Indiana legislature but could not find housing within miles of the capital because of discrimination against blacks. (I had known for years that the Crispus Attucks High in Indianapolis was the largest all-black school in the country.) Each year he spoke to my classes, often pleading for stricter standards in South Bend's all-black Linden School.

My life in South Bend proved to be more hectic than that in Mississippi. The book had brought a considerable notoriety and invitations to address hundreds of organizations followed. Unquestionably, I could have become of some importance in the civil rights movement, and at times I was tempted, but I decided early to play the game in low key. The result was that I clocked many hours on the platform talking about the good and the bad of Mississippi. I felt that many knowledgeable, well-intentioned listeners were close to the truth but often for the wrong reasons. I made a continuous effort to straighten them out. My approach was usually historical, reminding audiences of early nationalism in North and South, in Mississippi as well as Indiana. The fanaticism of some pre-Civil War abolitionists who refused to have meaningful social contacts with blacks, as Faulkner somehow knew, had parallels in the civil rights movement, and a few frenzied people still agreed with a Chicago Reconstruction paper that the final solution might appropriately be the fashioning of Mississippi into a gigantic frog pond. Questions from the audience invariably had to do with the course of the Meredith admission to Ole Miss, and while I made no attempt to gloss over facts, I tried the best I could to *explain* them. I had never assumed the old North-South controversy to be irrepressible, nor do I now think there is much choice between people because of where they live. As I moved quickly from a narrative involving recent events into a generalized historical discourse, I am sure my listeners were better informed on Mississippi's problems than they would have been after hearing the ideological missionaries sent forth by the Sovereignty Commission.

Within a few months of the publication of *The Closed Society,* I must have been solicited by every speaking bureau in the country. This was quite flattering and I'm a little ashamed that I didn't answer their inquiries. Also I turned down several chances to go to Washington to become a part of federal civil rights agencies because what I was doing seemed equally important. At this time, I still believed that I should spend the rest of my time in helping Negroes in their quest for the better life. But I wanted to remain my own boss, to speak or not to speak, as the situation seemed to demand. My best audiences were in colleges and universities, and I addressed numerous church groups and forums sponsored by newspaper and civic associations. Listeners in the synagogues were the most attentive (and asked the most intriguing questions) as their rabbis and other leaders had been in the forefront of the mobilization for improving the lives of blacks. At Tuskegee Institute I had the feeling that my message was old stuff to my receptive audience until I realized that it might have been unusual to hear it from a white Mississippian. I had the distinct feeling that my classroom had simply been extended and that it was up to me to perform in the most scholarly way possible. There was no place for demagoguery, nor do I believe I indulged in any during my three or four hundred appearances from Boston to Norfolk to Houston to Palo Alto.

I'm sure I could have done what my detractors in Mississippi claimed to expect—make a pot full of money out of the misery of the state where I had put in the best years of my life. This I know I did not do. I have little idea of my income in the period after I left Mississippi. Of course it would have been impossible to have earned less than my Ole Miss salary. There was never a fee beyond $500 for speaking, and only two or three of these. Many times I spoke for free, or for expenses only. I turned down numerous invitations, partly because of schedule conflicts but more often because I did not want to feel exploited nor did I desire to exploit Mississippi. I still have the tapes of many talks, and these will be available in the archives at Ole Miss.

In my search for comprehension of Mississippi culture, I had found over the years numerous books on race relations in areas adjacent to the great river, which I gradually absorbed and began to use in my teaching. With the advent of the civil rights movement the best of these were reissued in paperback and I was requested to write new introductions for several. This I did.

After his death I became fascinated with Faulkner's fiction, and at Notre Dame I began to use him as my chief interpreter of the South. Soon I was encouraging students to compare the imaginative prose of Faulkner with the "reality" of the sociological studies. But I must admit that I was somewhat piqued when a Faulkner scholar did exactly the same thing in a book which equated reality with *The Closed Society*.

The first and possibly the best of the volumes reissued was *Deep South: A Social and Anthropological Study of Caste and Class* by two man-and-wife teams of anthropologists from Harvard, one black and one white. It was a painstaking study of race relations in the Natchez area but could have been applied to the Delta.

The established classic on national black-white relations, issued during World War II by Gunnar Myrdal, the eminent Swedish sociologist, was reissued in two paper volumes in 1964. In my hectic days of travel I had fallen behind a few days with a promised review for the old *Herald Tribune*. After speaking at the University of Indiana, I stayed up the remainder of the night to complete the essay and early the next morning took it to Western Union for its dispatch to New York. When the manager of the office came in to find my piece already on the wire, he exclaimed, "I didn't think the game [Indiana vs. North Carolina] was until tonight." Apparently he thought that all such lengthy messages had to be of an athletic nature. My review appeared on January 10, 1965.

I sent in the introduction to Elizabeth Sutherland's *Letters from Mississippi* while I was teaching my last classes at Ole Miss in the summer of 1965. That same summer I wrote the foreword to Russell Barrett's *Integration at Ole Miss*. The following year the University of Indiana Press published James Meredith's *Three Years in Mississippi,* probably the most authentic historical account of his breaking the racial barriers in the state. I read the manuscript with great care and made some suggestions for change in a two-hour long-distance call to his editor in Bloomington while I was immobilized in a snowstorm near Buffalo on the New York Thruway. This is the only volume I may have influenced somewhat without having had a part in its publication.

One of my dearest friends in Mississippi, David L. Cohn, published *God Shakes Creation* in 1935 and brought it up to date in 1947 with *Where I Was Born and Raised*. The larger volume was republished in 1967 by the Notre Dame Press, with an additional preface by Jim Silver.

In my numerous speeches around the country after leaving Mississippi, I developed a propensity to recall the phrase or anecdote that found a receptive audience. It became customary for me to say that I had not been fired nor was I performing for the Citizens Council or the Sovereignty Commission—and to tell the apocryphal story of counting the votes in Yazoo City in the Dixiecrat election of 1948. A town official read out to the tally clerk the name of Thurmond a couple of dozen times and then came across a ballot for Truman. He hesitated but continued, entoning "Thurmond, Thurmond, Thurmond" a few hundred more times and then discovered Truman's name a second time. He exploded, "That son-of-a-bitch voted twice. Mark them both off." My wife objected to my remark that when I found the sales of my book flagging, I would wire friends in Mississippi, "Burn another church."

Aside from a few clumsy speeches made in Kansas, including a

Lincoln Day effort in which I refused to talk about the Great Eman-
cipator, my public speaking began in Mississippi. I was pleased to
address high school graduates in Hickory Flat and Baldwyn before
moving on to nonprofit talks mostly in rural areas sponsored by the
state Department of Education. Then I proceeded to service clubs
in Oxford, Holly Springs, Tupelo, Jackson, and Biloxi. In the meantime I watched closely the professionals who came to Ole Miss,
being especially intrigued by the wit and charm of David Cohn and
Sir John Wilmot. Of course the classroom can be a remarkable
source for the development of equanimity in public speaking for a
naturally timid person. As my own talks became more controversial—even those before Civil War round tables—I learned to be
cautious in public statements. So my carefully assembled presidential address to the Southern Historical Association may be considered my graduation examination in public utterance, preparing
me for the ordeal ahead.

I have my own theories as to the rise and fall of most grand
enterprises in this country. As a movement gains strength and
power, new leaders are attracted who feel the pressure to raise the
level of demands. As these are at least partially satisfied, increasing
numbers of opponents, who believe their territory to be threatened,
are antagonized, and in our democracy they bring about a political
backlash. Slowly at first but with increasing momentum the campaign reaches its peak and then goes down the other side of the hill.
There may be permanent gains, but the crest has been passed. Such
was the case with abolition, prohibition, organized labor, and perhaps women's rights. Certainly civil rights followed such a path.
Whether the Negro was better off as a result of the Civil War may be
debated as he moved from slavery to caste. The NAACP brought
about very slow changes, usually through legal channels, from 1910
to World War II when many of its members were still willing to
settle for separate *and* equal. As new groups were formed, demands
were elevated, the ante was raised. Intensive radicalization appeared in the sixties. I saw this formula being worked out in South
Bend, where for decades the Poles and Negroes had coexisted on
the west side of town, each with their own schools. Then the Polish

workers felt threatened by increased demands of the blacks, particularly on the economic front, so they kept Negroes out of the unions. As a member of the Human Relations Council, I was quite aware of the new antagonism. Black leaders were themselves worried that public-school integration would cause them to lose control of the all-Negro Linden school, in danger of being phased out completely. I remember talking with one youngster who returned from a national meeting in Detroit convinced that blacks were going to be assigned their own section of the country on the Gulf Coast, including Mississippi. Bob Moses talked of the inherent corruption of white society and espoused an all-Negro community where virtue might prevail. Blacks began to believe they could make it on their own. Some developed an arrogance that disdained white support. A friend of mine was ousted from the executive board of the Association for the Study of Negro Life and History because she was Caucasian. Stokely Carmichael raised the fist of Black Power. Perhaps all this is rationalization on my part, but particularly after going from Indiana back to the South and moving around Florida after retirement, I became less and less involved in civil rights. This has been on my conscience. But I have never lost concern with the movement, and I believe as strongly as ever that this country has the obligation to furnish all its citizens with "equality at the starting line" as well as fundamental rights.

In the middle and late sixties the black leadership became more and more demanding. In turn I changed directions somewhat in my support of their ambitions, as indicated by the following statements that I used as a basis for discussion with students at Notre Dame and later at South Florida:

United States Commission on Civil Rights (1967): "The longer Negro students are in desegregated schools, the better are their academic achievement and their attitudes. Conversely, there is a growing deficit for Negroes who remain in racially isolated schools."

Malcolm X: "My greatest lack has been, I believe, that I don't have the kind of academic education I wish I had been able to get."
"The true brotherhood I had seen in the Holy World has influenced me to recognize that anger can blind human vision."
"My friends today are black, brown, red, yellow, and *white*."

Militants such as Carmichael ask blacks to reject material values which of course is a denial of the claim of "a piece of the action."

Militants call for an end to our "sick" society with its emphasis on the "white man's capitalism." The greatest danger to the future well-being of the black man and the poor in general would be the malfunctioning of the present capitalistic system, as in a full-fledged depression.

Blacks *cannot* separate from our society. Militants speak for black capitalism which on its face is absurd if divorced from U.S. capitalism.

It may be that ghetto blacks have benefited least from the War on Poverty and other recent changes in the United States. Still, New York City now spends more on the relief of the poor than on education. Franz Fanon pointed out that African masses have not benefited from revolutionary changes on that continent, he says because of the new native bureaucracy—black "exploiting" black.

Black militants have been doing their best (with some success) to prove that the Negro has been an integral part of American history. It is inconsistent to do this and at the same time to disclaim that history, or to disclaim integration in U.S. society today.

American civilization *is* part Negro. It is also true that blacks are *part* African. Aside from being one-fourth European biologically, blacks are more American in heritage than African.

If, as they claim, only blacks can interpret correctly black history and black culture, who is to interpret black culture in the Caribbean and in South America where there is a biracial, integrated society? Do we leave out of black history William Lloyd Garrison, John Brown, Herbert Aptheker, John Fry, Michael Schwerner, and Andrew Goodman?

Militants call for black unity. But extremism begets disunity. Even the white southerners were not unified in the Confederacy. In 1965 6 percent of the blacks in the United States declared themselves as supporting Malcolm X. Black militants represent only a small fraction of blacks in the United States today.

Polarization *by* blacks leads to an acceptance of polarization by whites (who have shown an increasing acceptance of the black man). Inasmuch as the greatest need among blacks is for education and skills, polarization will make it much harder to get the required massive appropriations for education, housing, and relief.

The arguments of the militants for *separation* have for the past fifteen years been presented with vigor by the White Citizens Councils, the Ku Klux Klan, the Americans for the Preservation of the White Race, and the National States Rights Party. To say that the goals of these

organizations are different from those of the militants is not to gainsay
the similarity and even the identity of the arguments.

At Notre Dame I developed two new courses, one on black history and the other a seminar in which I used William Faulkner as a
chief interpreter of the South. After a few years I realized that
instead of teaching black history, I was holding a class in the evolu-
tion of white supremacy. In fact I had few black students (the fees at
Notre Dame are excessive for most Negroes) until a dozen or so
were signed up for the fall of 1969. My lack of understanding of the
thinking of blacks was one of the reasons I went to Jackson to teach
at Tougaloo College that summer. Notre Dame made me a small
grant to be used in getting to know blacks in central Mississippi, but
my hospitalization (twice) and constant problems with breathing
prevented me from getting much done. When I did not return to
South Bend in the fall my class was taken over by Sam Shapiro, who
at a Christmas history conference told me that one of the blacks
stood up in the back of the classroom after a rather heavy assignment to say, "Professor, you don't really think we're going to learn
all that shit, do you?" As I found out at Tougaloo, there were usually
repercussions when whites taught black history.

It was understood by those who visited in the Faulkner home that
there would be no discussion of his fiction, and I may have used that
as an excuse for having read little of Faulkner before his death. Then
I became an addict. To force myself to read his stories over and over
again, I began to discuss them in class, and subsequently this procedure became my major approach to the meaning of southern history.
Early in my Notre Dame experience I helped out the sophomore
class in a symposium on Faulkner, and I began to collect a small
library to go along with the memorabilia of my association with him.
I added films and each year I showed *Intruder in the Dust*. Many
Faulkner scholars visited Notre Dame, and I was instrumental in
introducing Carvel Collins to the faculty there. When I moved to
Florida, my interest was accelerated in William Faulkner of Oxford,
Mississippi, to the point that I wrote several papers about my association with Mississippi's great author.

I have been asked many times why I left Ole Miss. I'm sure I have given many answers, depending on my mood. It seems to me that I was too stubborn to have allowed myself to be driven away. Of course I had felt the need to get out of Mississippi several summers before the admission of Meredith, including that of 1962. When I finally decided to leave for Note Dame in 1964, it was definitely to be for one year though I had been offered a tenured position. I did return to teach at Ole Miss in the summer of 1965 before going on to Rutgers. For some time I had seen erstwhile friends in Oxford cross the street to avoid speaking to me. I knew I was only tolerated by many citizens, including some members of the board. The moment I crossed the Mississippi line my income was more than doubled, and it is difficult to return to genteel poverty of one's own free will. Outside of Mississippi I had no feeling of an enforced stricture on what I said or did. Unquestionably, one of the profound reasons came out of a long conference in a Chicago hotel room with Provost Alton Bryant, a long-time friend at Ole Miss, who suggested that the university administration would find it easier to deal with the legislature if I were not on campus. And then, I had been in and out of hospitals from South Bend to Ann Arbor to Boston for treatment of emphysema, which I now believe increased in virulence because of tensions stemming from a furious activity beyond my capabilities (my hectic schedule included full-time teaching and a heavy load of public speaking). I have believed from the beginning that what I did and said were in the ultimate interests of the university and the state of Mississippi, and therein I suppose lies my best answer. My thirty years in the state are precious to me, and I am grateful that the Ole Miss campus gave Dutch and me an ideal place in an ideal time to bring up our three children. This is more than mere sentimentality, as is evidenced by the sad certainty, as of those other expatriates, of a complete lack of desire to return. For whatever reason, Mississippi has made real progress toward equality for all its people, and I am well pleased. But I still prefer my life of retirement on an island on the west coast of Florida. Every day I seem to have less zeal for the fray.

In the summer of 1964 while I was doing the chores designed by Harcourt, Brace and Jovanovich, the civil rights movement reached

The Reverend Theodore Hesburgh

a climax in Mississippi. Almost as soon as *The Closed Society* reached the bookstores, it appeared that the changing times demanded its sequel. So, while teaching at Notre Dame and running around the country making speeches and giving interviews, I began collecting materials to bring my book up to date. Again, I went through the same process of painstakingly checking every detail, and after my stints at Ole Miss and Rutgers in the summer of 1965, I drove with my wife and younger daughter to Albemarle Sound on the North Carolina coast. There I wrote from early morning until late at night, not even seeing the Atlantic Ocean only three or four miles away until the day of our departure. Then we returned to Notre Dame via Ole Miss. The last writing on the revised edition of my book, now with an added hundred and twenty pages, "Revolution Begins in the Closed Society," was completed at Paris Landing State Park as we crossed the border out of the South.

The most remarkable person I encountered in my departure from the South was Theodore Hesburgh, president of Notre Dame. Though an administrator, he gave me the impression of being aggressively on the right side of most social questions. His facility for remembering names and faces was superior to that of any southern politician I have ever known. In my first days in South Bend, after Dutch and I had met him only in a receiving line for new faculty, we encountered him in the local airport, and almost at once he inquired as to the whereabouts of Bill and Betty, saying that he assumed Gail was still at home with us. This flattering question simply indicates his unfailing identification with even a casual acquaintance.

Shortly thereafter, he asked me to lunch with him at the Morris Inn. Somehow, I knew he would ask my opinion as to whether the United States Civil Rights Commission should keep its February date in Jackson, Mississippi, already postponed several times, the widespread rumor being that it feared violence. That night I called Wofford Smith, the involved Episcopal chaplain at Ole Miss who answered my inquiry with a vulgar affirmative. That is the message I carried to Hesburgh, and as the new governor Johnson reversed Ross Barnett in calling for cooperation with the commission, Father Hesburgh must have considered me as a minor prophet.

During our lunch, he produced a copy of my book, requesting an autograph. Pleased at this, I was a bit ill-at-ease while I debated about signing the volume to Father Hesburgh, Theodore Hesburgh, or maybe the more familiar Ted. Later I discovered that he had donated the volume to the library, as he apparently does with all his books. He led the simple life of the priest, if working eighteen hours a day could be called that—at least he slept on a cot in Corby Hall and ate in the college cafeteria. I remember too my embarrassment when a student priest half my age demanded that I address him "Father" in class lest I destroy his image. I never called him by name again. It seemed much easier to address the nuns as "Sister."

In any case I developed the feeling that Hesburgh and Silver were allied in a great cause. Of course, he made mistakes, and when I told him about one of them, his stolid reaction indicated, I thought, a somewhat grim sense of humor. An illuminated manuscript given to him by the Pope appeared in a glass case in the library with a dangling participle in the first paragraph of the history accompanying it. When I mentioned this to Hesburgh's secretary, she coldly responded, "Father Hesburgh wrote that." As I left the office I could not help remarking that he would never make Pope. I attended one meeting in which he quickly calmed down several hundred noisy demonstrators obviously out to provoke him. At times he appeared to be the strict disciplinarian. I still have the impression that nobody could talk with Hesburgh and look him in the eye without believing in his sincerity and his dedication to truth. Unquestionably, he has a special presence. Yet he was criticized by some faculty members, as all college presidents are, for administrative deficiencies, but I could find little fault in perhaps the greatest man I have known. He built the magnificent thirteen-story library; the mural on one side has a pivotal portrait of Jesus with arms outstretched as if (as seen from our seats in the stadium) asking, "Where's Hesburgh?" or simply saying "Touchdown."

An amusing story was told me by the president of Brandeis University. Hesburgh had approached him for financial help in securing manuscript copies from the famous Ambrosian Archives in Italy for the medieval collection in the Notre Dame library, with duplicates going to Brandeis. Abram Sachar tried to raise the funds but failed until he invoked the cooperation of Cardinal Cushing. When I arranged an enormous civil rights conference which took place in early 1972 at the University of South Florida, Father Hesburgh was the only nonsoutherner invited.

Republican Mayor Lloyd Allen appointed me to the South Bend Human Relations Commission, which saw to the enforcement of local legislation and court decisions dealing with civil rights. It had an overriding public relations function. The commission developed a close association with the police department and the school board. As a member I put in long hours meeting with the officers of local labor unions, though I must admit that we were largely unsuccessful in breaking down the regulations I believed were set up to keep out blacks. On the other hand, most blacks seemed unwilling to abide by lengthy and complicated apprenticeship rules. On the whole, the city fathers appeared more anxious to bring about complete integration in all facets of life in South Bend than were the town's citizens. Prejudice is where you find it.

In my fourth year at Notre Dame, I was lured into a debate about black power with Ron Karenga, a cultist leader from the West Coast. If I had seen the many leaflets and pamphlets sold by his aides before and after our meeting, I would have been better prepared to counter his onslaught of arguments which I considered unpleasant and rather stupid. Before our encounter, he requested that I speak first and then criticized me for talking without having heard his story. Two enormous blacks stood imposingly with crossed arms on the stage, whether to protect Karenga or to intimidate me and the audience I never knew. I'm not sure who "won" the debate, though I do remember that I refrained from using the strongest point in my carefully assembled arsenal, that Karenga could speak with difficulty for the blacks as he obviously had a larger number of white genes. Maybe Mississippi laws of race had taken charge of my mind, though I prefer to think it was plain decency that kept me from personal remarks. In any case, I came away from the debate thinking that charlatans get into every good movement and that sometimes they take charge.

James Silver at Notre Dame

President Hesburgh was talked into supporting a campus program of black power when he underwrote (but did not himself participate in) a week-long meeting of racial militants. I attended all the sessions, not minding so much the constant flow of obscenities and the derogatory references by practically every performer to those "mother-fucking whites," as I did the assumption that whites had been responsible for nothing of value in the history of the world. (All sessions took place in the splendid Notre Dame library.) Toward the end of the conference an extravagant banquet was held with a flourish. The Silvers were invited, we thought, because there were not enough blacks in that part of Indiana to fill the seats. Of course the dinner expenses were taken care of by Hesburgh, as was a last day's trip by bus to Detroit for all who desired to go. At the very first session I sat with a student from Nigeria who refused to attend further because, as he later told me, he had no time for indulgence in nasty frivolity. Conferences of this type may well have contributed to my further education about race.

As the civil rights movement reached its peak, I listened in surprise as an overflow audience at a national meeting of the Organization of American Historians in Philadelphia came to its feet to cheer Julius Lester *(Look Out Whitey, Black Power Is Going to Get Your Mama)*. As I saw it, two of his main points were that (1) American society had deprived the Negro of the chance to perform great deeds, and (2) historians had kept his large achievements out of their books, ideas mutually exclusive. Historians of this century have been traditionally liberal, and how many were taken in by these arguments I simply do not know. Skeptical as I was, I still did not have the nerve to speak out in contradiction of what I considered historical nonsense.

I never quite understood why the Episcopal church held one of its national conventions in the new field house of Notre Dame. In adjusting to black-power demands, the Mississippi delegation proved to be one of the most liberal. I happened to be present in the convention hall when a bearded black grabbed the microphone of the presiding officer and demanded millions from the church in "reparations" for historical injury to Negroes. Most churches (including the Catholic) turned their backs on this kind of blackmail, but the Episcopalians did vote two hundred thousand dollars to assuage the blacks. I presume that in time this obligation was paid off. Anyway the Mississippi delegates assembled each night after the meetings at the Silver home on Bader Avenue, where some of them were lodged, to talk over the day's events. We got acquainted with some remarkable Mississippians.

In South Bend I had the opportunity (which I did not have in Mississippi) to meet socially a considerable number of blacks. Many of these were fine people and a few were victims of their environment. Partly on account of my activity on the Human Relations Commission and I suppose a little because of *The Closed Society,* I was invited to numerous interracial gatherings and I attended those I could with an extremely busy schedule. I was unable to join the group of advisers of the black mayor of Gary though I did speak to a mixed group of educators in his troubled city.

The most impressive black family Dutch and I became closely associated with consisted of Roland and Dorothy Chamblee and their six remarkable children. Roland came from Georgia (with a pedigree superior to that of most whites), had obtained his MD at Meharry Medical College, and had moved to South Bend, where he interned and set up his practice. A kind of Renaissance man (reminding me of Bob Farley), he had an extensive local practice catering to blacks and whites alike. A large part of his time was devoted to bettering relations between the races; a first-class speaker, Dr. Chamblee was usually available for impromptu addresses. As physician to the Notre Dame seminarians, he was intricately tied up with the Catholic church. Shortly after we left South Bend, Roland Chamblee sold his big home in the country and his professional business in order to take off for Uganda where he and Dorothy set up a hospital for the indigent. In less than a year they were expelled from the country by Idi Amin who apparently did not take kindly to Americans, even if they were blacks dedicated to caring for his people. The Chamblees are now back in South Bend.

When I found difficulty in climbing the stairs to the fourth-floor class in the Administration Building, I turned to Roland Chamblee for help. As I moved more deeply into pulmonary disease, he put me

into St. Joseph's Hospital and then sent me to the university hospital
in Ann Arbor for various analyses. At the time I couldn't help pon-
dering the advisability of putting my life in the hands of a graduate of
Meharry; I concluded that Dr. Chamblee was not only a first-rate
physician but that I trusted him implicitly. He was always searching
out new knowledge. When his beautiful daughter was married to a
Harvard law graduate in an extensive Catholic service, Dutch and I
not only attended but had the reception in our Bader Avenue home.
I still marvel that a couple from the South would put on a sort of
garden party for more than a hundred guests, over half of whom
were black. In my fantasy mind I have often taken all the Chamblees
back to Mississippi to demonstrate once and for all the extraordinary qualities people can have when they are not deprived of the
chance by local custom.

For the spring term of 1966, I obtained a leave of absence from
Notre Dame to teach at the Massachusetts Institute of Technology.
This meant, of course, that an instructor from Mississippi had been
for a short while on the faculties of the two famous Cambridge
universities. At the same time Gail attended the local public school.
She was something of a lonely child, taken to bringing classmates
home for play in the afternoons. About half the time, I noticed, they
were black. Hodding Carter III at that time was a Nieman fellow at
Harvard, and so it was perhaps inevitable that he and I made joint
appearances before a few New England audiences. I suppose it was
somewhat normal too that at first I thought of the possibility of a
permanent place on the MIT faculty. But I soon gave up that idea, as
I learned that history had a secondary place among students who
unquestionably were perceptively bright but who seldom admitted
there was anything for them to learn, especially in the humanities.

The highlight of my Indiana experience came with the celebration
of Negro History Week, February 11–17, 1968. I still have the proclamation issued by Mayor Allen, whose cooperation played a considerable role in an extravaganza put on by the school system, Notre
Dame, the *South Bend Tribune,* radio and television stations, and
the Human Relations Commission. The climax came Thursday night

with a gala affair in the Morris Civic Auditorium, attended by more than two thousand people, about half of them white. Dutch and I attended with Roland and Dorothy Chamblee. Aside from the entertainment of choral groups from city schools, a distinguished array of speakers included Father Hesburgh, Mayor Richard Hatcher of Gary, Mrs. Frankie Freeman, member of the Civil Rights Commission from St. Louis, and, as the speaker of the evening, Charles Wesley, outstanding historian and college president. In the lobby was displayed a fine collection of books on race in America and an extended, annotated bibliography prepared by the Human Relations Commission was handed out as well. I am unaware of a more elaborate program for this week at any time in any place in the United States.

In the Notre Dame years I attended two White House conferences, one on civil rights and the other on education. To the first Bill Silver was a delegate also, because after having been turned down for entrance to the Harvard Law School, he had returned to Mississippi as the executive secretary of the Young Democrats and as assistant director of the Human Relations Commission (the following year he made it to Harvard Law, partly on the recommendation of Aaron Henry). I was not impressed with the busy work of either conference as their concluding resolutions seem to have been cut-and-dried and perhaps drawn up before the call-to-order, the procedure, I suppose, in all such meetings. Lyndon Johnson appeared unannounced at both conferences, and in the second a spread was put on for the visitors in a veritable tent city on the White House grounds; it reminded me of a medieval tournament. Johnson appeared with all his cabinet, but at the risk of seeming impertinent I should report that when the time came, I headed for the elegant repast rather than for the line formed to shake the hand of the president. Bill and I got to sit at a table with Walter Reuther whom I admired as a great labor organizer as well as a civil rights leader.

During the summer of 1968 Notre Dame sponsored a program in Austria to bring many Americans teaching abroad in such services as the Peace Corps up-to-date educational and historical developments in the United States. From the History Department Sam

Shapiro, Vince De Santis, and I were on the faculty of the program. So the Silver family had its second chance for a few months in Europe, this time without Bill and Betty, but with Gail. We visited Washington and New York before flying to Paris for a week, and then journeyed to the Mediterranean coasts of France and Italy by bus and train, finally arriving in Innsbruck.

In Washington Wofford Smith led me on an extended tour of Resurrection City, the muddy enclave on the Mall near the Lincoln Memorial. This dream of martyred Martin Luther King had been brought low by poor management and senseless competition among its directors. Such a dreary experiment in protest pretty well convinced me of the impending demise of the crusade for civil rights. In Paris we took in the usual sights, that is, until Gail rebelled at a superfluity of historical instruction. She was more in harmony with Beaujolais country and the French and Italian rivieras.

The school was a considerable success, with many mature students who had for years been away from home. There was a pleasant camaraderie, especially on trips to Germany and Switzerland. At the end of the summer the Silver family went on to Vienna where an American doctor (and Harvard graduate), who represented the American Medical Association, demonstrated his ignorance of both the race problem in the United States and developments in the treatment of emphysema. But he did suggest that we seek out the sunshine of the Adriatic instead of our scheduled trip to Prague (where we would have arrived with the Russian tanks) and the Scandinavian countries. I suppose we should have been grateful to the USSR, because fear of impending invasion of Yugoslavia swept the Italian summer visitors away and made room for us.

On our way home we had a magnificent train ride through the mountains of central Europe, a day's excursion on the Rhine, and a visit to Anne Frank's hideaway in Amsterdam. Together with a previous tour of Dachau, this last established in my mind Hitler's unintentional contribution to the cause of racial advancement in the United States. In Innsbruck we developed a close friendship with a Peace Corps veteran who, in the years away from his home country, had married a handsome black woman from one of the Dutch colonies. In Austria the young couple had one child with them and another on the way, and in Amsterdam we visited them all. They were quite apprehensive as to their coming reception in the United States. My only suggestion was that they stay out of the South and all rural areas. For several years we exchanged letters with them in Los Angeles where they seemed to have settled happily.

In my move from Mississippi to Indiana I did not relinquish what had become my favorite recreation, the weekly poker game. Since my sophomore year at Carolina, I had been under the illusion that I was one of the very best at it. But in South Bend I was introduced to a group of professionals who rather promptly took care of this assumption of superiority. As is said in farm country, they cleaned my plough. After this sad experience I transferred my card playing to a faculty group where I performed with more success. In the basement of our house on Bader Avenue we played on an elegant poker table. Some nights we performed in a professor's home on the other side of town. Often in the wee hours I would ride my bicycle home through a black enclave. Each time, I must confess, I pondered what I would do if I were stopped by hoodlums, especially when I was carrying a lot of cash. I finally decided it would be of no use to point out to my would-be antagonists that I had once been a friend of Meredith. Luckily, I never had to put that fear to the test.

For a few weeks I was under the impression that *The Closed Society* would be taken by the Book-of-the-Month Club. While this did not happen, some awards did come my way. I was honored by membership in the American Academy of Arts and Sciences and was given the Anisfield-Wolfe prize for the best book on the subject of race published in 1964. The next year Dutch and I flew to New York City where I not only received a Sidney Hillman award but was asked to make the main speech at the banquet. On the platform that night sat Oliver Emmerich, my old Mississippi friend and sometimes antagonist as editor of the *State-Times* and as chairman of the Board of Trustees of the Institutions of Higher Learning, who had intelligently searched for answers to our state's racial problems. He was honored by the Amalgamated Clothing Workers of America for his work in race relations in Mississippi. The event that gave me the greatest satisfaction of my academic career came when Benjamin Mays, the venerated president of Morehouse College, bestowed on me an honorary doctorate upon the hundredth anniversary of the college, the year of his retirement in 1968. That afternoon in Atlanta Mays awarded six honorary degrees, three to whites and three to blacks. The fascinating thing was that the white educators were all rather poor, while the blacks were successful businessmen who had made their fortunes while performing good works.

I was in a hotel in Norfolk when a call came through from Walter Johnson of the history department at the University of Chicago. Would I go on a civil rights march from Selma to Montgomery? I told him I would think it over, though I felt sure at the time that I would not participate. (I have never been an activist, and my one appearance on a picket line caused me considerable embarrassment.) My rationalization really was that one who had lived in Mississippi the previous years didn't have to prove himself by going to Alabama. Besides, a month or so before I had agreed in a meeting with a couple of civil rights lawyers in New York City to testify as an expert witness in a federal case coming up in Jackson. What intrigued me about the expert business was that all I had to do was to give my opinions. So, I waited until I returned to South Bend and only then discovered that this was to be a march of scholars in support of Martin Luther King. At once I could envisage a trial in which the segregation lawyer would ask me one question: "Professor Silver, did you march from Selma to Montgomery with Dr. King?" That question and my answer would discredit me with any Mississippi jury. Many of my historian friends did go to Montgomery, but not quite in the way the country may have believed. The group of scholars gathered in Atlanta but could not obtain public transportation to Alabama. They finally chartered a yellow Baptist bus in which they were driven to Montgomery, stopping off for the night at Tuskegee. On the way west, the vehicle swayed onto the shoulder of the highway, and a voice was heard from the back, "For God's sake, man, be careful or you will kill liberal history in America." So these men of academe only walked the last four or five miles on that famous march. I am reminded that as I listened on television to the King oration from the capital of the Confederacy, and I couldn't help wondering when he quoted from Vann Woodward's southern history what his listeners' reaction would have been had they known the author was in the audience. The trial in which I was to have testified as an expert witness regarding the intentions of the Mississippi legislature never took place.

Roland, Terry, Ruth, and Dorothy Chamblee of South Bend

CHAPTER SIX

Southerner Again

(1969–)

In January 1969, I traveled from South Bend to Greenville to testify in a suit against the Ole Miss administration in federal court presided over by Judge Coleman of the Fifth Circuit. To obtain expense money, I agreed to speak at the Social Science Forum at Tougaloo College, a meeting arranged by Kenneth Dean, executive secretary of the Mississippi Council on Human Relations. Out of this trip came the origin of my plan to teach a summer course at Tougaloo. It seemed appropriate for someone who had been on the Ole Miss faculty for the better part of thirty years to teach at a largely black college, even though my appearance would be late for participation in the more hectic civil rights activities. I was unaware at the time that in all my days in Mississippi I had not been allowed any real contacts with blacks on my academic level and that in my book I had written more about white supremacy than black history. Besides, this would be my chance to find out about the problems of black people. So I began an extensive correspondence with John Dittmer, the white dean from Indiana whose insights have helped me enormously to comprehend life at Tougaloo.

I was a little uncertain about my return to Mississippi. As a precaution, the first night I turned on all the lights and shuttered the windows in my small, air-conditioned apartment and walked around the dwelling to ascertain what would be observable within. The next apartment was occupied by a visiting professor from Nigeria who had custody of the only thermostat in the building—we never did agree on what might be considered an equable temperature. My most amazing learning experience of the summer was the close identification of the black radicals with white faculty; the black teachers had been there long enough to have adjusted to conditions in Mississippi.

My only class that summer consisted of ten blacks and one white. It seemed to me that these students were out to embarrass me even before they had an inkling of what I would teach. Thomas Jefferson, they claimed, should be removed from the history books because of his ecstatic adventure with a black woman. I could not understand why this might not be glorified as a great American romance. When I requested their substitute for our third president, the agreement was on Nat Turner. I tried quite gingerly to find my way and one day suggested that a handsome Negro woman who was married to a white civil rights lawyer must believe in integration. She exploded at the intemperance of the notion and later that year seemed to vindicate her outburst by getting a divorce. Except for mixed crowds at receptions given by President Owens, it was my experience that whites socialized with whites and, I presumed, blacks with blacks. An exceptional black student guided me to most of the local eating places; later he got his PhD from Princeton and is now teaching history at Tougaloo. In Jackson that summer the national meeting of the NAACP was held, dominated by Charles Evers. It was there that I congratulated the widow of Medgar Evers on her book, *For Us, the Living,* and she in turn thanked me for having written *The Closed Society.* I had met her martyred husband at Tougaloo almost exactly a decade before. That summer I visited Charles Evers in a local hospital where he had been placed in the maternity ward to escape from threats on his life. I did not get much done on my own investigation of black culture because I was troubled with emphysema, but teaching at Tougaloo was an exciting and rewarding experience.

My departure from Indiana and permanent residence in Florida resulted from a misplaced telephone call. The summer at Tougaloo was proving to be a trying one because of a general indisposition that landed me in hospitals several times. So when an invitation came to speak on the campus of the University of South Florida, I was glad to accept. Never having heard of the institution, I surely wouldn't have placed it on the west coast, in Tampa. In any case the summer evenings were balmy and I was impressed by the vigor of its youthful History Department. Already concerned about returning to the rigors of winter in South Bend, and after consulting with my wife and daughter in Oxford, I obtained a leave of absence from Notre Dame to take a post offered at USF. I was simply following in the wake of some very able faculty members at Ole Miss who had found sanctuary in Florida. The accidental death of the department chairman who had offered me the job caused some confusion, but I soon settled down to a ten-year stint of teaching, my last. Various fortuitous circumstances—including my selection by *People* magazine as one of the best teachers in the country and the general conception that I was a Faulkner expert—brought increments in salary so that by the time of retirement, my income had reached three times that of my best years at Ole Miss. In time my wife became executive director of the Democratic party in Hillsborough County, and Gail followed her sister to college in New England after completing King High School in Tampa. In 1984 she is in her senior year of medicine at the University of Washington in Seattle.

In spite of continued problems with my lungs, I was able to carry on normal collegiate activities, appearing occasionally on historical and civic programs and writing articles and reviews for area papers and journals. At one point I put together a lengthy piece for *The Floridian,* the Sunday magazine section of the *St. Petersburg Times,* about the place blacks had achieved in Florida higher education. At no time did I feel it necessary to defend my point of view before the bar of public opinion in my adopted state. University authorities must have been pleased with my work for they granted me both emeritus status and an honorary doctorate.

I quickly became adjusted to the good life in Florida, partly with the purchase of a power boat for fishing in the Gulf of Mexico. In my middle years here, we bought an apartment on Honeymoon Island off the coast of Dunedin, where I wrote this account of our Mississippi adventure.

Even my most conscientious enemies should concede that *Missis-*

sippi: The Closed Society was an honest attempt to get at the facts. To the utmost of my ability I used the same procedures I had learned in graduate training and had developed in my writing at the University of Mississippi. Of course, *The Closed Society* presented my own point of view, which had been largely formed from the exigencies of life in Misissippi for a quarter century. It would have been impossible to have told the whole story. I had not had the chance, nor did I develop the opportunity, to talk at length with many of the participants in the Meredith imbroglio. There were no interviews with Ross Barnett, Paul Johnson, John Kennedy, Bill Simmons, Burke Marshall, Senator Eastland, Judge Brady, or dozens of others concerned with the historic events in Mississippi, and therefore my book was not completely researched. I am not impugning my own integrity for I believe as I did twenty years ago that I made an unusual effort to search out the truth in *The Closed Society*. At the same time, I have not been sure that presenting a completely balanced account ever was possible. Nor did I attempt it.

While still at Notre Dame, I was delighted to be invited to put together a documentary history of the Meredith Case, to be used as a supplementary text in classrooms across the country. At the time I was plagued with emphysema and was in the process of moving to Florida. In the academic year 1969–1970 I took up teaching at the University of South Florida and continued my policy of occasionally obtaining leaves of absence from local hospitals to meet my classes. Too ill to work on the book of documents, I returned to South Bend to spend most of the summer of 1970 recuperating in the backyard of the home we had been unable to sell. For the first time in ten years I was under no pressure, and so I was able to put together four hundred and fifty pages of documents from my own collection of materials and from the Law Library at Notre Dame. I sent the completed volume to the editor, who seemed gratified with the result.

In the fall I returned to Tampa, this time with Dutch and Gail. The galleys for the book of documents never arrived. The manuscript apparently was lost on the shelves of a company involved in bankruptcy. Several years after its completion, the work was returned to me. Upon the recommendation of a friend of mine, the University of Notre Dame Press took a look at it but decided the time had passed for such a publication. It was the same story at Memphis State University. So, still convinced of the usefulness of a collection of the Meredith documents, I forwarded my manuscript to the archives of the University of Mississippi, assuming that one day it would be discovered and at least used by historians. I am sure that the people of Mississippi have a right to know precisely what happened and what was said in their state's confrontation with the federal government.

For the second half of the year after I returned to Florida, I devoted three or four hours each day to putting together, under the sponsorship of USF and the Southern Regional Council (SRC), the most imposing symposium on civil rights ever to take place in Florida and perhaps in the country. Under the rubric of a "Symposium on the Contemporary South," twenty-five participants, each with a dramatic experience in the field of human rights, held a series of addresses and forums for a five-day period beginning Sunday, January 9, 1972. The sessions were divided into four main categories: "Two Decades of Human Rights," "The New Southern History," "The New Southern Politics," and "The South Tomorrow." Major speeches were delivered by Benjamin Mays, president emeritus of Morehouse College and the dean of black leaders in the South; John Hope Franklin, chairman of the department of history at the University of Chicago; Eugene Patterson, former editor of the *Atlanta Constitution* and a Pulitzer Prize-winning editor of the *Washington Post* and now editor and president of the *St. Petersburg Times;* and Reubin Askew, governor of Florida. Julian Bond, veteran Georgia legislator and former Communications Director of the Student Nonviolent Coordinating Committee; Howard Lee, mayor of Chapel Hill; and John Lewis, head of the Voter Education Project of the Southern Regional Council, completed the roster of blacks on the program. From Mississippi came Frank Smith, William Winter, Pat Derian, and Hodding Carter III. Foundations were represented by Leslie Dunbar (Field), Harold Fleming (Potomac Institute), and Pat Watters (Southern Regional Council). I was particularly pleased about the specialists in southern history who came: Vann Woodward (Yale), Paul Gaston (Virginia), Dewey Grantham (Vanderbilt), Bell Wiley (Emory), and George Tindall (North Carolina). Besides

its chief executive, Florida was represented by former Governor
Leroy Collins; George Mayer, author of *The Republican Party;* and
the president of the University of South Florida, Cecil Mackey. The
list of panelists was completed with Charles Morgan of the American Civil Liberties Union who wrote *A Time to Speak;* Reese
Cleghorn, coauthor of *Climbing Jacob's Ladder* and editorial-page
editor of the *Charlotte Observer;* and Joel Fleishman, director of
Policy Sciences and Public Affairs at Duke University.

The meetings, packed with students, faculty and townspeople,
were covered extensively by the area's news media and the southern
press generally. Feature articles about the symposium appeared in
the *Atlanta Constitution* and the *Baltimore Sun;* another article became a chapter in *The Americanization of Dixie* by John Egerton.
Through funds provided by the SRC and the Ford Foundation, the
Southern Educational Communications Association (SECA) promised four hour-long documentaries as well as copies of each paper as
actually delivered. Because of a mechanical breakdown in the recording machinery, SECA furnished only two half-hour films, which
appeared on national public television. The failure to produce copies
of the speeches as given prevented me from editing the proceedings
of the symposium. This had become the story of my publishing
career, as much the same thing happened with the Carrier biography
and the papers of the Fifth Annual Civil War Conference at Gettysburg College. Still, the "Symposium on the Contemporary South"
may well have been the highlight of my academic life, if only for the
reason that I had been associated in one way or another with all of
the participants in the program.

When I began the collection of data and ideas for my speech in
1963 to the Southern Historical Association, the speech that grew
into a book, I entered into an extensive correspondence with knowledgeable people in Mississippi and traveled about the state to gather
further information. Still, life at Ole Miss implies partial isolation,
and as my excursions to the capital, the Delta, and the Gulf Coast
were of necessity sporadic, I was forced to depend on a close reading of the local press, which often told more than was intended. In
the spring of 1963 my wife and I made an extended journey through-

out Mississippi, conversing mainly with whites of a similar disposition to our own.

Thus I failed to learn the details of the Jackson Movement (1962–1963) until I read John Salter's spirited volume entitled *Jackson, Mississippi: An American Chronicle of Struggle and Schism* (1979), which so impressed me that I bought copies for my children who had departed from their native state. Salter is a community organizer who at 27 came into Mississippi in the late summer of 1961 to teach sociology at Tougaloo. His story of the systematized grass-roots activities in Hinds County is a splendid narrative which fills many gaps in my own experience. Though Salter and I have yet to meet, we wrote about many of the same people: Bill Higgs, Ross Barnett, Tom Johnson, James Meredith, J. P. Coleman, Aaron Henry, and the Women for Constitutional Government, to mention a few. In the period of Salter's most frenetic activity, I was teaching at Emory in Atlanta and trying to compose my address. I find it difficult now to recall the exact dates when I visited Jackson State, the headquarters of COFO, the Fairgrounds stockade, and emotional gatherings in the Masonic Temple, but they were surely after Salter left Mississippi and were therefore outside the Jackson Movement.

I write these words to suggest only minor incompatibility between Salter's book and *The Closed Society*. But the key postulation of both Salter and Ed King (who wrote the introduction) has disturbed me beyond agreement. It is that the Jackson Movement was largely brought down by pressures from ostensible allies, the NAACP and the federal government. I just don't know. I am aware, of course, of the fierce competition between the NAACP and its more leftist rivals (Southern Conference Educational Fund, Student Nonviolent Coordinating Committee, CORE, Southern Christian Leadership Conference) which sprang up in the radicalization of the modern civil rights crusade. Unquestionably, the federal government as well as the NAACP put its faith in accommodation, in voter registration, and in the slow legal process. After all, it did take Meredith almost two years to work his way via the courts from Jackson to Oxford, and then he prevailed only because of federal power. The national bureaucracies of black leadership and the federal government had developed a certain stodginess and were extremely cautious about antagonizing public opinion. On many occasions I perceived that the children and the aged among the disinherited were the fearless ones in their eagerness to involve themselves in direct action.

Nevertheless, I am inclined to go along with the assurance of Burke Marshall that the Justice Department always kept in mind that after intervention it had sooner or later to return the responsibility for law and order to state authority, and therefore it was unwilling (as well as unable)—unless irreparable damage was anticipated—to protect those militants consenting to risk their lives in civil rights activity. His assertion deserves better than a cynical dismissal as a patent fabrication.

Though our ultimate goals mesh, I am by nature more conservative than Salter and King. They are doers, activists willing to put their lives on the line for what they believe. Perhaps long residence in the South has influenced me. I see *The Closed Society* as an attempt to explain a momentous change in Mississippi by reference to its past and by the avoidance of deliberate indoctrination. I do find it extremely difficult to believe that Marshall, John Doar, Arthur Schlesinger, and the Kennedys, with whom I worked closely and admire enormously, could have conspired to destroy the mass involvement of the Jackson Movement. Certainly they were not extremist. Perhaps the controversy can be reconciled as a jurisdictional and family dispute among travelers on the road to the same destination.

In 1972 I summarized my views on Faulkner in a paper read at a Southern Historical Association meeting in Miami Beach. The society had already devoted one of its most successful sessions to a discussion of W. J. Cash's *Mind of the South* thirty years after its publication. Subsequently I was asked to evaluate William Alexander Percy's *Lanterns on the Levee,* another famous book published by Alfred Knopf in 1941—hence my last scholarly paper read before an association meeting in Washington in 1975.

I decided early in my gathering of data not to visit Greenville for fear of having my interpretation challenged by the charm of the Percy family. My wife and I had once been guests, along with David and Lillian Cohn, at an elegant dinner at the home of LeRoy Percy, and I had visited the city later to assist two excellent graduate students who were writing their Ole Miss master's theses on the life of Cohn. My own conclusions regarding Percy posed the same problems as "The Closed Society" for here again I was undertaking a judgment on my home state and its people. I think it will stand the test of time.

Afterword

Before the showdown came between the federal government and Ross Barnett's official Mississippi, I had received dozens of letters from the state's expatriates who were burdened with a feeling of responsibility for Mississippi's medieval caste system but who would not or could not think of returning home. Not only had these people transcended their early environment but apparently they were filled, as James Street was, with an abiding love for their birthplace. Sometimes, too, I have encountered the bitterness of an editor of a widely circulated national magazine who returned in the later fifties after an absence of twenty-five years to write a feature story about the taxing of the illegal sale of alcoholic beverages. He reached Oxford with a basketful of pints of whiskey purchased at five dollars a bottle from bootleggers throughout Mississippi. Later he discarded his extensive notes with the wry comment, "It's like coming home after all these years and finding that your mother is a whore."

Every white southerner since the beginning of slavery, I believe, has had the Negro on his conscience in greater or lesser degree. For a generation I had known that the whites most sensitive to racial injustice were southern-born men and women who somehow came to see the enormity of the crime against the black man. Their only solution to an intolerable personal problem—once it was established that the segregation barrier could not be breached—was to leave the South. A few rugged individuals I could name have chosen to stick it out in Mississippi to fight the good fight against intolerance and

135

prejudice at home. Such as these have from the beginning made a
mockery of "black power."

Most of the concerned persons who have talked with me have
marveled at their youthful incomprehension of evils inherent in their
heritage or even of the existence of a caste society. They have been
likely to recall an incident, petty or glaring, that awakened their
conscience a little or emancipated them with a wallop. Travel outside the South, military experience especially since the start of the
Korean War, reading some writer like Baldwin or Faulkner or
Wright or Lillian Smith, or even contact with an enlightened teacher
have on occasion brought the young whites into touch with reality.

To remain in small-town Mississippi and speak out against the
"system" has been to invite ostracism and economic suicide if not
physical reprisal. Every legal, social, political, educational, and economic institution has been used to perpetuate and fortify white
supremacy. Negro parents had long since learned to teach their
children to make the most of life as culturally deprived, inferior
citizens. In the first half of this century for either black or white to
protest the sanctity of custom was only so much heroic nonsense.
The value of Meredith's *Three Years in Mississippi* lies chiefly in its
documentation of the degree of corruption and self-deception within
the state's leadership whose single aim was to keep one qualified
Negro out of the University of Mississippi. For further proof, all one
needs to do is to check the behavior of those in charge in the fifties
and early sixties.

It should be remembered, though, that when the civil rights movement really began to menace the Mississippi way of life after the
1954 Supreme Court decision, the possibility of local acquiescence
in the new liberalism was minimal indeed. For Mississippians were
being told with increasing shrillness by outsiders that what three
generations had accepted as historical truth was so much mythology. Furthermore, separation of the races and absolute control of
every facet of society by the whites—universally assumed to be not
only constitutional but the work of God—were not being challenged
from within as evil and immoral. It is no wonder that a proud and
religious people resisted for a decade or that their defiance was
successful. The breakthrough came in the summer of 1964 with the

invasion of civil rights workers as well as with federal laws and court decisions, and since then the revolution in Mississippi's closed society has been moving with deliberate speed toward color blind democracy.

I have never really left Mississippi. For a year or so at Notre Dame I subscribed to the *Clarion-Ledger,* perhaps as a kind of penance. In both Indiana and Florida I was able to use William Faulkner as a chief interpreter of the South. In 1973 I was invited back to address the students of Ole Miss in an ODK-Mortar Board forum I had helped to initiate more than thirty years before. It seemed appropriate to read my paper on Faulkner, and the result was an ovation in Fulton Chapel. Still later, I returned to the campus to receive a copy of *What Was Freedom's Price?* dedicated to me by the history faculty. I have also journeyed to Jackson to address the annual meeting of the American Civil Liberties Union and to participate in a program at Millsaps College commemorating the freedom summer of 1964. From time to time I have contributed books from my library to Rust and Tougaloo colleges, and have donated papers of various kinds to the archives at the University of Mississippi. Our children have made regular pilgrimages to the land of their birth. I have never felt out of touch with the state of Mississippi. I look upon it even now as my home.

I have been reading once again thousands of letters received in the 1960s but see no use for them in this narrative. If anyone is interested, they will soon be placed in the archives at Ole Miss. It seems to me that they were favorable to my conduct in those years in a ratio of fifteen to one. Many messages sustaining my position were postmarked in Mississippi while a few from the state excoriated me for my views. Unquestionably, most of those whose feathers I had ruffled chose not to become my communicants. It is only natural that I have most respect for those who came down on my side.

Having read all of my available correspondence going back to the early thirties (including my extant carbons), I feel confirmed in the general thesis of this reminiscence that until some moment in the Meredith affair I had been running through life scared, desiring above all to be accepted in my work and play by my contemporaries.

This should be easily comprehensible, even as a partial cause of my apparent assumption of authority and occasional brusqueness. Certainly I wished to avoid my appearance of being obsequious. What I had learned in college and graduate school became the basis for independent analysis of Mississippi's culture. I believe I showed signs of mental growth. Surely I tried.

While I make no profession of understanding the intrusions of the dream world, it could be of some significance that often over the years while I slept, my mind has come up with graphic pictures— failure in the classroom, losing my job, joining the unemployed, not being able to feed and educate my family, and living in cabins with dirt floors without the usual facilities, and more. These visions still trouble me once in a while.

Of far greater import has been the impairment of my naturally strong body. In my high school years this emerged as an irritating skin rash apparently caused by poison oak. There may have been a physical reason for my sluggishness at Carolina. In the thirties my physician suggested that I was victimized by various allergens, and I hastened off to St. Louis to consult a specialist in the field. Back in Mississippi I remember taking showers between classes, the water as hot as I could tolerate it and then shifting to the chillingly cold. This procedure seemed to drive the blood from the surface and thereby soothed the skin. In Montgomery a doctor experimented by injecting blood taken from my arms into my hips. Many a time I have played poker throughout the night with both arms loosely bound with bandages soaked in Vaseline. God knows how many foods and condiments were placed on my forbidden list and how many grasses I tried to avoid. In Scotland my weekly visits must have helped the National Health Service toward bankruptcy. But while in the Marshall Islands during the war I conducted a few tests on my own. For several weeks I consumed *only* those foods excluded from my diet, and still maintained excellent health. At that precise time Dutch was struggling with two small children on the Ole Miss campus and wondering when the big tree in the backyard would come crashing down on the house. As I reconstruct the picture there was no way for me to help solve her problems simply because I was stuck on a small island with quite nominal chores. A few years after my return to the states, I was introduced to the healing properties of cortisone.

After a decade of troublesome decisions I arrived as if by the wave of a magical wand at the point where there was no doubt as to my course. As I see it, shortly later, during the period of what might be considered enormous stress, my health was close to perfect. No longer was it necessary to suppress my views in any degree; right or wrong, it was full speed ahead.

Admittedly, I am theorizing about my health and my life. For years I had been in attendance at hospitals in Mississippi, Missouri, Massachusetts, and Tennessee. At Notre Dame I began to develop shortness of breath, the beginnings of emphysema, and subsequently I found myself hospitalized in Indiana and Michigan and finally in Florida. My lungs were decimated, I think from more activity over the recent years than my body could safely encompass. While my diagnosis may not coincide with that of the medical profession, it is one I believe to be most accurate. In the early seventies, I was close to death three times in the Sunshine State, but now all I have to contend with are the normal ills of old age, plus a considerable intake of assorted pills to ease my shattered lungs.

I am as at ease with the world and with myself as it is possible for a naturally contentious man to be. When I finish this volume, I plan to return to leisurely fishing, swimming, beach walking, watching television, reading fiction, the *St. Petersburg Times,* and a news magazine, and in general enjoying the balmy weather of the Gulf Coast. I hope these words explain satisfactorily the thesis of this little book and the course of my life in Mississippi.

There is one more item. I am greatly concerned with the land where our children were born and raised. In 1965 I wrote "Revolution Begins in the Closed Society." Since then I have returned to Mississippi on many occasions and have kept up a desultory correspondence with some of its citizens, primarily of a mind similar to my own. My feeling is that in spite of the low rank economically (and thus culturally) of the state in the nation, the land of the magnolias has made great progress in its quest for equality before the law for all its people. To substantiate this claim, one has only to reflect on conditions prevailing in the middle years of this century and to take a good look at the massive resistance to progress then espoused by the state's weak leadership. The nation finally demanded that its unfinished business of the previous century be completed even to the intrusion of federal power, and the state has been forced to what its people in their hearts must have known to be right.

The masses of people in Mississippi are relatively poor. The last few decades have seen only a handful of blacks achieve prosperity, and yet their outflow from the state has been reversed.

It is probably true that "equality at the starting line" is an impossible goal, but many barriers faced by blacks and poor whites a short time ago have been reduced. Whole classes of people need no longer believe that they are inherently inferior.

Each of us has a tendency to generalize from his own limited experience. I make no effort to list the improvements that have taken place among the people of Mississippi. Suffice it to say that I am greatly encouraged. I feel that Mississippians are moving rapidly toward that moment when my children will be capable of reversing Faulkner's famous statement made in the early 1950s that—involved in a love-hate relationship with his birthplace—he found it necessary to hate Mississippi a little more than a couple of decades before. They now must surely acknowledge that they are more proud of their native land than when they were growing up on the Ole Miss campus. Here is one small evidence of remarkable change: it would not have been possible two decades ago for this volume to have been published by the University Press of Mississippi.

In early November of 1982, I flew to Memphis to participate in a Southern Historical Association gathering, commemorative of the 1955 meeting (which I had arranged). Of the original speakers Faulkner and Sims had died, but Benjamin Mays, then 88, was alive and present. This grand old man charmed an overflow audience as he had twenty-seven years before. Tom Clark from the previous cast also returned. The new speakers were Sam Cook, president of Dillard University; Claude Sitton, civil rights reporter for the *New York Times* and now editor of the Raleigh *News and Observer;* and Willie Morris, former editor of *Harper's* and an eminent Mississippi author. Frank Smith presided. Bill Silver arrived from the Virgin Islands, and we drove to Oxford for a couple of days with friends, and then on to Jackson where William and Elise Winter hosted a dinner for us in the governor's mansion with some seventy guests, most of them former students of mine. I found the occasion somewhat reminiscent of the dinners we had put on at Ole Miss preceding the ODK-Mortar Board forums. Each of the guests seemed ready to praise the progress their Magnolia State had made in race relations, and I found no reason to disagree. This experience was indeed heartwarming for the former Ole Miss professor of history.

Many have indeed run scared, but the goal is in sight.

Appendixes

A. Report from Britain (1950)

B. We're Going back to Mississippi (1952)

C. Response to "A Professor's Crackpot Talk" (1956)

D. The Tragedy of Southern Leadership, 1820–1860 (1961)

E. Mississippi Must Choose (1964)

F. Correspondence Related to James Silver and the Board of Trustees (1964)

G. Faulkner and the Teaching of History (1972)

H. William Alexander Percy: The Aristocrat and the Anthropologist (1975)

Report from Britain
(1950)

Among the pieces I sent back from Scotland, the one I dispatched on February 12, 1950 was concerned with Mississippi. Here it is:

It's beginning to look as though professors in southern universities may one day be considered as human beings, even important humans like football coaches. I'm not thinking, of course, in terms of comparative salaries but in the amount of abuse that may be hurled at them without fear of recrimination. Perhaps the fact that I am writing from the campus of a British university where for a long, long time academic freedom has prevailed causes me to see the picture back home in clearer perspective. Over here where a professor is looked upon as an individual with certain inalienable rights—such as are guaranteed to every American in the federal Constitution—it is as difficult to explain the silly antics of a small minority of red baiters and professional patriots as it is to combat the notion that all Americans are rich.

Such observation is prompted by the receipt in this morning's mail of a clipping from the Jackson (Miss.) *Daily News* of February 2 which proclaims in two-inch headlines: Solons In Secret Session Here to Hear 'Red' Names. It seems that the author of a subversive activities bill in the state House of Representatives, after requesting an executive session and having charged that Mississippi colleges "are infested with Communist fellow travelers," accused three professors at the University of Mississippi of "molding the minds of Mississippi students" along biased political lines of thought. The legislator included me in his list of "undesirable professors," along with another Fulbright grantee who is in the Philippines, even further from home than I am.

I am inclined to believe that the general public, which seldom gets behind such press stories, might be interested in the feelings of a professor who may as well have gone through the past dozen years with the slogan "Big Brother is Watching You" pasted on his office door.

Put yourself in his place if you will. What would have been your reaction if a senior in your department had been invited to the home of a prominent Mississippi politician where she was continually pumped for evidence of

144

your subversive teaching? What if a former county sheriff, who claimed access to the Board of Trustees, had threatened you with being fired because you had gone to his home town and had given, in an adult forum, as requested by the State Department of Education, both sides of a controversial labor question?

How would you feel if informed by your chancellor that an administrative officer of the university (who had previously written that you were one of his "favorite" professors) was getting up a "file" on your background at the request of a Congressman who objected to your advocacy of federal aid to education—a bill, incidentally, introduced by the beloved Senator Pat Harrison? If a forum speaker who had accepted the hospitality of your home had, without your knowledge, denounced you to the Governor as a "red" after a discussion into which you had not even entered?

I think I know what your reaction in this and similar cases would have been because, believe it or not, a professor has feelings too. You may ask: "Why has he not previously protested against these things?" Because none of the information had come to him "officially." Because he realized that any fuss stirred up might harm the university to which he has devoted fourteen of the best years of his life. Because by nature he is peace loving and because he did not want his wife and two children, born almost on the Ole Miss campus, to become involved in nasty disputation. But because, most of all, he believed firmly in the basic intelligence and sense of fair play of the Governor, the great majority of the Legislature, and the members of the Board of Trustees. They have shown many times that they would come to no snap judgment based on *ex parte* evidence.

Obviously, this is no place for the professor to debate his beliefs. For the record, though, he would like to state that he is no more a communist or fellow traveler than his brother Rotarians in Oxford, or, for that matter, the honorable members of the Legislature. In fact he had never knowingly seen a Communist until he ran into a rather unkempt fellow selling the *Daily Worker* on the streets of Aberdeen. He thinks of himself as being a "middle of the roader" who may lean slightly to one side and then to the other. He believes firmly in the capitalistic system. But he has long since attempted to get away from doctrinaire views and has tried to make up his mind on problems affecting the South by asking himself a simple question: "Is this thing good for the South as a whole?"

The professor has been wondering most of the day as to the supposedly reliable evidence on which the young man who denounced him as "undesirable" based his reputation-shattering charge. Apparently they had been together on the Mississippi campus for a number of years. Had the legislator been in one of his classes? Had he read any of his writings? Had he made a genuine effort to obtain first hand information which the accused himself would gladly have given? The professor can't be certain because he doesn't remember the gentleman, but he thinks the answer in each case is "no." He has no desire to impugn the motives, intelligence, or integrity of the legislator, but he surmises that the youngster has confused presentation of all sides of a question with un-Americanism.

This is the first time that my name has appeared in the press in such fashion. What I do and what happens to me is of little significance. But I wonder whether the University of Mississippi can ever become more than a trade school, whether it can ever achieve greatness, as long as its faculty has to keep in mind the whims and prejudices of the nearest legislator. I have been brought up with the notion that the primary function of any university is to seek and disseminate the truth. I am perfectly aware that truth may never be found but I do know that it is absurd to look for it in an atmosphere of suspicion and distrust where academic freedom does not exist.

It is my considered opinion that the great majority of Mississippians want their University to be free. The time has come for a mature and civilized people to frown upon adolescent and irresponsible outbursts to the point where they would no longer be looked upon as political assets.

We're Going back to Mississippi
(1952)

After two very valuable years "abroad," the Silver family re-
turned to Mississippi in the summer of 1952. The following arti-
cle was written on 1 June and appeared in several Mississippi
papers and in the Richmond Times-Dispatch.

Northern friends smile in amiable disbelief when we suggest
that, having spent one year in Britain and another in Boston, in the last
three, we are eagerly awaiting the end of our "sentence" so that we may
return to Mississippi. Incredulity merges into amazement when it is further
disclosed that we might have taken advantage of a chance to climb a rung or
two on the economic ladder, outside the South. In spite of all that has been
written about Dixie, these friends are still the victims of grave misconcep-
tion as to what has been happening down there.

For sixteen years I have taught as I pleased, without the slightest interfer-
ence from those in authority, in my history classes at the University of
Mississippi. I have talked freely in speeches from Byhalia to Clarksdale and
Pascagoula. Certainly political leaders and some businessmen have disagreed with my expression of sometimes unorthodox convictions on the
Negro question, labor, states' rights, and the New Deal. It is true that a
congressman, a newspaper columnist, and various and sundry local politicians have tried to get me fired. Despite such occasional flurries, intelligent
citizens have, for twenty years, supported a superior Board of Trustees'
insistence on a decidedly high degree of academic freedom in Mississippi.

Much of the North still seems to dream peacefully in a twilight of ignorance concerning constructive developments in the South. The meaningless
but belabored poll tax (which most southern states have abolished), opposition to a moral-enforcing FEPC, a rare piece of violence quite similar to the
staid New England brand as reported in the Boston press, and the antics of a
congressman or two endowed with the southern type of demagoguery, remain the antiquated grist for the ever monotonous chant of antagonism
toward an assumedly backward section.

Since coming to Boston I have attended two Ford Hall forums on the race
question, one led by the judicial William H. Hastie, and the other by a
courageous southerner, Lillian Smith. Only one point of view has been
presented, which is probably as it should be inasmuch as a large part of the

clientele, regardless of the speaker or his subject, week after week asks the same loaded questions on the Negro problem. The only Harvard Law School forum of the year having to do with the South presented two brilliant speakers, professional advocate Thurgood Marshall and scholarly Marion Wright, with the NAACP party line, as opposed to an eager but inept defender of gradualism, an editor from North Carolina. These were not the only performances which led me to believe that the shades of William L. Garrison were still carrying the torch for partisanship at the expense of enlightenment.

Then I conducted a few discussions of my own in the Winthrop area only to discover that the average run of citizen, faced with reality, reacts to a race situation about as does the same kind of person in Mississippi. Several women belligerently addressed themselves to the potential calamity, from their point of view, of Negro neighbors. It appears that Winthrop itself, like many New England communities, has had its own race problems and its prejudices too. The original Yankee Protestants have been plagued with swarms of Irish, Jews (after the Chelsea fire of 1908), Italians, and now all these elements are fearful of the possible influx of Negroes.

The continued preaching of the gospel of racial tolerance, in the schools, the churches, and the press, has been, it seems to me, an absolute *must* in a region populated with such a heterogeneous family. This may explain in part the intense concern up here with southern racial problems.

At the colorful St. Patrick's Day parade in South Boston, my children noticed several all-Negro bands, one of which proudly displayed the emblem of championship of the diocese of Archbishop Cushing. In New York several of the waterfront locals of the International Longshoremen's Association are made up of Negroes, by their own choice—and, too, these have been the only ones with guts enough to testify against port racketeers. Much segregation, North and South, seems to be self-imposed.

Four articles in the Boston *Globe* last January depicted graphically the inferior status of the educated Negro in this area. We ran into a Negro from Arkansas who had worked his way through Boston University's law school and who is now earning his living as a clerk in a Boston department store. Not only are the average colored people likely to be found in slum districts but in the factories and shops where they work in low-paying jobs with heavy manual labor.

On the other hand it should be said that one of the old New England towns has this year elected a Negro as its meeting moderator. But I have been told that this deserved honor came in part because there were few voters of his race in the community. Which reminds me that I have noticed less antisemitism in the South than anywhere else in the country.

We have been painfully aware that a young, New-Dealing congressman who has announced for the Senate has indulged in demagoguery, in regard to the South, that would do justice to the mental gymnastics of John Rankin.

One of the saddest tragedies in this enormous nation of ours is that we have not frowned into oblivion the politician who would make political capital by fighting imaginary dragons which always seem to abound just over the horizon. Southern dragons, perhaps unfortunately, don't vote in Massachusetts.

Even an eminent Harvard professor of economics, chairman of the New England governors' committee on the textile industry, has demonstrated symptoms of localism which are sure to bring spots before the eyes. In the cloistered seclusion of the academic seminar, he serenely testifies to an easing of conscience based on the concessions which he claims New England has made to the southern economy through tariff reduction, with the implication that the South should be rhapsodically content with being socked on the head with an economic hammer six times daily instead of the traditional dozen.

The whole southern industrial picture has been distorted in the New England press. Those who cry for racial equality in the South are seemingly unwilling for it to come in the only practical manner possible, through economic abundance. For, historically, the South's "waywardness" has resulted in the main from her poverty (submerged whites without hope in the past have been easily led—remember Hitler, the Germans, and the Jews?—into frightening excesses against their colored neighbors), and the recent amazing gains in racial tolerance have paralleled an increasing prosperity.

It would seem that many a northern crusade to "free" the Negro in the South has been based on the fantastic idea that it might be achieved while the South remained in its old state of colonial dependency. (We have learned, I hope, that hungry bellies require food before their owners are receptive to notions of liberty.) This is reminiscent of the choleric insistence of the abolitionist ever panting to free billions of dollars worth of property in slaves sold in large measure to the South by New Englanders who had closed out their equity and had become moral. Southerners need to learn, of course, that today's inflamed precursor of the millennium is no more representative of northern opinion than was his ancestor of a hundred years ago.

I am not suggesting that the people, by and large, of New England are different from those in Mississippi. They aren't. I am not implying that New Englanders should be unconcerned about racial problems in other parts of the country. They shouldn't be. They have an enormous stake in developments in the South, and, for that matter, in California. But surely, reform should be plugged for its own sake rather than for the specious reasoning that it will be of propaganda value in combatting Communism in Ethiopia or Assam.

The articulate formers of public opinion in New England need to inform themselves of the tremendous and revolutionary changes taking place in the South. They should glory in the gradual bringing of Mississippi's standard of living up with that of Massachusetts. Only when that is achieved, and it is coming more quickly than most people suspect, can this nation speak as a unit. They must realize, also, that the frenzy of the professional reformer is not conducive to the settlement of age-old problems of which the South is not only aware but is deeply concerned with solving.

All of this may indicate why one family (of mixed North and South antecedents) which has had the good fortune of living "abroad" for a couple of years, is impatiently awaiting its return to the most delightful part of the country in which to live. We suggest in all humility that those who would understand the "New South" had better not stay away too long for it is undoubtedly the most exciting and most rapidly changing region of these United States.

Response to
"A Professor's Crackpot Talk"
(1956)

On October 17, 1956, I addressed the Rotary Club of Jackson, Tennessee, on the subject "The Lunatic Fringe and the Moderates," which seemed to cause some little furore among patriotic Mississippians. According to witnesses, including Seale Johnson, president of the McCowat-Mercer Press, who had requested that I make the talk in the first place, my words were well received by the audience. Such was not the case with sundry members of the press and the Jackson Daily News *headlined its lead editorial on November 1 with "A Professor's Crackpot Talk." Perhaps by this time I had learned a bit about adversarial relations in Mississippi, for I not only answered the inquiry of the Board of Trustees in some detail but forwarded copies of my reply to the governor and various friends. Former students and eminent historians (Arthur Schlesinger, Thomas D. Clark) came to my rescue. Here is a copy of the letter I wrote to the Board on October 29, 1956:*

The University of Mississippi
College of Liberal Arts
University, Mississippi
October 29, 1956

Dr. E. R. Jobe, Executive Secretary
Board of Trustees
Institutions of Higher Learning
1007 Woolfolk Building
Jackson, Mississippi

Dear Doctor Jobe:

In answer to your letter of October 17, I am pleased to write you about a speech I made to the Jackson, Tennessee, Rotary Club on October 17, 1956. Unfortunately, I cannot send you an exact copy of what I said because I spoke from rather incomplete notes. But those notes are before me and I am able to give you, without distortion, the substance of what I said.

First I ought to say that I was rather shocked at the report of my talk as it came out in the *Jackson Daily News* and other papers. I do not think there was an effort at misrepresentation but it does look as though the reporter tried hard to find something sensational in an otherwise rather dull historical essay. I am enclosing a copy of the report of the speech which came out in the Jackson (Tennessee) *Sun* and which is reasonably accurate. Also it might be in order to quote from a letter which I received from Seale Johnson, president of the McCowat-Mercer Press in Jackson: "The reaction to your talk was most favorable. I am sorry that the Associated Press saw fit to pick up the story and distort it. You certainly said nothing that would be offensive to anyone who would take time for a moment's thought. It was provocative, but heaven knows that's what we need in these times of 'never say anything that anybody could possibly disagree with.'"

As for the talk itself, it was simply a plea for freedom of thought, backed by sound historical fact. First I spoke of what I called "Mississippi's tragic blunder in 1861." I *emphasized* that I thought that Mississippi had legal right on her side and that she was probably morally right but that *judged by results* her action could be considered nothing less than a "tragic blunder." The results, of course, were millions of blasted lives, a people who had to suffer physical, financial, economic, etc. degradation for at least two or three generations. I suggested that Mississippi in the 1950s was just coming back to its relative economic prosperity of the 1850s. And I think no historian or man who has read the history of his country would take issue with this. [I used Mississippi, of course, as a prototype of all the states that seceded.]

Next, I suggested that Mississippi's secession was based on certain beliefs of the people that turned out to be illusions. These were: 1) the idea of peaceful secession (there would be no war and it would be wise to get out of the union in order to make a better bargain to return), 2) the notion that Yankees wouldn't fight, 3) the belief that abolitionists controlled the North, 4) a mis-interpretation of the significance of Lincoln's election (Lincoln had a heterogeneous party, both Houses of Congress were controlled by the Democrats until secession, and the Supreme Court was favorable to the South, and Lincoln himself turned out to be a reasonable man), 5) the notion that King Cotton was supreme and would force the British and French to action favorable to the South, and 6) the idea that the slave states were unanimous in thought. I made it clear that these thoughts were not believed by all Southerners but that most Southerners believed some or all of these things.

Then I tried to point out how such a situation had developed in the thirty years before the Civil War and how the South had moved from the accepted ideas of freedom of thought as expressed by Thomas Jefferson to the insistence on orthodoxy of thought in the 1850s. I made it plain that it all went back to the abolition attack and that the South, a minority section in a country run by majority rule, in order to defend itself, had increasingly stifled dissent within its own region in order to make its power stronger in national councils. Thus there developed the "passion for unanimity," the insistence on a "United Front." The orthodox doctrine consisted, in the main, of states' rights thinking in politics and the proslavery philosophy in social matters. After some thirty years of slow but accelerating indoctrination, most southern politicians at least, accepted this kind of thinking. Especially in the 1850's, journalistic, church, and political leaders made little effort to present other than the southern point of view.

I then pointed out that the danger of enforced orthodox thinking and the refusal to listen to dissenting voices, is that important decisions may well be made on a completely doctrinaire basis. And, as Dr. Avery Craven points out so well, southern politicians fought against internal improvements at national expense and against free lands, both of which were wanted desperately by people in the Northwest, because these things did not fit in with states' rights doctrine. Dr. Craven believes, and I think reasonably so, that these doctrinaire southern decisions alienated the Northwest, previously tied closely to the South by family, economics, and the Mississippi River system, to the point that the South lost her natural allies in the Northwest. However good this may have seemed in the 1840s, it undoubtedly turned out tragically for the South in the 1860s.

This was the basis of my argument. The subject is controversial, no doubt, but I am sure that the vast majority of southern historians will go along with me on the general thesis. Admittedly it is speculation but speculation backed up by meticulous historical research. I think it the duty of any historian worth his salt to get these ideas before intelligent people.

Having made what I considered my main talk, but finding that there were about ten minutes left, I launched into a summary of a paper by Professor George Tindall of Louisiana State University, a paper having to do with bringing up to date a famous essay written by Ulrich B. Phillips back in 1928. I had read this paper of Tindall's a couple of days before, thought it highly provocative and worthy of consideration, and had prepared my notes so that I could use it or not, as time permitted. In my short summary I made it extremely clear (three times, in fact) that these ideas came from a South Carolina born historian. In my short summary I made it extremely clear (three times, in fact) that I thought these ideas were worth serious attention, but that I had not thought through them enough to know whether I could completely endorse them. My audience, I am sure, understood what I had in mind. I would guess, from your letter, that you are not interested in a summary of Tindall's general thesis, but I have decided to send you an exact copy of my notes and you may judge from them something of the nature of Tindall's ideas.

You and I both know how difficult it is for a newspaper reporter to get accurately the substance of a thirty-minute talk. Indeed, I am quite aware of the whole difficulty in communicating ideas when words are interpreted in so many ways by different people. My whole notion in making this talk was to bring before what I considered an intelligent audience some of the thinking of southern historians generally. I had no intention of being a propagandist but was concerned solely with a serious, sober, conscientious examination of an explosive but tremendously important subject.

Because of the obvious possibilities of misunderstanding, I shall be delighted to come before the Board of Trustees of the Institutions of Higher Learning at any time to answer whatever questions its members might have.

I am sorry that I could not send you an exact copy of the talk, but I have done my level best to send you an accurate summary of its contents.

Sincerely,

James W. Silver
chairman, history department

cc: Chancellor J. D. Williams
    Provost W. Alton Bryant
    Dean Victor A. Coulter

The Tragedy of Southern Leadership, 1820–1860 (1961)

At the Fifth Annual Civil War Conference at Gettysburg College on November 19, 1961, I read my paper "The Tragedy of Southern Leadership, 1820–1860." At the time I had no notion of being elected to the presidency of the Southern Historical Association, though I had thought of expanding the essay into a book, partly because of the influence it might have on the situation in Mississippi.

The people of South Carolina, Mississippi, and five other states of the lower South would not have seceded had they foreseen four long years of a bloody conflict they were destined to lose.

It has been persuasively argued, moreover, that they would never have withdrawn from the Union without a careful preparation for such an eventuality by short-sighted and blundering leaders. In effect, the people had been conditioned to make the proper response to the correct stimulus, the election of Abraham Lincoln in this case. By February 1, 1861, seven of the fifteen slave states had quit the Union.

Granted that these southerners could not have looked into the crystal ball to see surrender at Appomattox. Nonetheless they did make their fatal decision on the basis of what soon proved to be gross misinformation. However good the intention, however high the motive, however faultless the principle, the result was what Gerald Johnson has described as four years of blood and agony, "ten years of military occupation, thirty years of poverty and grinding toil, ninety years of harassment, anxiety, frustration, and moral deterioration."

By 1860, as Wilbur Cash saw it, the South had become a land of fantasy. Perhaps there was no particular harm in the illusion that every planter was a gentleman, in the glorification of southern womanhood, or even in the romanticization of slavery. There was cause for alarm, however, in the southerner's estimate of the Yankee, and in his belief in a solid South, "the last great bulwark of Christianity," whose tribal God would never let His chosen people down.

It was generally believed that secession, being perfectly legal, would take place without "a jostle or a jar." Southern politicians vied with each other in their eagerness to drink or wipe up with their handkerchiefs all the blood that might be spilled. There was little comprehension of the fierce devotion to the Union of millions of Americans in the rest of the country, nor, for that matter, of the North's enormous industrial potential. Out of the Union, southern states would be in a fat bargaining position for a triumphant return, on their own conditions.

Britain and France needed southern cotton so desperately that they would use powerful naval forces to brush aside any blockade the North might be presumptuous enough to establish. Cotton was indeed King. Or, so it was assumed.

The Yankee ("low-bred, crass, and money grubbing") had no stomach for man-to-man encounter in the open field with the chivalrous southerner. Governor Pettus of Mississippi was making plans of an evening to ambush invaders of his sovereign domain with shotguns, as his grandfather had successfully ambushed the Indians. When the war did come, college students from all over Dixie clamored to be sent to Virginia ere the opposition fade away or the picnic be rained out. They could hardly be expected to see quite so far into the future as Shiloh where farm boys from Alabama would be locked in death embrace with farm boys from Illinois, to the greater glory of both.

Nobody in the South, at least nobody articulate, acted as though he had the faintest glimmer of an understanding of Lincoln. A Montgomery paper lampooned him before and throughout the War as Abraham Hanks. The South had never been allowed to forget his house-divided speech, and apparently unaware of his repudiation of Helper and Brown and his express determination not to interfere with slavery in the states, considered his election a terrible and instant menace to the southern way of life.

Mounting the bandwagon, the professional politicians in Washington ignored Lincoln's unenviable position as a minority victor whose maverick party was made up of so many discordant elements that some of his supporters would begin to howl as soon as he opened his mouth. Disregarding a resolution of the House Committee of Thirty-Three that the South be cheerfully granted reasonable and effectual guarantees, southern Congressmen proclaimed to their constituents that all hope of relief had been extinguished and honor demanded a new Confederacy by way of separate state action. This a week before South Carolina seceded.

Had Lincoln been the rogue the South had been disciplined to believe him, he could have done little immediate damage. (Of course he turned out to be a reasonable sort of fellow, as southerners discovered somewhat late.) If the slave state representatives and senators had not pulled out of Congress, the Democratic party would have controlled both the House and the Senate. Forgotten was the resolution of the previous May in which Congress had explicitly stated, with the concurrence of Republican members, that it had no right to interfere with slavery in the states. That resolution had been sponsored by Jefferson Davis of Mississippi.

To crown this strange confusion of circumstance, the Supreme Court had not long before awarded to the South her last inch of demand in the western territories. In time Lincoln would unquestionably make new court appointments but as a minority President he must act cautiously in view of the control of Congress by the opposition (assuming the southerners remained) and the chances were that he would be hard pressed.

The truth seems to be that the people of the deep South, under severe provocation it is true, had nevertheless been thoroughly prepared for secession by their bungling politicians, their chauvinistic press, their political preachers, and their blind philosophers. They had been seriously misinformed, and on the basis of this misinformation, caught in the hysteria of the moment and plagued by a rapidly closing mind, they made a terrible decision which their descendants have been paying for even to the present generation.

It may be overly harsh to say, as Allan Nevins has said, that the South was tricked into secession by leaders who "lacked imagination, ability, and courage." Jefferson Davis, himself a reluctant secessionist, claimed that the people "were in advance of their representatives throughout," which was true enough in his own state, but he failed to add that the emotional explosion of the people in secession climaxed thirty years of ceaseless indoctrination.

For her own good reasons the South drew back from the spirit of nineteenth century movements directed toward freeing the human mind and body from restraint and upholding the divinity of the individual. It is of little concern here whether this rejection of the new liberalism resulted from a simple realization of its incompatibility with slavery, from agricultural depressions in the 1820s and 1830s, from a recognition of the South's evident minority political status, from vigorous outside attacks on the peculiar institution, or from a genuine fear of slave insurrections. The important thing is that the South developed her own Orthodoxy which came into full bloom in the 1850s.

This Southern Creed consisted of the pro-slavery argument, states' rights and religious fundamentalism. It categorically denied the validity of much of classical economics and the need for social experimentation. It finally emerged from a defense of the status quo to an aggressive southern imperialism which logically included the revival of the slave trade.

In 1831 Calhoun, recognizing the slave states as "a fixed and hopeless minority," openly launched his crusade for a united South. Although he had largely failed two decades later, at the time of his death during his losing fight against the Compromise of 1850, his devoted partisans never faltered in their impassioned drive for southern unanimity. In the fifties the Orthodox View was brought to perfection and generally accepted in principle, though there was more talk than accomplishment in the promotion of southern industry, southern shipping, southern literature, southern education, and even southern recreation.

More aggressively in the Deep South, the newspapers and magazines, the colleges and churches, the legislatures and Congressional delegations, the commercial and agricultural conventions, were lined up almost solidly to preserve and expand the accepted southern way.

As it gained in power, the southern majority protected itself by ruthlessly suppressing minority dissent within the section. When expedient, southern rights associations and vigilance committees made their appearance. The threat of violence was usually sufficient and by 1860 thousands of moderate southerners had departed from their native land or had acquiesced in help- less silence. This is not to say that a reign of terror prevailed in the im- mediate antebellum South but waves of pathological fear did sweep across the land whenever a crisis developed. The chief intellectual exercise of the time consisted of super-patriotic exhortations designed to terrify an exag- gerated radical opinion in the North and to destroy a feeble subversion in the South. In such a model society there was little call for critical analysis of social problems so petty tyrants played a frivolous game called "Stand Up and Be Counted."

The South's retreat from reality, its invention of a civilization resting on hallucination, its willingness to override individual rights, its renunciation of the doctrine of progress, and its insistence on thought control, sprang con- sciously from the minds of her leaders. These were the second class men who deigned to walk in the footsteps of Mason, Jefferson, Madison, Pendle- ton, and even the early Calhoun. Perhaps the challenge of their times was more perplexing than that of the founding fathers but the melancholy cer- tainty is that they failed to meet it. Universal manhood suffrage and democ- racy in religion may explain but not excuse their political and religious demagoguery; in any case the new southern leaders patiently coached their constituents along the path to inevitable disaster.

The statesman who, twenty years before, had accepted "a large part of the disgrace of slavery," and who had frowned upon "refined arguments on the constitution," in 1836 saw slavery as "the most solid and durable foun- dation on which to rear free and stable institutions." Calhoun was not the first apologist to present slavery as "the most perfect agreement ever known in Anglo-Saxon history." He demanded absolute acceptance of the superior civilization of his section whose people quickly learned to regard slavery in a "rigid, single-minded, and doctrinaire" way.

It may be that the South refused to think at all about the morality of slavery as it extended the slave codes and accepted its institution as provid- ing a dreamily contented society, except in those rare instances when out- side agitators stirred up the happy and carefree blacks to cut their masters' throats. The philosophers continued to tie up the loose ends in their denun- ciation of Jeffersonian liberalism and their sanctification of the proslavery argument. More and more they engaged in the wearisome doubletalk of George Fitzhugh who somehow discovered that southern slaves were not

only the happiest but also the "freest people in the world." To him the
wealth of the North was "little but a fiction," and as degrading materialism
had brought only suffering to the northern masses, it would soon give way in
the western world to some modification of domestic (black and white) slavery, "the normal condition of society."

The fitting epilogue to normality was achieved in the Confederate constitution which, according to the Vice-President, "put at rest, *forever,* all the
agitating questions relating to the peculiar institution. . . ." For once and for
all Jefferson was specifically repudiated as the new nation's cornerstone
rested "upon the great (physical, philosophical, and moral) truth, that the
negro is not equal to the white man."

The historic use of states' rights by every section of the country as a
defense mechanism against supposed national injury need not detain us
here. Its identification with the South and conservative groups generally,
however, may remind us that a states' righter is, by definition, anyone
whose enemies are in power in Washington. Georgia and Alabama professed undying devotion to the principle when honest John Quincy Adams
thought it proper to live up to solemn agreements with the Indians, but
quickly shifted their allegiance to nationalism when the terrifying Jackson
came into office. Mississippi added her condemnation of states' rights in the
nullification crisis and as late as 1851 declared in convention that "the asserted right of secession . . . is utterly unsanctioned by the Federal Constitution."

Although the doctrine of state sovereignty has traditionally been a major
part of the South's armor, it followed a devious path in the period between
the introduction of the Wilmot Proviso and the Civil War. In those days as
Professor Bestor has shown, the proslavery leaders unblushingly asserted
that state sovereignty immutably directed the use of federal authority to
enforce the *rights of the slave states only* in the territories and to nullify
state legislation in the free states in the matter of fugitive slaves. In this
sleight of hand the South was concerned with "the flagrant pursuit of immediate advantage," as it should have been. With the election of Lincoln the
states' rights fetish, never abandoned, was dusted off and with a flourish
made ready for spectacular use.

Long before 1860 religious orthodoxy had laid its paralyzing hand on the
South. In the years before Garrison began his crusade, volumes of Paine,
Hume, and Voltaire had been cast into the flames in which deism and
skepticism were being consumed. Waves of evangelism swept over the
common man whose personal religion soon contemplated a Devil loose in
the world and man's only hope the intervention of a righteous God.

Literal scrutiny of the Scriptures was accepted as the gateway to salva-
tion. A perverted Puritanism became the guide to moral conduct. Evangel-

ical denominations which had first denounced slavery were soon defending
it with Biblical authority. Such primitivism became an integral part of the
sacred teachings of southern Protestantism. Anti-intellectualism replaced
tolerance and reason.

At the laying of the cornerstone for the University of the South, Matthew
Fontaine Maury stated, "The Bible is authority for everything it touches."
And the Bible taught that the southern social order was designed by God for
His own purposes. As Benjamin Morgan Palmer sermonized, the "provi-
dential trust" of the South was "to conserve and perpetuate the institution of
slavery as now existing. . . . The position of the South at this moment is
sublime."

Religious fundamentalism denied to the South its only intellectually
sound defense of slavery, the new anthropology. Investigations of Morton,
Gliddon, Squier, Nott, and Agassiz indicated that the races of man were of
plural creation and distinct species. Physical anthropology thus not only
challenged the Jeffersonian idea of equality but also, unfortunately, the
Biblical account of creation, as well as "all the strong arguments" for slavery. To accept the new heresy, even though it apparently proved the inferiority of the Negro, was considered a strategic error "more dangerous
than all the ravings of the abolitionists." The pious southerner kept his
fundamentalism and lost his science.

Until after the Mexican War there may have been no certainty of the
destination, but, as Cash wrote, "The south was *en route* to the savage ideal
. . . whereunder dissent and variety are completely suppressed and men
become, in all their attitudes, professions, and actions, virtual replicas of
one another." In such a situation, as Harvey Wish has pointed out, men are
likely to "clad their prejudices with the majesty of eternal moral principle."

This is not to imply that all southerners reached the savage ideal or that
most southerners engaged in extravagant cant about moral principle. There
never was southern unity, in Calhoun's day, or any other. Moderation
existed in the border states down to the war and there were some rugged
souls in the deep South who defied the mandates of public opinion. Still,
there is considerable truth in Stanley Elkins's conclusion that:

> . . . the Southerner faced a situation in which all the hostile criticism was
> coming from the outside. A whole series of loyalties was thus automati-
> cally called into question. . . . There was no longer generally to be found
> the man best equipped to deal with slavery intellectually—a man such as
> Thomas Jefferson whose mind operated under the balanced tensions
> created not only by a repugnance to the system but also a commitment to
> it.

Patriotism became the first duty of the citizen. A ban was placed on
analysis and inquiry; there was little hospitality to new ideas; complacency
reigned. The South was morbidly sensitive. A Tennessean commented that

everyone "felt the crushing power and the omnipotence of this despotism of public opinion. The least suspicious of disloyalty to slavery . . . brought infamy and the curse of social outlawry." Little wonder that impressionable teachers and preachers left the South, not always of their own volition.

Freedom of speech, of the press, freedom in schools and churches, freedom of anyone who would criticize the social order, were watered down things at best. Social experimentation did not completely die out, but the innovator must needs keep himself clear of any taint of antislavery.

Universal white manhood suffrage was achieved in Louisiana, Virginia, and North Carolina between 1845 and 1857, but more in the spirit of Henry Wise than Thomas Jefferson. A delegate to the Louisiana convention of 1845 prophesied that the new democracy would "raise a wall of fire kindled from the united souls of freemen, around our state and its institutions, against the diabolical machinations of abolitionism."

There was little in the college curriculum of that day to direct a student's attention to current problems in any case, but after 1845 expression of unorthodox views carried the threat of expulsion. From 1832 students at the University of North Carolina were not allowed to discuss party politics from a public stage. As if he weren't already sufficiently supplied, Representative Brooks received yet another cane from the University of Virginia. The ousting of a few professors from time to time must have had a salutary effect on faculty conduct. As one of them in 1857 left the University of North Carolina, he fired a parting salvo that should have been heard around the world: "You may eliminate all the suspicious men from your institutions of learning, you may establish any number of new colleges which will relieve you of sending your sons to free institutions. But as long as people study, and read, and think among you, the absurdity of your system will be discovered and there will always be found some courageous intelligence to protest against your hateful tyranny."

There is, indeed, a contrast between this defiance of enforced conformity by Professor Henry Harrisse and a temper-of-the-times editorial in the Richmond *Examiner* on the care and treatment of Yankee schoolmasters.

The South has for years been overrun with hordes of illiterate, unprincipled graduates of the Yankee free schools (those hot beds of self-conceit and ignorance) who have by dint of unblushing impudence, established themselves as schoolmasters in our midst. These creatures, with rare exceptions, have not deserved the protection of our laws. They bear, neither in person nor in mind, a very strong resemblance to human beings. So odious are some of these 'itinerant *ignoramuses*' to the people of the South; so full of guile, fraud and deceit, that the deliberate shooting of one of them in the act of poisoning the minds of our slaves or our children, we think, if regarded as homicide at all, should always be deemed *perfectly justifiable; and we imagine that the propriety of shooting an abolition schoolmaster, when caught tampering with our slaves, has never been questioned by any intelligent Southern man. This we take to be the unwritten law of the South.* . . . Let all Yankee schoolmasters who propose invading the South with a strong nasal twang, a long Scriptural name, and Webster's lexicographic book of abominations, seek some more congenial land, where their lives will be more secure than in the vile and 'homicidal Slave States.'

In the 1820s the southern press did not generally defend slavery; twenty years later it did so almost unanimously. (The Richmond *Enquirer* described the institution in 1832 as "a dark and growing evil," in 1855 as "a natural and necessary element of society." More shameful still, in 1845 the fourth estate of Dixie heartily supported the suppression by mob action of Cassius Clay's *True American*. Soon the moderate Charleston *Courier* felt it necessary to cry, "We must transmit a heritage of rankling and undying hate to our children." In fact the southern press became so alarmist in time of crisis that one of its own number warned, a month after the election of Lincoln: "We respectfully submit that it is the duty of southern editors to be entirely satisfied of their truth, before they publish flaming accounts of contemplated insurrections."

By the decade of the fifties slave state legislatures had imposed severe penalties for the criticism of slavery. Postmasters and justices of the peace were granted inquisitorial power over the mails. To argue that these laws, along with the slave codes, were leniently executed is to miss the point; the laws themselves served their purpose.

The gentle Fitzhugh summed it all up. "We must meet agitation by counter-agitation; propagandism by counter-propagandism. We must establish and support presses, deliver lectures and write books and essays, to sustain the course of government against anarchy, or religion against infidelity, of private property against agrarianism, and of female virtue and christian marriage against free-love."* Give the people "the sanction of religion. Well directed superstition is the best prop and stay of law and government."

An effective propagandist, Fitzhugh fell victim to his own dialectic. After some indecision, he concluded that prosperity and civilization required the revival of the slave trade. Even the terrors of the Middle Passage melted away as he contended that the white European immigrant was more terribly exploited than the black African because his passage was paid and "the sooner he is thrown to the sharks, the better for the owner of the passenger ship." A revival of the trade would give the North cheaper raw materials and "it is more probable that New York, Pennsylvania and the whole North-

---

*Fitzhugh looked upon woman's rights with scorn. "So long as she is nervous, fickle, capricious, delicate, diffident and dependent, man will worship and adore her. Her weakness is her strength, and her true art is to cultivate and improve that weakness. Woman naturally shrinks from the public gaze and from the struggle and competition of life."

west would also become slave-holding." "Now if the missionaries, instead of feeding and clothing and making presents to the savages, would catch them, enslave them, and put them to constant work, they might speedily and certainly civilize and christianize them." And with Garrisonian heroics, Fitzhugh declared that if legal niceties forbade the slave trade, "we should speedily dissolve our unequal union and get rid of a partial and oppressive Constitution."

The last steps to the savage ideal were taken in stride by the sage of Port Royal as he went into his song and dance about war as a character builder and commended his fellow southerners as having "the lofty sentiments and high morals of a master race, that would render them unconquerable."

In the thirty years before the Civil War the South was victimized by its own authoritarian special pleading. Southern leaders proved themselves intellectually inferior to the great Virginians, in considerable degree because expansion of the suffrage and religious evangelism made it more likely that demagoguery and mere popularity would be rewarded with high place. Educational opportunity lagged far behind voter responsibility. There was a leveling down of the quality of the participating membership of state and church. With the broader base for office holding, those who got to the top were the ones who could best manipulate or appeal to the masses. Military heroics and log cabin theatricals were at a premium. Chauvinism and bluster led to a glorification of the status quo and rationalization changed slavery from an institution to be ashamed of to one to contemplate with pride. By the time the preachers got through with slavery it had become a sacred fellowship, the sublime basis for all southern society. Most tragic of all the Southern Creed became fixed, static, an article of faith to be accepted, not examined. A generation grew up in a myopic society, not universally agreed upon, but with the dissenters quieted in one way or another. Instead of approaching a difficult problem with an open and inquiring mind, southern leaders first looked to see how potential solutions fitted in with the prevailing wisdom. Neither the leadership nor the wisdom was adequate to the crisis of 1860–61. The South had undermined itself from within.

From the War of 1812 to the Civil War the United States could have been divided, at any given time, into at least five distinct sections, no two of which had identical interests. New England, the Middle States, the Southeast, the Southwest, and the Northwest were constantly shifting their attitudes on such timely questions as internal improvements, the tariff, the national bank, humanitarian reform, popular education, Indian removal, western lands, the federal ratio, slavery and a host of lesser items. No section by itself could enact or block federal legislation. Of necessity the country was run by a coalition, like the one which left New England out in the cold for the first quarter of the nineteenth century.

Rapid population changes made it rather evident that after 1820 the South was destined for permanent minority status. Slave state rights and privileges and ambitions might be protected by equal voting power in the Senate, by presidential veto, by court action, but most surely by close political association and good public relations with other parts of the country, particularly the friendly Northwest. This sometimes was and should always have been the guiding principle behind southern political strategy. Bargaining, compromise, concession, toleration, and a sympathetic concern for problems confronted by people in other areas were clearly indicated as enlightened self-interest. In 1820 Calhoun suggested, "If we systematically oppose the North, they must from necessity resort to a similar opposition to us." It was clear to him that the Missouri Compromise was saved when eight representatives from the Middle States and seven from New England, together with a few northern senators, joined the South. The vote of one northern senator defeated the obnoxious tariff bill of 1820 and the pleasing Walker tariff of 1846 was passed only with the help of northern Democrats.

It is almost inconceivable that, following the leadership of Calhoun, the South would, after 1830, demand total victory by way of a state rights doctrine with its constant threat of disunion and a solidly unified section zealously devoted to a strict party line. When, after the introduction of the Wilmot Proviso, Calhoun urged the South to ignore party and united on a southern candidate, even Zachary Taylor had the foresight to see that such action would result in a northern President, "The free states having the majority of the voters." Virginia's Senator William Roane could not comprehend Calhoun's "learned jargon about *minorities*. I have never thought that they had any other *Right* than that of freely, peaceably and legally converting themselves into a *majority* whenever they can." Obviously the South could not achieve a majority on any issue without outside assistance which would hardly be forthcoming if she pursued an inflexible policy of state sovereignty and southern unity.

An early example of the intrusion of what was rapidly becoming the South's orthodox view to thwart a southern political victory occurred in 1830 after the introduction by Senator Foot of Connecticut of a resolution calling for the restriction of the sale of western lands. A verbal battle between the West and New England created a conspicuous opportunity for the invigoration of the Southern-Western axis and the return of the Northeast to minority status. Under the leadership of Daniel Webster, New England maneuvered the debate away from western lands and New England recalcitrance into a classic argument on the nature of the constitution. According to Charles Sydnor, "At this point the Southern Senators made a grave tactical error. Instead of disregarding constitutional questions and pushing ahead into the breach between East and West, they accepted the challenge and rushed to the defense of state rights." The South let New England escape from the trap of its own making, being "more anxious to prove the correctness of its constitutional interpretation than to win in the practical game of politics."

Since that time the South has been proving the correctness of its constitutional principles—the true faith—with such fanatical inflexibility that it has sacrificed hundreds of chances for political and economic advantage, and what is of greater significance, it has denied itself, again and again, the luxury of examining questions on their own merits. From a simple defense dogma, states' rights has been transformed into an inviolable creed.

Thus, instead of playing the political game on a day-to-day give-and-take basis, Calhoun, considering himself the masterful politican he was not, attempted to build in the South a sectional party backed by an impregnable constitutional defense. His unimaginative, all-or-nothing policy of conformity was repudiated in his lifetime, for in the 1840s the South developed its only virile two-party system. As Gerald Capers has ably demonstrated, Calhoun's straitjacket thinking led to one blunder after another. He was influential in wrecking the Whig party in the South, in furthering the alienation of the Northwest from its southern alliance, and in liquidating his own last gamble for the Democratic nomination in 1848. His friend, Senator Dixon Lewis of Alabama, was constrained to say that Calhoun "reminds me of a great general who wins battles and then throws away his life in a street fracas."

The togetherness which Calhoun called for in vain was nearly achieved after his death through the instrumentality of the Democratic party. In the fifties the South dominated the party and the national government. It used federal power not only to secure its own immediate objectives but at the same time to humiliate the Northwest, anxious to exploit the country's natural resources with positive assistance from Washington. Democratic vetoes of homestead and internal improvement bills deemed essential by the Northwest were used effectively by clever politicians such as Joshua Giddings to convince would-be capitalists that the slave power not only intended to forestall economic progress but to hold the free North "politically bound, hand and foot." Those in national control failed to be guided by the imperative Democratic necessity of holding the South and satisfying the Northwest. As Avery Craven sees it, the election of 1860 turned on the relationship of government to business. Only Stephen Douglas seemed able to cope with the Republicans on the issue of progress and he was repudiated by a dogmatic South following its orthodox persuasion.

A surprisingly good case can be made for the contention that the abolitionists were mightily assisted in arousing northern opinion by their deadly enemies, the southern leaders. In the early 1830s, Yankee hostility was directed against abolition, not slavery, as abolition was first aimed at the slaveowner, not northern opinion. When Senator Robert Hayne demanded that the mayor of Boston take action against William Lloyd Garrison, his Honor wryly admitted that he had never heard of the fellow. Locating him "toiling in a barren Boston loft," Mayor Otis wrote Hayne that Garrison's zeal "has not made, nor was likely to make proselytes among the respectable classes of our people." At that time Garrison had to offer only the "impotent fury of his own poisoned pen."

But the South innocently expected the North to suppress its lunatic fringe. In 1836 the legislatures of Virginia, South Carolina, Georgia, and Alabama requested northern laws against newspapers and tracts which might excite slaves to revolt. The Massachusetts legislature received the memorials cordially enough, referring them to the proper committees. Open hearings were held which abolitionists skillfully turned into spectacular displays for civil rights and freedom. William Goodell claimed, for instance, that the southern proposal was a brazen effort to "rob the free states of those liberties brought to Massachusetts by the Pilgrims." The legislature took no action and the abolitionists had gained a tactical victory at the expense of the South.

The same blunder, on a national scale, was perpetrated by those irritated and emotional southerners in the House of Representatives who gained a witless eight-year gag rule while handing the cause of respectability on a platter to the abolitionist. In 1836 95 percent of the antislavery petitions were presented by Whigs who were more concerned with embarrassing the Democrats in an election year than in protesting the inequities of slavery. The resulting gag rule fanned the flames the South hoped to extinguish. Abolition now had gained a popular tenet of faith, the protection of civil rights, and an embattled leader, ex-President Adams, who considered the resolution "a direct violation of the constitution of the United States, the rules of this House, and the rights of my constituents." Overnight abolitionists were no longer meddlesome fanatics but champions of a great constitutional right. John Minor Botts remarked in disgust that the battle for the gag rule "made more abolitionists in one year, by identifying the right of petition with the question of slavery, than the abolitionists could have made for themselves in twenty-five years."

According to Professor Elkins, "Showers of antislavery petitions . . . were circulated by thousands of voluntary workers, including substantial numbers of women who had for the first time a satisfying mode of civic activity in which they could engage with reasonable propriety. To all these newly recruited citizens, inspired by the spectacle of the ex-president defending a question of manifest right, theirs seemed an enterprise sanctioned by the soundest of constitutional principles."

Calhoun who a few years before 1836 had ridiculed the abolitionists as possessing "little or no personal influence," now exaggerated their power by suggesting that they had "the disposition of almost unlimited funds." It would not be long before he would demand that the North "cease the agitation of the slave question." On the eve of the Civil War, William Seward was still deriding with great effectiveness the Democratic party for having "denied the right of petition, and effectively suppressed the freedom of speech."

As the abolitionists pressed their relentless attack, the South hardened its heart and its laws concerning slavery and the possible critics of slavery. Not only was the circulation of antislavery literature pronounced a felony but the slave codes were tightened beyond all reason. In a time when the most moral southern practice might have been written into law, as proposed by Thomas R. R. Cobb, the church and state were moving away from the amelioration of the conditions of slavery. Not until the first year of the Confederacy did there materialize a minor crusade, in the main directed by Presbyterian laymen, to humanize the institution of slavery. The point here is the confession of these Confederate humanitarians that in the fifties they had felt it unpatriotic to speak out for fear of acknowledging dissension within the South and seeming to be making common cause with abolition. They had indeed been caught in an impasse, for the very absolutism of slavery against which they longed to protest had emerged as one of the strongest intellectual weapons of the abolitionists. In thus being unwilling to risk the designation of fellow travelers, these churchmen abandoned their ethical responsibility.

Nowhere was the failure in spiritual leadership pointed out with more cogency than in the April 1860, issue of the moderate, conservative *Presbyterian Quarterly Review* of Philadelphia. This church magazine spoke for gradual, compensated emancipation, it is true, but it also bitterly denounced abolition and called for enforcement of the fugitive slave law. The editor, Benjamin J. Wallace, wrote of "the impulsive generosity, the frank bearing, the gentlemanly courtesy, the high sense of personal honor and chivalrous courage" of southerners. At the same time he warned that the only way to prevent slavery from causing "unpleasant excitement" in the North was for them to divest it of laws and incidents offensive to Christianity. "This would at once take the wind out of the sails of agitators and fanatics." Abolition, he contended, had raised only a corporal's guard until Calhoun tried to unite the South, assuming the North would be divided. "Here originated that reign of terror at the South by which a great political party not only crushed out its opponents, but hushed down the southern conscience, and compelled its clergy and churches to say *aye* to every proposition deemed orthodox, for the security, the perpetuity and the expansion of human bondage." By 1860 the southern conscience had, indeed, been hushed down.

It has long been routine for demagogues in this country to call out absurd and meaningless charges against their opposite numbers in other sections. In the speaker's own day, Congressman John Rankin of Mississippi's first district accumulated considerable political capital by fulminating against New York's Victor Marcantonio, and *vice versa*. In the same pattern southern extremists built up a bogey-man in Garrison and treated him and his kind as representative of the North, while their northern counterparts performed the same kind of service for Fitzhugh. In this pleasant exchange the South played a losing game for its very existence was at stake.

The South "must meet agitation by counter-agitation," cried Fitzhugh. "We can throw firebrands as well as the abolitionists." This rabid propagandist ignored the great evils he saw in slavery and professed to believe that freedom of the press, speech, and religion were more dangerous "than all the robbers and murderers and malefactors put together."

Take one aspect of his attack on northern society—his claim that Europe was disposing of her oversupply of labor as "human cattle" on American shores. Long continued, such traffic would build up the surplus of northern workers to the point of depressing the market and destroying the price. This grim Malthusian concept may have tickled the southern fancy, but it also led a Britisher, Charles Mackay, to charge in 1859 that Fitzhugh would enslave the Irish and German immigrants "as fast as they arrive." A New York Methodist editor did not need to elaborate on Fitzhugh's disparagement of "countless millions of paupers and criminals who build up and sustain the cowardly, infidel, licentious, revolutionary edifice of free society." Senators Sumner, Wade, Wilson, Seward, and Doolittle, Representatives Egerton (Ohio), Waldron (Michigan), and Windom (Minnesota), as well as hundreds of editors and churchmen entered into the sport of passing Fitzhugh's choicest comments on to their northern public. Lincoln used Fitzhugh in every speech he made in 1856. And it would appear that the Irish and German immigrants, the workers, the paupers, and perhaps even Fitzhugh's criminals, made their own response in the election returns of 1856 and 1860. (Fremont and Fillmore together got almost a half million more votes than Buchanan.)

An 1856 Republican pamphlet was entitled, *The New Democratic Doctrine: Slavery not to be confined to the Negro race, but to be made the universal condition of the laboring classes of society.* Certainly, this was the essence of *Cannibals All!* and of such assertions as the *Examiner's* "the principle of slavery is itself right, and does not depend on difference in complexion."

Attributed to Governor Wise, Senator Mason, and the Muscogee (Alabama) *Herald* was perhaps the most quotable quote of all: "Free society! We sicken of the name. What is it but a conglomeration of greasy mechanics, filthy operatives, small-fisted farmers, and moon struck theorists?" Opponents of Senator Douglas in Galesburg paraded a huge banner which declared: "Small-fisted farmers, Mudsills of Society, Greasy Mechanics for A. Lincoln." One of the authors of the 1860 Republican platform claimed with considerable truth that southern Democrats considered northern society a failure because greasy mechanics, etc. had "political rights accorded to them." He might also have commented later that they performed yeoman service at Vicksburg and Chattanooga and Atlanta.

It was reported for years that Robert Toombs had bragged that one day he would call the roll of his slaves on Bunker Hill. This kind of bluster was not exceptional. Henry Foote invited New Hampshire's abolition senator to visit Mississippi where he would be hanged from the highest tree. John P. Hale replied that if Foote came to New Hampshire he would get a respectful hearing. Davis, Yancey, Fitzhugh, and many others did speak in the North while no free-soiler was tolerated in the South. In 1848 Douglas charged that southern extremists had doubled the abolition vote that year. Later President Buchanan was convinced that Seward's preposterous prospect of the rye and wheat fields of Massachusetts and New York being surrendered to slave culture "produced serious apprehension in the North." What he forgot was that this was only a re-statement of the house-divided thesis which Lincoln had in turn borrowed from Fitzhugh.

Harvey Wish has concluded that Fitzhugh's "words shocked men and women of unquestioned integrity . . . who considered the Virginian to be representative of the pro-slavery South." Industrial workers and small farmers, particularly those recently arrived from Europe, rather indifferent to the moral side of slavery, were easily aroused to apprehension over the prophecy of the loss of their own liberties and their hopes for economic advancement.

Southern leaders who defended their own superior society by challenging that of the North, at least those extremists who demonstrated their willingness "to infringe upon basic civil and personal rights, free speech, free press, free thought, and constitutional liberty," played with amazing ineptitude into the hands of the abolitionists and the Republicans. There is reason to think that they were responsible for some of the narrow victories of Lincoln over Douglas in the crucial 1860 election.

After the Compromise of 1850 scuttled the secession movement for the moment, John R. Thompson threw down the gauntlet to the North—"the continued existence of the United States as a nation, depends upon the full and faithful execution of the Fugitive Slave Bill." As justifiable as this must have appeared, it seems unbelievable that any shrewd southern politician would have handed to the abolitionists such a deadly weapon with which to belabor the South. Almost a hundred major cases in which the power of the federal government was used in melodramatic fashion to drive home to moderate Yankees the most iniquitous aspects of slavery, led Garrison to say that the law swayed more neutrals to abolition than anything since the assassination of Lovejoy. A single runaway incident brought from the pen of the most widely read poet of the day, the pious and militant Whittier, lines of untold propaganda impact:

But for us and for our children, the vow which we have given
For freedom and humanity is registered in heaven;
No slave hunt in our borders,—no pirate on our strand!
No fetters in the Bay State,—no slave upon our land!

The northern people would not obey the law. To many it was a simple case of befriending the underdog. The speaker remembers with what pride, more than forty years ago, an old maid aunt pointed out to him a former underground station on Cauga Lake in upstate New York. Seward called the law "unconstitutional, cruel and humiliating," and a Universalist paper declared, "The Clergy are making the blood of the people boil with indignation." The underground railway was most influential for what it did to the people who assisted the runaway slaves. It did little to weaken slavery, especially in those states from which came the most uproarious protests, but it did a great deal to strengthen the antislavery movement. Like the insistence on the maintenance of slavery in the nation's capital (where it was on display for all the world to see) and the imprisonment or quarantine of Negro seamen whose ships entered southern ports, the most noteworthy results were in the propaganda value to the cause of abolition.

Southerners might profitably have looked into Lincoln's failure to protest against the enforcement of the Fugitive Slave Law. "A professional politician looking for votes," Lincoln may have accomplished his most masterful stroke in the conciliation and merging of the forces of antislavery and negrophobia. The Republican was unquestionably a white man's party. While some members hated slavery, the vast majority was most concerned with the prevention of competition from the Negro in territory or free state. Lincoln was adroit enough to dramatize at every turn the danger of slavery in the free states; he told the laborer and small farmer who aspired to middle class economic status that they should not be willing to go where they would be degraded or have their families corrupted by rivalry with Negroes. He wanted the territories "for homes for free white people."

In the 1830s de Tocqueville pointed out that "in those parts of the Union where the Negroes are no longer slaves they are in no wise drawn nearer to the whites. On the contrary, the prejudice of race appears to be stronger in the states that have abolished slavery than in those where it still exists; and nowhere is it so intolerant as in those states where servitude has never been known."

Frederick Douglass once recalled a revival in New Bedford, Massachusetts. "Another young lady fell into a trance. When she awoke, she declared she had been to heaven. Her friends were anxious to know what and whom she had seen there; so she told the whole story. But there was one good old lady whose curiosity went beyond that of all the others and she inquired of the girl that had the vision, if she saw any black folks in heaven? After some hesitation, the reply was, 'Oh! I didn't go into the kitchen.'" Another famous fugitive slave, Harriet Tubman, said she was discriminated against in the South as a slave and in the North as a Negro and a woman.

Leon Litwack has thoroughly documented the fact that the Negro in the antebellum North enjoyed few rights and privileges. "He was disfranchised in every state, denied the right to settle in some, and confined to menial employment in all. Extralegal 'Jim Crow' regulations systematically separated him from the white community. There was an organized movement to remove him to Africa or Central America. Even professed friends of the Negro, advocates of the abolition of slavery, saw no hypocrisy in subscribing to popular notions of white supremacy." Northern politicians "tried to outdo each other in declarations of loyalty to the antebellum American Way of Life and its common assumption that this was a white man's country in which the Negro had no political voice and only a prescribed social and economic role."

At this late date, it seems to the speaker that in the almost universal Yankee negrophobia the South ignored a weapon potentially more devastating than the proslavery argument was to the abolitionists. With only a little flexibility in its thinking, instead of the idiocy of Fitzhugh, the South might have presented a position something like this: "Slavery in the South is the most powerful protector of the white man in the North. Abolish it and free Negroes will move northward en masse (as indeed they did later). The South will voluntarily keep its slaves out of the territories above the old Missouri Compromise line (as nature has decreed in any case). As the southerners of Jefferson's day assumed, slavery is a theoretical but necessary evil and it will be a long time before the black man can be turned loose on white society. While his process of education is taking place, the institution will be reformed to the extent that the slave will receive certain basic protections from state and church. Free society has many problems of its own and the South will refrain from adding hers to those of an already overburdened North. North and South should unite in a truly American way of life."

This proposition might have sounded ingenuous in the 1850s, though it wouldn't have seemed so to Washington, Mason, Madison, or Monroe. The melancholy fact is that since the era of these men the southern people had been run into a pocket. Over a period of more than thirty years they had gradually succumbed to a doctrinaire gospel and a stultifying atmosphere in which clear thinking was outside the realm of possibility. Instead of controlling her own destiny the South was being controlled by circumstance and directed by mediocre leadership.

In the decade before the war, a series of unforeseen and calamitous events shook the country with an impact comparable to the artillery barrage before Pickett's charge. The reception of *Uncle Tom's Cabin,* the violence of bleeding Kansas, the crisis of *The Impending Crisis,* the brutality of the Sumner-Brooks affair, and the impact of the incident at Harper's Ferry, all created high tension and all were staged over and over again by propagandists, free and slave. In each situation, the South reacted as a capricious adolescent rather than as a calculating, mature adult.

At any other time *Uncle Tom's Cabin* might have been greeted solemnly but with an amused tolerance. Certainly it was no *Mandingo* or *Tobacco Road*. A civilization which had produced Uncle Tom and Little Eva could not have been so bad, and, after all, Simon Legree hailed from Yankeeland. Yet, according to the New Orleans *Crescent,* Mrs. Stowe had whetted "the knife of domestic murder and shakes over the innocent head of every matron, maid or babe in the South, the blazing torch of midnight conflagration, the brutal and merciless instruments of death, that are struck to the heart or dash out the brains of the sleeping or the helpless, in the bursting out of a slave insurrection."

The editor of the *Southern Literary Messenger* requested from his ranking reviewer, George Frederick Holmes, an analysis "as hot as hellfire, blasting and searing the reputation of the vile wretch in petticoats who could write such a volume." As specified, the Virginia professor excoriated Mrs. Stowe's "criminal prostitution of the high function of the imagination to the pernicious intrigues of sectional animosity and the petty calumnies of willful slander."

Little boys calling each other nasty names! At least one southern editor, with his feet on solid ground, saw that "the Southern press, with few exceptions have rendered Mrs. Stowe a most acceptable service, by their united and zealous efforts to kick her work into consequence and notoriety."

Avery Craven has shown that while the Kansas-Nebraska Law did not originate in the South, most Dixie Congressmen, with only the slightest hope for Kansas as a slave state, voted the party line. Kansas was abandoned by the southern people, not the politicians. The express repeal of the Missouri Compromise turned out to be a serious error, for it plunged the South into an impossible contest and did inestimable damage to the Democratic party. The meaning of it all was clear to Walt Whitman who in 1856 asked the slave holders what they would do with Kansas if they got it. "Then would the melt begin in These States," he wrote, "that would not cool till Kansas should be redeemed, as of course it would be."

Hinton R. Helper turned to the *Impending Crisis* because he had been forced to delete his antislavery sentiment from an 1855 travel book. His economics faulty, his recommendations too severe to secure the least hearing in the South, Helper was denounced as a renegade and his book as "incendiary, insurrectionary, and hostile to the peace and domestic tranquility of the country." Almost a calm reception. But when the Republicans endorsed Helper's treason, the South wrathfully turned to burning the book and imprisoning its circulators despite the plea that such action would play into the hands of the abolitionists.

Senator Sumner's diatribe, "The Crime Against Kansas," was thought by Lewis Cass to be the most un-American and unpatriotic speech he had ever heard. Douglas questioned whether Sumner's object was "To provoke some of us to kick him as we would a dog in the street, that he may gain sympathy upon the just chastisement," and deemed his speech unworthy of a reply. The South's reply, by Preston Brooks, created the sympathy Douglas had despaired of and converted the zealot into a martyr. One southern paper suggested that the assault on the Massachusetts senator would be worth a thousand speeches and arguments to the abolitionists. "An unwise friend is more terrible than a score of enemies," it said. The moderate Mobile press was certain that Brooks had inadvertently strengthened both northern abolitionists and southern fireeaters. Once more the South was pushed into the Northern consciousness as a "land of bullies who silenced opponents with revolvers, clubs, bowie knives."

John Brown was no menace to the South; his raid was not much more than a local disturbance. Buchanan thought that "considered merely as an isolated act of a desperate fanatic, it would have no lasting effect." But the South considered Brown as the legitimate offspring of the aberrant forces that had given birth to the Republican party and proceeded to help transform him into a legend which still goes marching on.

As the South, over the years, worked itself beyond the point of no return, some men always suggested the right direction, the road that was not taken. Maybe it is more accurate to say that in the thirty years before 1860 there were always simultaneously at least two contrary trends in evidence. Because secession and the war have distracted us, we have a tendency to forget the sturdy economic gains, including the industrial, made in the South in the prosperous 1850s. We are likely to forget the agricultural revolution which was aligning the South with progress. A South able to commit itself to the mainstream of western civilization might have been the alternative to withdrawal and defeat.

A militant Quaker, editor of the Greensboro *Patriot,* spoke out strongly in 1834 against the new demagoguery: "We would rather bask for one hour in the approving smiles of an intelligent and undeceived people, than to spend a whole eternity amidst the damning grins of a motley crew of office seekers, despots, demagogues, tyrants, fools and hypocrites." In 1835 Benjamin Franklin Perry suggested that "The course which the Southern people ought to pursue is one of profound silence on the subject of slavery." When abolition petitions inundated the House of Representatives the next year, many southerners—Bedford Brown, Grundy, King, Clay, Preston—feared the consequences of interfering with the right of the petition. Instead of suppressing the abolitionists, as Calhoun demanded, these moderates wanted to ignore them. Fifteen years later, Joel Poinsett argued that "the interests of the slave holder and the slave . . . will best be promoted by calming as early and as far as possible the dangerous agitation, which originated and has been kept up by political Demagogues for their own sordid purposes." In the 1840s John Hampden Pleasants, George Tucker, Henry Ruffner, and other Virginians were defending freedom of the press and attacking slavery as a menace to the whites.

Just before the war several Nashville papers pleaded with the South to reject the fire-eaters and requested the southern press to stop quoting extremist northern statements to the neglect of more "representative opinion." In New Orleans at least a few editors suggested giving up the abstractions and consolidating slavery where it was. At this time Jefferson Davis spoke as a southern moderate, of disunionists as mosquitoes around an ox, annoying but never deadly.

The ministers of the gospel who identified slavery with the cause of God lacked that touch of humility possessed by the Reverend Mr. Caskey, a Confederate chaplain who wrote after the war:

> Some of my preaching brethren told the soldiers that our cause was just and that God would fight our battles for us. I never did feel authorized to make any such statements. I believed our cause was just, of course, but I could see as clear as a sunbeam that the odds were against us, and, to be plain, I gravely doubted whether God was taking any hand with us in the squabble. I told some of the preachers who were making that point in their sermons that they were taking a big risk. I asked them what explanation they would give if we should happen to get thrashed. I told them such preaching would make infidels of the whole army, and put an end to their business if we should happen to get the worst of the fracas. I wanted to do my duty as a preacher in the army, but I didn't want to checkmate the ministry in case we should come out second best. I think a preacher should always leave a wide margin for mistakes when it comes to interpreting the purposes of God beyond what has been clearly revealed in the Scriptures. It is not good policy for a one-horse preacher to arbitrarily commit the God of the Universe to either side of a personal difficulty anyhow.

On June 18, 1865, John H. Caldwell preached at Newnan, Georgia, a sermon entitled, "The Slavery Conflict and Its Effect on the Church." Acknowledging that he had ever been convinced of the multitudinous wrongs in slavery but that no minister would have been permitted by the slave power to speak out against them, the Reverend Mr. Caldwell came to a logical conclusion: "If the institution of slavery had been right, God would not have suffered it to be overthrown. . . ."

But these lonely voices were lost among the trumpets and the moderate Davises quickly capitulated. The mind of the South was crippled and its people were looking to authoritarian doctrine for positive answers to their problems. There was hardly a chance, in the lower South, for an objective appraisal of the situation created by the election of Lincoln. In Georgia, for instance, slaves were not running away and slavery was in no danger. Yet an Atlanta paper could editorialize: "Let the consequences be what they may—whether the Potomac is crimsoned in human gore, and Pennsylvania Avenue is paved ten fathoms in depth with mangled bodies or whether the last vestige of Liberty is swept from the face of the American Continent, the South will never submit to such humiliation and degradation as the inauguration of Abraham Lincoln." And the Reverend James Wilson addressed his congregation at Gonzales, Texas:

> It may be that if you behave yourselves very circumspectly and give them no cause to be angry with you, lie still where they have thrown you—though they now have the power to overwhelm you . . . with destructive laws, hot as the hellish passions of their own black hearts . . . they will not be cruel, they will defer your utter destruction yet a little longer, . . . upon good behavior. If you will cringe and fawn and smile, perhaps they will not kick you . . . I think that perhaps the philosopher who first made the discovery of Southern effeminacy viewed the world through glasses of Northern manufacture.

The leaders were crying for action and the people had long since been made ready. Both felt rather than reasoned. One is reminded of the sad commentary by the late Charles Ramsdell who was "tempted to reflections upon what has long passed for statesmanship . . . but I have not the heart to indulge them."

We have taken a quick look at the "statesmen" of only one side, the South—the reverse of the coin is even more dismal, for the North, certain of her destiny, could have been indulgent—the South whose leaders failed the people. It may well be that southerners since the Civil War, for all their flamboyant dedication to the Lost Cause, have subconsciously repudiated the extremists who led them into three generations of tribulation, for the South's authentic heroes are those who offered their lives on the field of battle, the Lees and Jacksons and Johnstons, the ones who had overwhelmingly opposed secession as the proper course of action.

Mississippi Must Choose
(1964)

*In the years after my departure from Ole Miss I was called on
dozens of times to write reviews of books having to do with civil
rights and to put together articles on the events in my home
state. In the summer of the publication of* The Closed Society *I
wrote for the* New York Times Magazine *a timely piece entitled
"Mississippi Must Choose." This was probably my most arduous essay for at that time I was so encumbered by interviews
and appearances in the eastern area of the country that I found
difficulty in putting two consecutive sentences together. Here is
what I came up with:*

In this hot summer of 1964 Mississippi has been singled out as
the main objective of an assault dedicated to the proposition that it, too,
must participate in the common decencies and routines of American social
and political life. The reaction within the state to this obvious intrusion has
been fierce, the response of an aroused citadel in which the alarm has been
struck. That known majority which is always ready to stand fast and fight to
retain Mississippi's ancient customs has been called to the colors. It has
rallied to maintain the "closed society," or what Aaron Henry, president of
the state organization of the National Association for the Advancement of
Colored People, has called Mississippi's "affinity for the bottom."

The united front that has been strong enough to nullify the United States
Constitution since 1875 is officially as solid as ever. But every knowledgeable Mississippi segregationist looks to the future with foreboding. He
knows, in short, that the time is fast running out when the country will any
longer tolerate this enclave of feudalism within the United States and that
his only choice is to make the inevitable transition peaceable or bloody.

More than most other Americans, the people of Mississippi have been
victimized by history, poverty, ruralness, constant expatriation of bright
young minds, by a dedicated white-supremacist press and by a chronic lack
of leadership. Until the relatively recent discovery of oil and gas, Mississippians (of whom four out of ten are Negroes) have had to look primarily to
the soil for their living. The prosperity of the 1850s was destroyed by war
and the prosperity of the 1950s is now endangered by the battle to sustain an
outmoded caste system.

Although beyond the state's borders, Memphis and New Orleans,
through historical accident, are Mississippi's principal urban centers. The
state never has had a chance to create an Atlanta, a Nashville, or even a

176

Birmingham. This is relevant on the fair assumption that intellectual fer-
ment, when it does occur, occurs in cities. Some observers like William
Alexander Percy, the author of *Lanterns on the Levee,* claim that if Mississippi ever has produced an aristocracy (like South Carolina) that aristocracy
never has been powerful enough to carry the day in time of crisis. Certainly
as a frontier community (half the state was settled within a generation of the
Civil War), the land of the magnolia and the mocking bird missed the period
of extended apology for slavery. The early Mississippi hero was Andrew
Jackson, who always came out fighting and who eagerly despoiled the Indian. In its antebellum heyday, Mississippi so cherished the duel that newspaper editorializing was indeed a precarious business. The Civil War
correspondent of *The Times* of London, William Howard Russell, noted
that casual local conversations had "a smack of manslaughter" about them.

It is significant that Mississippians are proud of their martial record
against the red man, the Mexican, the Yankee, the Spaniard, the German
and the Japanese. But their most hapless victim has been the Negro. Violence and the threat of violence played the major role in the somewhat
belated shift from the institution of slavery to the caste system and, during
the twentieth century, in the maintenance of white supremacy. The culture
of the state is still predominantly physical and elemental, as evidenced by
the preoccupation of leading citizens with athletic prowess, feminine pul-
chritude and evangelical religion.

The best young men born between 1825 and 1845 were lost in battle and
many of those who returned after Appomattox quickly deserted their homes
for the economic opportunities which beckoned from North and West. Intelligent, sensitive natural leaders have been leaving in large numbers ever
since. Today ex-Mississippians play a phenomenal part in the world of
business, in the professions and in the arts, and while they maintain a love
of their native soil, they do not return.

A society in which most of the people, black and white, go along with the
well established orthodoxy—white supremacy backed with religious fundamentalism and a professed belief in states' rights—demands adherence to
a noncontroversial one-party system in which the road to political prefer-
ment is usually paved with demagoguery. Wild-eyed personalities, odd
enough to attract a following among a frustrated electorate receptive mainly
to low forms of entertainment and gargantuan braggadocio, capture the
highest office. In such a state the patrician occasionally successful at the
polls dares not contemplate tampering with the racial picture; the more
likely eventuality in politics is a Bilbonic plague or a Barnett blight.

The prime beneficiaries of the system are the Bourbon businessmen who,
through their financial investments in political opportunities, are able to
thwart the legitimate economic and social desires of small farmers, tenants
and industrial workers. All whites make at least short-time economic, social
and status gains from the debasement of the Negro. For a hundred years
since the Emancipation Proclamation and the post-Civil War amendments

to the Constitution, the black man has been forced to accept the place of subservience and poverty. Since the Depression of the 1930s Mississippi's agricultural revolution has driven the little man of both races from the land, but the state's avid pursuit of industrialism has borne the label "For Whites Only." Because there are not enough janitorial and yard-boy jobs to go around, Negroes make up about 85 percent of the relief rolls.

What, then, are the distinguishing marks of the closed society that characterizes Mississippi? The social order that former Governor Barnett defended with such satisfaction rests upon the stubborn determination of the white population to keep Mississippi a white man's country. Those in power or near it refuse to acknowledge any serious challenge to the doctrine and system of white supremacy. Their beliefs are sustained by the unconditional and unwavering acceptance of an interlocking sequence of discredited assumptions:

1. The biological and anthropological "proof" of Negro inferiority (which would keep him a second-class citizen forever).

2. The presumed sanction of God as extrapolated from the Bible.

3. The present state of affairs as one that is desired and endorsed by Negroes and whites alike.

4. The repeated assurance that only through segregation can law and order prevail.

5. A view of history which declares that there has been a century of satisfactory racial experience in Mississippi.

6. A Constitutional interpretation which denies the validity of the Supreme Court desegregation decisions and the 1964 Civil Rights Act.

Nowhere in the prevailing thought is there admission that nearly everyone in the civilized world has long since abandoned these premises without which the Mississippi way of life founders in its own absurdity.

A philosophical foundation, even if intellectually respectable, would not furnish the massive support necessary for the continuation of the closed society in an antagonistic world. Beyond its fundamentalist creed, then, the society has two engines designed to insure the maintenance of white supremacy: the distortion of Mississippi's past and the distortion of Mississippi's present.

The first of these is composed of the *antebellum myth*—the Old South as a classical Golden Age; *the Confederate myth*—the south as a humane society risen in spontaneous self-defense of its sanctified institutions, its family and country life, against wanton Northern aggression, and *the Reconstruction myth*—a society laid waste by an unprovoked war, become a Federal garrison, oppressed by an insolent Yankee inquisition and finally redeemed by virtuous Southern patriots (the intruder is expelled and the Negro is saved from himself by returning him to his old security through segregation and new and beneficent forms of his old tasks).

The present view of life is distorted by the claim of Negro contentment, by the notion that all racial troubles originate outside the state, by the politics of segregation (the asserted usurpation of Mississippi's sovereignty by a Federal civil-rights-and-school-desegregation conspiracy based in Washington and not so obscurely related to the international Communist plot to destroy America), and by the almost absolute support of the status quo by the makers of public opinion—the press, the pulpit and the politicians.

With such powerful forces of indoctrination at work, it would be strange indeed if whites and blacks alike did not grow up prepared to accept and extol their heritage. But there are still stronger means by which the closed society is entrenched. Every lawmaking body and every law-enforcing agency is completely in the hands of those whites who are faithful to the orthodoxy. From governor to constable, from chief justice to justice of the peace, every officer of the society is dedicated to upholding and maintaining the status quo by whatever means are necessary.

The white man is educated to believe in his superiority and the Negro is educated to accept his position of subservience and inferiority. In the civic and service clubs, the educational institutions, the churches, the business and labor organizations, the patriotic, social and professional fraternities— all individuals who would advance themselves in any of these are oriented from infancy in the direction of loyalty to the accepted code. In times of stress the Legal Educational Advisory Committee, the State Sovereignty Commission, the Citizens Councils, the Women for Constitutional Government, Patriotic American Youth and dozens of similar new groups spring up to man the ramparts against outside encroachment and internal subversion. The nonconformist learns the advisability of keeping his mouth shut, or is silenced in one way or another, or he finds it expedient to quit the state.

The closed society of Mississippi thus swears allegiance to a prevailing creed with over a hundred years of homage behind it. Based on antique assumptions no longer tenable and on a legendary past, the doctrine of white supremacy is guarded by a bureaucracy, by ceaseless, high-powered and skillful indoctrination employing both persuasion and fear, and by the elimination, without regard for law or ethics, of those who will not go along. Within its own borders the closed society of Mississippi comes as near to approximating a police state as anything we have yet seen in America.

And yet the closed society is not absolutely closed. In Mississippi there are legislators (very scarce), editors, lawyers, labor leaders, ministers, educators and businessmen who sometimes protest against the prevailing orthodoxy. It has always been so. In his inaugural speech last January, Gov. Paul Johnson told his listeners that "we are Americans as well as Mississippians," and further declared that "hate, or prejudice or ignorance will not lead Mississippi while I sit in the Governor's chair." Six months later Johnson is something of an enigma, but he is obviously a remarkable improvement over his inflexible, racist predecessor, and it is possible that he will go down in history as the man who led his people out of the wilderness.

Mississippi's greatest white supremacist, former Gov. James K. Vardaman, thought that to educate the Negro would be "to spoil a good field hand and to make an insolent cook." He never seriously considered alleviating the black man's ignorance, nor did The Man Bilbo nor any other successful politician in the first half of the twentieth century. But with participation in two world wars and increasing contact with friends and relatives who had fled the state, as well as some access to expanding news media, the Negro grew more and more restless within the caste system, and Negro leadership began to emerge.

In fact, the most remarkable development in Mississippi history is the indigenous Negro leadership in evidence since 1954 when one hundred Negroes flatly refused to endorse Gov. Hugh White's plans for separate but really equal school facilities. It is not just Medgar and Charles Evers, the Robert L. T. Smiths, not just Aaron Henry, J. H. Meredith and Clyde Kennard, but hundreds of developing leaders such as the three hundred social science teachers I talked with in Jackson a few months back. By themselves these stalwarts could do very little, but it is increasingly evident that they are not alone, that indeed the rest of the country is rapidly throwing its weight behind them. And this phenomenon is not just a summertime thing.

The outlook for assistance from white moderates who see the future with some degree of optimism, because increasing numbers of colored citizens are becoming eligible to vote, is not so promising. Open help from these men of goodwill probably will not be forthcoming. It is not that they disagree but that the combination of the old social paralysis, fear, and the real difficulty of breaking out of the pattern of the social life they have known all their lives—even though many have long made the break so far as conviction is concerned—is simply too much for them without massive support from the society they work and live in.

The voter registration drives are all conducted by local Negroes and "outside agitators" of the Student Nonviolent Coordinating Committee, the Congress of Racial Equality, the NAACP and other organizations, like the National Council of Churches and the Voter Education Project of the Southern Regional Council. In the courts the chief defender of first-class citizenship for colored Mississippians is the United States Department of Justice. (Not a single white native lawyer will take a civil-rights case.) The Mississippi Civil Rights Advisory Committee, which seeks to protect the rights of all Mississippians, has found it well-nigh impossible to recruit members. But *it is functioning,* as is the biracial Council on Human Relations.

Mississippi's great hope economically is the industrialization of the state. Here some progress has been made. The businessman, however, has been too engrossed in making money to think clearly about the consequences of industrialization, but neither he nor anyone else is magician enough to freeze the social status quo while revolutionizing the economic order. Many now regret the turning over of the Negro problem to the extremist leadership in the Citizens Councils and are beginning to understand that a healthy modern industrial structure cannot be raised upon the sands of segregation, minimum wages (for whites only), poor schools, anti-intellectualism, Negrophobia, meager social services, antiunionism and a general policy of "hate the Federal Government." The pressing need now is for a substantial number of prudent and imaginative representatives of the power structure—which has, until now, failed the state—to become sufficiently aroused by recent events to band together for the purpose of withdrawing their support from Mississippi's self-inflicted closed society.

Several years ago the Mississippi Economic Council (the state's chamber of commerce) spoke out strongly for keeping open the public schools even with integration. The Jackson Chamber of Commerce has recently advised the local owners of hotels, restaurants and theaters that they must obey the new Civil Rights Law (though the Robert E. Lee Hotel chose to close its doors) in spite of the anguished cries and threats of the white supremacists. Sons and daughters of Northern owners of industry brought into the state by its famous Balance Agriculture With Industry program are now teaching in the summer Freedom Schools and this is bound to have an eye-opening effect.

Our country is now in the midst of an authentic revolution. The promises of the Declaration of Independence and the Emancipation Proclamation are beginning to become reality for 20 million black Americans. These promises will not be denied to a million citizens just because they happen to live in Mississippi. The long predicted turn is upon us.

As the tensions of the long summer ahead accumulate in both North and South, the outlook is divided between the certainties of concealed resistance and sporadic terror and the more distant "new society." Perhaps in Mississippi the new society can be seen only as a matter of faith, as something beyond a wide and temporal Jordan. If this is the case, the fault, while Mississippian enough, is shared beyond the borders of my state.

The shock around the nation over the disappearance of the three S.N.C.C. workers and the continuance of their work by their colleagues and others make it inevitable, however, that Mississippians will one day break out of the blind patterns of resistance required by the convulsive imperatives of white supremacy.

The ultimate question for Mississippi is whether these words William Faulkner wrote on Dec. 1, 1955, will take native root and flourish:

> The question is no longer of white against black. It is no longer whether or not white blood shall remain pure, it is whether or not white people shall remain free.
>
> We accept contumely and the risk of violence because we will not sit quietly by and see our native land, the South, not just Mississippi but all

Correspondence Related to James Silver and the Board of Trustees (1964)

Board of Trustees
Institutions of Higher Learning
1007 Woolfolk Building
Jackson, Mississippi
Office of the Executive Secretary
April 27, 1964

Dr. James W. Silver
The University of Mississippi
University, Mississippi

Dear Dr. Silver:

A subcommittee of the Board of Trustees, composed of M. M. Roberts, H. G. Carpenter, and Tally D. Riddell, wishes you to appear before them at the University or at the office of the Board of Trustees in Jackson at the earliest possible time that your health would permit. On that appearance, you will be requested to state under oath before a stenographer or reporter such comments and responses as you may care to make concerning the following specific matters and any similar or related matters, together with any other or additional comments or remarks you may wish to have become a part of the Subcommittee's investigation report to the Board of Trustees concerning your fitness as a member of the faculty of the University of Mississippi. Should it be your desire, you may have counselors or attorneys with you at the time of your appearance.

The specific matters which will be inquired about are:

(1) The basis for your alleged statement "The genesis of the deception which shifted the blame for the insurrection from Mississippians to federal officials came from the University administration. A singularly inaccurate story blaming the 'trigger-happy, amateurish, incompetent' marshals, and suggesting examples of diabolical brutality toward male and female stu-

dents, was in the hands of Barnett and Eastland within an hour or so of the firing of the gas,"—Speech of James W. Silver, Asheville, North Carolina, on November 7, 1963, and any action taken by you related to such statement since it was issued including but not limited to its reissuance, modification or retraction.

(2) The basis for your alleged statement "Long after it was made abundantly clear that many faculty members had witnessed the inception of the riot and knew for a certainty about the fraud against the federal government, the administration did not deviate from its original position but, on the contrary, continued to search for evidence condemning the marshals,"— Speech of James W. Silver, Asheville, North Carolina, on November 7, 1963, and any action taken by you related to such statement since it was issued including but not limited to its reissuance, modification or retraction.

(3) The basis for your alleged statement "By seven all observers knew that for whatever reason, the Mississippi Highway Patrol had abandoned its enforcement of law and order and was in fact in some cases encouraging the restless crowd to demonstrate against the marshalls,"—Speech of James W. Silver, Asheville, North Carolina, on November 7, 1963, and any action taken by you related to such statement since it was issued including but not limited to its reissuance, modification or retraction.

(4) The basis for your alleged statement that the witnesses who testified before the Legislative Investigating Committee of the Mississippi Legislature "would have small compunction about lying to a legislative investigating committee, especially one that made perfectly clear what it wanted to hear,"—Speech of James W. Silver, Asheville, North Carolina, on November 7, 1963, and any action taken by you related to such statement since it was issued including but not limited to its reissuance, modification or retraction.

(5) The basis for your alleged statement that "The people of Mississippi have thus once again been victimized, this time by a gigantic hoax perpetrated on them by their own time-serving leaders whose sense of loyalty is only to the false orthodoxy of the closed society,"—Speech of James W. Silver, Asheville, North Carolina, on November 7, 1963, and any action taken by you related to such statement since it was issued including but not limited to its reissuance, modification or retraction.

(6) The basis for your alleged statements that "Ole Miss at best has but a mediocre faculty." "Nobody in his right mind would go to Ole Miss for an education in the first place." "In all fairness to Chancellor Williams, I must admit that he has occasional good days." "We are faced with at least ten years of extreme mediocrity at Ole Miss, all of which could have been avoided by able administrative leadership,"—Speech of James W. Silver, Atlanta, Georgia, on August 1, 1963, and any action taken by you related to such statement since it was issued including but not limited to its reissuance, modification or retraction, together with any prior or subsequent similar public or private utterances.

(7) The basis for your alleged statement that "The search for historical truth . . . has become a casualty in embattled Mississippi,"—Speech of James W. Silver, Denver, Colorado, on November 8, 1963, and any action taken by you related to such statement since it was issued including but not limited to its reissuance, modification or retraction.

(8) The basis for your alleged statement that "the ultimate result will be violence which will last a long time. I would almost predict Federal occupation."—Speech of James W. Silver, Memphis, Tennessee, on October 5, 1963, and any such action taken by you related to such statement since it was issued including but not limited to its reissuance, modification or retraction, together with any prior or subsequent similar public or private utterances.

(9) The basis for your alleged statement "I think we're in, in the next three or four years, for a holocaust,"—Speech of James W. Silver, Atlanta, Georgia, on January 16, 1964, and any such action taken by you related to such statement since it was issued including but not limited to its reissuance, modification or retraction, together with any prior or subsequent similar public or private utterances.

(10) The basis for your alleged statement "I rather suspect there's going to be somebody killed,"—Speech by James W. Silver, Memphis, Tennessee, on October 5, 1963, and any such action taken by you related to such statement since it was issued including but not limited to its reissuance, modification or retraction, together with any prior or subsequent similar public or private utterances.

(11) The amount of time which your public speaking engagements have required, including preparation and travel. The dates and places you have made public appearances outside the State of Mississippi in the past six months. The amount of time spent in teaching, consulting with students, graduate students and fellow faculty members about subjects you are teaching and research in your current teaching field.

(12) The number of doctoral dissertations you have counseled or advised. Your support or opposition to a doctoral program in your department. Your endeavors in recruiting new doctoral candidates, students and faculty members.

(13) Your activities on September 30 and October 1, 1962.

(14) Any published writings or public speeches by you relating to the University, its administration or faculty during the past 6 months.

(15) Any and all records or appearances before or written reports or complaints to committees of the University faculty or members of the University administration concerning your duties as a faculty member or the condition or conduct of the University.

Such other matters as your comments or responses may disclose would warrant further information or inquiry.

A copy of the report of all remarks at this appearance will be made available for your inspection as promptly as possible. Please arrange to have with you any reference material you may need at the time of your appearance. The cooperation of the promptest reply possible would be appreciated.

Very truly yours,

E. R. Jobe

ERJ: na

John Emmerich
13 Dunkird Rd.
Baltimore 12, Md.
April 29, 1964

Dr. Verner Holmes
Holmes Clinic
McComb, Mississippi

Dear Verner:

Two things:

First, I want to congratulate you on your election as chairman of the Board of Trustees of Institutions of Higher Learning. In my opinion, this is one of the highest honors Mississippi has to offer, and it offers one of the best avenues of service and for responsible leadership. I can't think of a man better qualified than you for such a job.

Second, I've been reading about the wolves howling after Dr. Jim Silver at Ole Miss. And if I haven't told you before I want to tell you now that Jim Silver did more for my education at Ole Miss than all the other professors combined. He was and is one of those rare men who make a college education worth all the time and expense. And there weren't that many at Ole Miss like that.

Jim's main problem is that the Mississippi Legislature—or at least some members of that body—don't really understand what higher education is all about. Jim's talent is in getting students to do some independent thinking— and he couldn't care less whether anyone agrees with his own views. Some people in our state, of course, stand in mortal terror of people who think for themselves.

I note that Rep. Jim Mathis seems to think Silver has somehow or other violated Mississippi's Constitution (conduct which the Legislature itself frequently follows). But Silver hasn't violated any laws, of course. He just speaks his piece, from time to time, saying the things that more educated Mississippians should say. I read his carefully prepared address before the Southern Historical Society, and while his tone was perhaps pessimistic, I couldn't find a word there which wasn't true. We have built a closed society—and if anybody needs any evidence, or I should say more evidence, of it, consider this effort to "get" Jim.

In any event, you know all this as well as I do. But I wanted to let you know how I feel about Jim, as one who benefited greatly by his presence at Ole Miss.

If we're so all-fired afraid of ideas, then it would have been just as well for Ross Barnett to have closed the University. If all we want is a glorified grammar school which can produce good football teams, the state may as well save the money.

Congratulations again on your high honor.

We're holding a continuous open house for all McCombites en route to the World's Fair. Jackie and Diddle Enochs spent a few days with us a week or so ago, and my mother and father were here just after that.

Give Emma our regards,

Cordially,

(signed) John

April 29, 1964

Mr. John de J. Pemberton, Jr.
American Civil Liberties Union
156 Fifth Avenue
New York 10, New York

Mr. William P. Fidler
American Association of University Professors
1785 Massachusetts Avenue NW
Washington, D.C. 20037

Mr. Clarence H. Yarrow
American Friends Service Committee
160 North 15th
Philadelphia, Pennsylvania 19102

Gentlemen:

As I am still confined to my home after last week's surgery, I am writing the three of you a sort of joint letter, with copies going to Burke Marshall of the Department of Justice, Robert J. Farley, former Dean of the Law School here, and Miss Garnet Guild, executive secretary of the American Friends Service Committee, in Houston, Texas. The occasion is the receipt of a letter (copy enclosed) from E. R. Jobe, executive secretary of the Board of Trustees.

The American Civil Liberties Union, the American Association of University Professors, and the American Friends Service Committee have all indicated an abiding interest in my case and there has been some interchange of ideas about it. For instance, Mr. Yarrow has recently talked with Bertram Davis and Louis Joughin of the AAUP, and I have just heard from Alan Reitman of the ACLU. It seems to me that the best procedure is to work out some kind of a joint program in the near future. But my immediate concern is advice from you gentlemen as to my answer to Mr. Jobe. After giving the matter a great deal of thought and having conferred with several faculty members here (mainly officers of the local AAUP chapter), I think it wise to request of the Board committee a clarification of Mr. Jobe's letter. Perhaps questions similar to the following should be asked:

> Is this to be a hearing within the meaning of the tenure system? Is this to be the hearing which will be used as the basis for the discharge or retention of Silver? Does the Committee have the right to request answers to its queries or should it present formal charges? Would it not be better for all concerned to have a full Board hearing, with formal charges and answers? Does the Committee want Silver's testimony to include sworn affidavits or should these be held for a hearing after formal charges have been presented? Will Silver or his counsel have the right to call witnesses and cross-examine them, including members of the Board, Administration, and public officials? Does Silver have the right to ask for a public hearing, now, or later? Are the fifteen queries to be considered as charges? Will Silver have access to Board and Committee minutes concerning his own case? Will Silver have access to files and papers collected by the Board, including such as the "sworn testimony" regarding Senator Yarbrough's communication with Barnett forces in Jackson on September 30, 1962 and the communications between Hugh Clegg and Senator Eastland on September 30–October 1, 1962? In other words, can Silver examine the Committee's evidence as the Committee is apparently asking to examine that of Silver? Will Silver have access to recommendations already made by the Committee to the Board? Will Silver have access to requests made by the Board formally or informally of the Chancellor? Who and under what circumstances alleged that Silver made statements (6), (7), and (9)?

It seems to me that the Committee is asking me to supply the information with which to convict me. This would appear to be nothing more than a fishing expedition violative of my basic rights. The communication from Mr. Jobe is the first written word I have had from a committee which has been investigating me for months.

On March 12 Mr. Jobe called to ask me to appear the next day before the Committee in Jackson. As I was speaking at Southwestern College in Memphis on the 13th, I agreed to come to Jackson to meet the committee on Saturday, the 14th. I got home from Memphis at 2:30 in the morning of the 14th, got up to teach a morning class, and then drove with an ailing back 170 miles to Jackson to appear before the committee. At this meeting the chairman, M. M. Roberts, suggested that proceedings (what they were was not divulged) against me would be dropped if I would agree to stop making speeches outside Mississippi. I refused. Then for an hour and a half the three committee members and Mr. Jobe plied me with questions and comments about my conduct. This came without warning and it would appear to me that the committee committed procedural errors and violated my basic rights and certainly has had no warrant to act on the basis of my impromptu answers. If the press is to be believed, the Committee recommended to the full Board that I be fired, as also the press has intimated that the Board or members of it have informally requested of the Chancellor that he fire me, which he has consistently refused to do. Until this afternoon, the Chancellor has not received a copy of the Jobe letter. In any case, I think the Board has violated its own rules by dealing with me directly rather than through my superior officers here, the Chancellor, the dean of the College of Liberal Arts, and my departmental chairman. Mr. Jobe himself made a trip to the campus to inquire of my department chairman and others as to activities of mine which might be used in charges against me.

The basis of all charges against me stems from my presidential address to the Southern Historical Association on November 7, 1963. The Committee has taken almost six months to get to its first written request of Silver. It now indicates a sense of urgency but this case is too important for me to proceed without due thought and advice. I do need legal advice, whether from a Mississippi attorney or an outsider, or both, I am not sure. I will need a considerable time to collect the evidence to substantiate my case, perhaps from as many as fifty people now living in all parts of the world. I am elated at the prospect of carrying my case to the people of Mississippi (and this may furnish my best chance at breaking down Mississippi's closed society), but I will need a good deal of assistance. At the present moment I have access only to a very limited amount of departmental secretarial assistance. There is a very loyal but small group of dedicated people in the AAUP here, the Administration appears at least to be neutral in my case, and intelligent people in the state fear loss of accreditation of Mississippi's colleges and universities. I think the charges made against me are frivolous and that I can so prove to reasonable men. I do have great strength, though it is also true that my cards are on the table face up.

At the present moment I need and request advice as to how to answer Mr. Jobe's letter. Beyond that I hope that the ACLU, the AAUP and the AFSC can find a way to act in concert in my case. I want to proceed intelligently and I can assure you that I am prepared to carry this case to whatever conclusion may be reached.

Sincerely,

James W. Silver

American Friends Service Committee, Inc.
160 North Fifteenth Street,
Philadelphia 2, Pennsylvania
April 30, 1964

Dear James Silver:

I recall with appreciation our visit in January when Ezra Young and I saw you on his first trip to Mississippi. Through Ezra Young and Garnet Guild, recent word has come to appraise us of developments in your situation. I am sorry this included news of your recent illness. I hope your recuperation is progressing nicely and that the worst of your physical ordeal is now passed.

Mike Yarrow and I went to Washington, D.C., on Monday, April 27th in your behalf for a special appointment with Mr. Bertram Davis, Deputy Executive of AAUP in their national office.

We were very cordially received by Bertram Davis of AAUP. He proved to be a very charming host and had us as his luncheon guests. Besides, he was leisurely and open in his discussions with us following lunch as we had the visit continue in his office. It became clear early in our conversation that we shared common concern for the integrity of higher education and the meaning of academic freedom and the relation this has to university teaching generally. This interest became specific as it related to the situation surrounding you at the University of Mississippi. Mr. Davis shared with us the work that AAUP national office has been engaged in wherein they have been making a very careful study of the situation in the state of Mississippi. This study has been under his supervision. He shared with us the information that they appointed a national committee with the following persons as members:

Professor Richard P. Adams, Professor of English at Tulane University; Professor Francis Brown, Professor of Chemistry at Duke University; Professor Forrest Lacey, Professor of Law at the University of Tennessee. This committee with persons they have called on in various campus situations has been involved for the past several months in a careful study of institutions in the state of Mississippi. They have had very real cooperation with the local chapter of AAUP at the University of Mississippi and felt that their presence there during the course of the study had a salutary effect throughout the state. It was evidently known that the AAUP was taking the situation in colleges and universities seriously and was able to pursue its inquiries about conditions with cooperation of very many faculty persons. The report will be published in due time and will then become a part of the public record. He found that the time at the University of Mississippi was made very profitable by cooperation of the officers of AAUP in that institution. He gave very strong endorsement to President Truss of the University of Mississippi AAUP and to Russell Barrett, Secretary of AAUP at the University of Mississippi.

He indicated that this was a very strong committee that had been appointed although it was clear that by design they were all from Southern institutions. Richard P. Adams, who is chairman of the study committee, is also a member of the National Committee on Academic Freedom for AAUP and Francis Brown is second vice president of the national AAUP.

Mr. Davis indicated that the procedure for the national AAUP was that it would work through its local chapters. He gave every indication that he felt that the local AAUP at the University of Mississippi could be counted on to work with the national office in the situation there. He stated that the national office was able to provide observers when there were inquiries and hearings of faculty persons so that no faculty person should go alone and that they provided counsel when this was needed and charges had been placed against a faculty person. He indicated that persons wanting this kind of help should ask directly for help and that then it would be considered seriously and provided. He indicated that when charges had been made that the AAUP would insist on knowing the charges and would provide a legal panel for assisting the faculty in such situations.

It seemed clear to all of us that in any developing situation for you that you should not go before a faculty committee or the board alone, that you should request an observer to go with you. This person might well be a member of the local AAUP. If this proved to be unworkable, this should be indicated to the national office. Both Mike and I had the feeling that if such a request came to Mr. Davis that it would be given serious consideration. If after such a hearing charges should be placed, then a request should come for legal counsel. This is a reasonable request and AAUP can meet such a request. This gave us confidence that support was forthcoming for you if you would follow the suggestion of trying to work through your local AAUP chapter.

I am sure that through Ezra Young we will all be kept close to your situation. We want to make known that all resources of AAUP can be made available to you. We urge that you make full use of its facilities as your needs require.

It was good to have Mike Yarrow call you from Washington to give you immediate word about our visit and assure you of our concern and support.

Sincerely yours,

Mary Moss Cuthbertson
National Director
College Program

May 2, 1964

Professor Vincent de Santis
History Department
Notre Dame University
Notre Dame, Indiana

Dear Professor de Santis:

This morning I taught my first class in three weeks and though I'm still somewhat wobbly I think that I'll be back to normal in a week or two.

I'm sorry that I missed the chance to talk with you in Cleveland. In the main this letter is to confirm my statement over the phone: I am making my plans and this is a commitment for my coming to Notre Dame in the fall, for the year. As a matter of fact I am entranced with the idea and I am looking forward to the experience.

The day I called you I had received a letter from the Board of Trustees suggesting that it would be happy to give me a hearing before firing me. All it proposed was that I furnish the Board with the information with which to hang me. This is a long and complicated fight, the substance being that the Board is afraid to fire me for my speech and is now looking around for other excuses. It all rather pleases me for it is proof positive of the correctness of my analysis of the closed society in Mississippi. But we are all in for a real fight. The ACLU, the AAUP, and the American Friends Service Committee have all rushed to my defense, with legal aid, etc., and I rather imagine that the Board will be surprised when it finds out what it has got itself into. The ramifications of all this amount to a great deal more than I can write in a letter.

The point I have made several times before is that I can't very well ask the Board for a leave of absence. This would play right into its hands, and would get the members off the hook. But our chairman, Joe Baylen, has agreed that he will recommend a leave of absence even as late as July and says that he has the course work so arranged that I can leave. In fact, he asked, informally, the secretary of the Board if I would be given a leave if requested and the secretary responded with a relieved *yes*. Next week the Provost of the University will be on the campus. He is an old and trusted friend, through whom any leave request would move, after July 1st. I will talk with him in confidence, and I am sure he will go along. This morning I talked for two hours with the Chancellor but did not dare tell him of my plans. But granting leaves of absence has never been more than a formality and I see nothing that would hold it up even as late as July. Of course it is possible that I'll be fired by that time but I doubt if the fight will be more than well started.

I had had an arrangement with Joe Frantz last year that if I were in trouble here during the year I would come to Texas. I had rather planned to go to

Texas next year (I *am* worn out with this place), partly because my daughter and her husband will be in school in Austin. But the chance to teach at Notre Dame appeals to me more and I am very happy to take advantage of it.

Sincerely,

James W. Silver

The University of Mississippi
College of Liberal Arts
University, Mississippi
May, 1964

Department of History
(after May 6)

Enclosed is the kind of letter I would write to Mr. Jobe in answer to his communication of April 27, 1964 if I were to do this without assistance. But I am asking for assistance, both because of the importance of this case and because of my own lack of knowledge of the legal, academic, and procedural aspects of it.

Dear ——:

I have given much thought to your letter of April 27, 1964 and naturally since you have mentioned counsel, I have consulted counsel.

The "specific matters" which you have stated to be the subject of the inquiry are in the main the views and opinions I have expressed, particularly in a lecture as President of the Historical Association before my fellow academicians in Asheville, N. C. on November 7, 1963. I believe my views and public comments on current events are constitutionally protected by the Fourteenth Amendment to the United States Constitution as it incorporated the protections of the First Amendment to the same.

Moreover, I claim that your projected course represents action by a State authority directed against my participation as a professor and citizen in the current struggle over the application of the equal protection clause of the Fourteenth Amendment.

I do not believe it is right or proper that you should persist in this inquiry. After 28 years on the faculty of the University of Mississippi, I enjoy tenure. The projected inquiry would violate my rights of tenure, academic freedom and free speech. It would also damage the institution which I have served for almost three decades.

If you persist in this inquiry, I shall ask that every proper procedure be observed and I shall appear as demanded with counsel.

I, of course, realize that an investigation "concerning (my) fitness as a member of the faculty of the University of Mississippi" puts into issue my retention or discharge from the faculty.

In order that I and my counsel may be fully advised, I request that you state the origin of the proceedings and the relevance of each of the 15 enumerated paragraphs in your letter of April 27, 1963.

Respectfully,
JWS

May 24, 1964

Mr. George Rogers
Teller, Biedenharn, and Rogers
Box 22, Vicksburg, Mississippi

Dear George:

Enclosed is a copy in my miserable Sunday morning typing of the letter that Mr. Abram and the others I talked with in New York City last Thursday suggested I send to the Board in response to the statement from Mr. Jobe on April 27.

I will not attempt to go into all the ramifications of my lengthy conferences with the AAUP people in Washington and the AAUP, ACLU and others in New York. This would require an extended meeting, I would think.

I have been authorized by the AAUP in Washington to enter into negotiations for the services of a Mississippi lawyer or firm. On the recommendation of Bob Farley and others your firm is the one I would prefer.

It does not seem proper for me to urge Mr. Teller, Mr. Biedenharn, and yourself to get yourselves involved in my case. I would, obviously, like very much to have your services. It is possible that this could become not only an interesting but an important case, as you well know.

In any case, as I understand it, you will get this in the morning, and will talk it over, after which you will call me. If you do become interested, I would plan to come to Vicksburg at the earliest possible moment so that we could clear up the complicated problems which are too numerous and bulky for me to discuss in this letter.

The very first problem that must be attacked and settled is the question of counsel and the parts to be taken by those who will be in advisory positions.

I shall do nothing in the case until I hear from you.

Sincerely,
James W. Silver

Law Offices
Teller, Biedenharn & Rogers
1205 Monroe Street-Power Company Building
Vicksburg, Mississippi
39161

May 30, 1964

COPY

Dr. E. R. Jobe
Executive Secretary
Institutions of Higher Learning
1007 Woolfolk Building
Jackson, Mississippi

Dear Dr. Jobe:

Professor James W. Silver has recently consulted with us, requesting that we, as attorneys, represent him in the protection of his rights and the maintenance of his earned status as a professor with tenure at the University of Mississippi.

Dr. Silver furnished to us the published excerpt from the minutes of the meeting of the Board of Trustees of State Institutions of Higher Learning dated November 15, 1962, as the same pertains to "Employment and Tenure of Faculties of Institutions of Higher Learning in Mississippi" and also supplied us with the "Statement on Procedural Standards in Faculty Dismissal Proceedings" of the American Association of University Professors as reprinted from the bulletin of that association, Volume 44, No. 1, Spring, 1958.

Your letter to Dr. Silver of April 27 indicates that a sub-committee of the Board of Trustees is now making an investigation concerning his "fitness as a member of the faculty of the University of Mississippi". Quite obviously the proceedings contemplated by your letter are not governed by the regulations which have been furnished to us. Consequently we must assume that there are other regulations of uniform applicability to all professors with tenure with which we are not versed.

In order to be placed in a position to properly counsel with Dr. Silver, we shall thank you to either advise us where we can obtain, or to furnish us with, the rules and regulations which are deemed apt together with a specification of the particular charges affecting Dr. Silver's fitness as a professor which form the basis for the sub-committee's investigation.

We shall further desire to be advised of procedural standards. If the conditions precedent to a hearing are met, then, in advance of such hearing, Dr. Silver should certainly know what opportunity and right he will be accorded to produce witnesses and evidence in defense of such charges as may be specified against him.

You may be assured of our client's desire to cooperate with the Board, as indeed is our sincere wish and purpose, with the hope that this matter may be soon and properly clarified consistent with the legal rights of Dr. Silver and the best interest of the institutions of higher learning of the State.

Sincerely yours,

Landman Teller

June 3, 1964

Mr. Melvin Wulf
American Civil Liberties Union
170 Fifth Avenue
New York, New York

Dear Mel:

Although I think that you have been informed of some of my activities since our meeting on May 21st in New York City, I feel that I should catch you up on the story as a whole.

I reached home on Saturday, May 23rd and fell into about a solid week's work with examinations and final grades. On that same Saturday, though, I had a long talk with Ezra Young and a companion of his from the American Friends Service Committee, as well as with some University people.

That night I called George Rogers of Teller, Biedenharn & Rogers, a well known Vicksburg law firm, to find out if they would represent me before the Board of Trustees. George called me back on Sunday, requesting me to come to Vicksburg on Wednesday, May 27. On that day I flew to Jackson and met with William Winter, state treasurer, who drove me to Vicksburg. The three members of the firm, Winter, and I conferred for most of the day.

As a result of this meeting I called both Mr. Morgan and Mr. Sands on the following day. On Friday, Mr. Teller came to the University, talked with me, then with Chancellor Williams, and again with me. He was to have talked with Mr. Sands yesterday, by phone.

From all this discussion it became clear to me that I needed to make a few important decisions (along the line brought up by Mr. Abram in New York). I have practically agonized over my next moves but have decided to do and in fact have done the following: 1) arranged for Teller, Biedenharn & Rogers to represent me before the Board, 2) agreed that this firm would respond to the April 27 letter of Mr. Jobe, and 3) requested a leave of absence so that I may teach at Notre Dame next year.

My major premise is that I am simply trying to establish my right to remain on the faculty of the University of Mississippi. I have made it very clear to Mr. Teller that to do this I am willing to go as far as necessary in the federal courts (and he has agreed to go with me) but if my situation here can be retained without this procedure, it would be best for all concerned.

I have many misgivings about requesting the leave of absence before the case was decided by the Board, but time has been running out on me and it is necessary that I give Notre Dame the assurance that I will be there in September. My decision to go to Notre Dame has been based primarily on the fact that in normal circumstances that is exactly what I would like to do.

I am well aware that some people will compare my case to that of Professor Murphy. Despite the similarity I do not think that this applies for I am determined not to voluntarily resign from my position here. Neither do I think that I should make a decision as important as this on the basis of the reaction of those who would like to get rid of me. I want to make it clear that there has been no pressure on me from the Board or from the University administration to request the leave of absence. This leave has been on my mind for almost a year and has no connection with my "case" before the Board.

Salary raises at the University normally come once every two years. I am convinced that the administration will in this matter treat me exactly as they have in the past.

Enclosed is a copy of Mr. Teller's letter to the Board. It is a good letter and I approve of it. What the Board will do I have no way of knowing and I don't think it wise to try to anticipate their action. This Friday I am going to attend a meeting of the Mississippi Council on Human Relations at Tougaloo College, and Saturday, the 6th, I leave with my family for three weeks in the East. From June 15 to the 22nd I will be at the Algonquin Hotel in New York City, primarily for the promotion of my book which will be published on the 22nd. After that I plan to return to listen to the Mississippi music.

I hope that those who think I have made wrong decisions in this whole matter will realize that I have gone over every alternative with the greatest of care, and that I believe I am following the proper course. It will never be possible for me to express my deep appreciation for the counsel and friendship shown to me by everyone concerned. I think that my right to say and do what I believe to be proper is being protected and that I shall be able to retain my position here with the least amount of harm to the University.

Sincerely,
James W. Silver

American Association of University Professors
1785 Massachusetts Avenue, N.W.
Washington, D.C. 20036
June 3, 1964

Professor James W. Silver
c/o Mrs. Chris Little
34 Irving Street, Apt. #32
Cambridge, Massachusetts

Dear Jim:

Thanks for your letter of "June 1, 1964 (glory be)."

I trust that you will be in Cambridge or en route while this letter is being typed and transmitted.

Do you really think the Board is going to give you a raise? I hope so, but if that happens I really do wish you could spend a portion of it to purchase me and Abram straw hats to wear. Wearing one would be more of a burden for me than having it served as a main course.

For heaven's sake don't worry about hurting peoples' feelings. Abram, Wulf & Co. will certainly understand even if the *Clarion-Ledger* will not. But then, you never have altered the patterns of a lifetime for the momentary convenience of Mississippi's voice of unreason.

You know what is best for you and your own desires. At any rate, you know that however your case develops, we are prepared to assist and advise you. I am certain that Landman Teller knows the ins and outs of Mississippi better than any of us do and I trust that he can and will capably shepherd you along your course.

Have you talked with Harcourt, Brace and World or their attorneys about the selection of local counsel if libel suits develop? Have you discussed this with Teller?

Have a nice trip and a good rest (this is not to indicate that publishers' schedules are conducive to this) and I will see you here in three weeks.

Good luck with the book.

Kindest regards,
Sincerely,
(signed, Chuck)
Charles Morgan, Jr.

Law Offices
Teller, Biedenharn & Rogers
Vicksburg, Mississippi

June 15, 1964

Dear Jim:

One day last week Jim, George and I were discussing the attorney-client relationship which exists between us, based on the understandings had at the time of your call by our offices on May 27. Since that time, and on May 29, I came up to the University and made the opportunity to talk with Chancellor Williams as well as to visit with you.

George, as you know, has had a general discussion with Dr. Jobe, which followed ours to Dr. Jobe of May 30, copy of which you have.

You were advised, by virtue of my telephone call to you over the past weekend, of the substance of Mr. Roberts' contact and you will herewith find enclosed a copy of my letter of even date, the original of which is going forward to Mr. Roberts. This last mentioned enclosure I am sure you will find to be self-explanatory and to be strictly in accordance with the understanding reached on the occasion of my telephone call to you.

In our inter-office conference of last week, we agreed that it would be wise, for your benefit and ours (not that we anticipate any misunderstanding), for me to set forth our understanding relative to this employment and our representation of you, which is to the following effect:

(a)That, as our letter to the Board of Trustees of May 30 discloses, our employment involves the protection of your rights and the maintenance of your earned status as a professor with continuing tenure at the University of Mississippi;

(b)That it is recognized to be in the best and mutual interest of yourself and the State to avoid controversy over this feature and, if possible, to enable a disposition to be accompanied by no fanfare or publicity;

(c)That, since you had determined many months ago to ask for a leave of absence so as to teach the coming year at Notre Dame in accordance with an offer from that institution, you authorized us to so advise the Chancellor and you have carried through on this feature, notwithstanding any misgivings which you may have had and notwithstanding that it can be anticipated that some news analyst or writers may erroneously suggest or wilfully infer that you were prompted to this action for other reasons;

(d)That we have naturally accepted this matter on the basis of the actions of which we are advised, largely referred to in letter addressed to you by the Board on April 27, plus our awareness, on the occasion of your trip here to see us on May 27 and since, of the fact that you have authored a book which will be released for publication on June 22;

(e)That in the preservation of your rights we expect to do that which in our opinion, according to our best judgment and without association with any others (unless we shall between us later so agree), determine upon those legal steps and that course of action thereby indicated which we believe to be prudent and best, concerning which action you will, in every instance where the opportunity exists, have advance notice.

As you know we have no fee arrangement other than that we shall look to you individually and shall undertake to make, under all of the circumstances, a reasonable and fair charge. We understand that you may expect to be reimbursed for these expenses by others, but that is a matter to be settled between you and the parties concerned. While we have not yet called upon you for a retainer fee, we shall feel at liberty to do so.

We assuredly respect and want to protect and shall protect to the best of our ability your academic freedom and your right as an individual and professor at the University within the orbit of your calling and the laws and regulations uniformly apt to express your views and to advance these contentions which you feel are proper and just. We all must recognize that the relationship of attorney and client as it exists here would not extend, either from your standpoint or ours, into unknown matters or unpredictable occurrences, so necessarily our relationship, which we hope will be a pleasant and successful one, is confined to those matters of which we have been made reasonably aware.

We feel that we have an understanding that your primary purpose is to secure your right to have made the public statements embodied in your North Carolina speech and your book and retain your status as a professor at the University with all of the rights, privileges and emoluments attributable to this office. Both you and we are aware that these statements have created and will create a political situation which might provoke the Board of Trustees into taking a course which, from the point of view of the best interests of the University, would be unwise and irrational.

While we recognize that we are without right to dictate or even influence your personal actions, we cannot refrain at this stage from strongly suggesting that you curtail any activity which would jeopardize your primary objective, an objective which we believe we have above correctly stated. We believe that you ought to be able to justify the observance of such a prudent course on the basis that while other groups and individuals may have aims and objects with which you are personally sympathetic, you already have enough problems with which to cope.

Jim and George join me in sending kindest regards,

Sincerely yours,
(signed: Landman Teller)

June 15, 1964
COPY

Mr. M. M. Roberts
Attorney at Law
Hattiesburg, Mississippi

Dear Mr. Roberts:

Dr. James W. Silver is presently out of the State; however, I managed to contact him over the weekend and to communicate to him the substance of your telephone call to me of this past Saturday morning.

Dr. Silver was specifically advised of your suggestion that he place you in a position to advise the other members of the Board of Trustees that, while he was on leave of absence for the 1964–65 school year, he would agree to seek employment elsewhere than in Mississippi. Dr. Silver is not agreeable to the making of such a commitment.

It is our understanding that Dr. Silver's present request for a leave of absence has been regularly made, duly processed and approved through channels, and thus recommended and presented, would ordinarily be routinely granted; but, if it is not, then Dr. Silver, a professor with tenure (with 28 years of service), expects to actively continue and serve as a member of the faculty at the University of Mississippi.

With kindest regards, I am

Sincerely yours,
(original signed: Landman Teller)

M. M. Roberts
Attorney and Counselor at Law
Citizens Bank Building
Hattiesburg, Miss.

June 16, 1964

Mr. Landman Teller
Teller, Biedenharn & Rogers
Vicksburg, Mississippi

Dear Mr. Teller:

Your letter to me of June 15 about Dr. Silver has been received.

Some of the information contained in your letter is new to me; but the matter will be brought up before the Board of Trustees at its meeting to be held during this week. What your client has done in trying to get a leave of absence is not known to me, but I personally cannot see how Dr. Silver will want to continue at the University of Mississippi if he continues critical of the University and its administration and all of the ongoings there and in our state. That approach on his part is simply wrong. He should be loyal to the forces which act for the good of the University and if he cannot do this, then he is failing to do what should be expected of you or me in our own area of activities. Your letter surely sounds like one that Dr. Silver has written himself.

Sincerely yours,
(signed: M. M. Roberts)
M. M. ROBERTS

August 10, 1964

Mr. Landman Teller
Teller, Biedenharn & Rogers
Power Company Building
Vicksburg, Mississippi

Dear Landman:

I was out of town when your long letter of June 15 came and I have been out of town a great part of the time since. Even so, at the time I had no disagreement with the contents of your letter and I did anticipate that within a short time we would have some business to transact.

This business has not developed and I am sure that we are both glad that it has not. Just what the Board committee reported to the full Board I haven't the slightest idea but I suppose all concerned decided to let sleeping dogs lie. Certainly, I see no reason to anticipate action of any sort from the Board or its committee until I make it plain that I am coming back next spring.

Enclosed are a couple of documents, a letter to Professor Adams of Tulane, an investigator for the AAUP, and a copy of the statement from the Chancellor granting my leave of absence. It does seem to me that the Board included an unnecessary slap at me in suggesting that it had not waived any rights to continue its investigation, etc. I don't know anyone who would have thought that the Board was waiving anything. A bit more serious is the fact that while every member of the history department was given a raise in salary for next year, and while the chairman of the department recommended that my salary be raised from $9600 to $10500, my salary officially remains as it was. The Provost assures me that this is normal procedure. While I have my doubts, I see no need to raise such an academic issue at this time.

I am sure that at times you have wondered whether I have paid any attention to your admonition to stay out of the spotlight. You may be surprised to learn that I have turned down a number of requests that I appear under the auspices of this and that organization. I need not be more specific but I can assure you that I have, for Old Silver at least, used some restraint. The LIFE piece was, I thought, innocuous. In May I did not know, of course, what a commercial publisher expects of an author of a book it is trying to sell. In any case the publisher, or Silver, or LIFE, or more likely the extremists in Mississippi have made a best seller, for the time being at least, of the book. The first printing of 10,000 copies is gone.

I'll be here about another month. You may not have guessed this but I have had very few official relationships with lawyers in the past. Mine with you and Jim and George has been most cordial and enjoyable. In any case I suppose, in fact that we are not expecting immediate problems, and that this would be a proper time for you to send me some kind of statement. I have just completed the payment for my back operation, and I may as well look into the abyss once again.

Yours,
Jim Silver

Board of Trustees of
Institutions of Higher Learning
Jackson, Mississippi
Office of the Executive Secretary
August 14, 1964

Mr. Landman Teller
Vicksburg, Mississippi

Dear Mr. Teller:

Thank you for your letter of May 30, 1964. At the outset, let me emphasize that the subcommittee immediately concerned with this matter has not requested Dr. Silver to appear before them to respond to any charges made against him. No formal charges have been presented against Dr. Silver. Rather, the subcommittee has requested Dr. Silver to appear before them with his counsel in the interest of making a thorough and complete and fair investigation of the various areas outlined in my letter.

As an attorney, you are, of course, familiar with the statutory and constitutional provisions which define the powers, duties, responsibilities and limitations of the Board of Trustees in connection with the employment of personnel. These matters cannot be modified or abrogated by the Board. You may be sure that within their framework the Board will accord due process both to the Institutions of Higher Learning of the State and to professors and others employed by it. Certainly a spirit of fair play prompted the subcommittee conducting this investigation to ask Dr. Silver to appear before them to make available such facts and information as he might be willing to present to them concerning the various areas of inquiry outlined in my letter while the matter was still under investigation and prior to the formulation of any specific charges, if any should be felt warranted at the conclusion of the investigation.

I do not believe that there is any procedural information pertinent to the subcommittee's investigation which is not contained in my letter of April 27, 1964. If no charges arise from this investigation, the matter will obviously end there. If charges are made, they will be presented to the Chancellor of the University with directions to refer the charges to a committee of University personnel for formal hearing and study, with reports to the Chancellor and thence to the entire Board. If charges are made, copies of these charges will be handed to you immediately and an adequate period of time (at least one month) will be afforded to you to make such defense as may be desired. Your client will be afforded the opportunity to appear before this University committee, if he desires to avail himself of such opportunity, and a full stenographic record will be kept and made available to you.

I trust that this response gives you the information necessary to enable you to advise us whether or not your client desires to appear before the subcommittee in accordance with my letter of April 27, 1964.

Very truly yours,
(signed: E. R. Jobe)
E. R. Jobe
Executive Secretary

Law Offices
TELLER, BIEDENHARN & ROGERS
Vicksburg, Mississippi
39161
September 3, 1964
COPY

Dr. E. R. Jobe
Institutions of Higher Learning
Jackson, Mississippi

Re: Dr. James W. Silver

Dear Dr. Jobe:

This acknowledges with thanks receipt of yours of August 14 which was in response to ours to you of May 30.

Since we wrote you on May 30, Dr. Silver applied for and, as we understand it, was by the Board granted a leave of absence effective this September 1, 1964, so that he may serve as a Visiting Professor at the University of Notre Dame for the 1964–65 session.

When Dr. Silver first contacted us in May, 1964, requesting that we accept employment as his counsel in this particular connection, he advised us of his appearance before, and his interrogation by, the Board's sub-committee on March 12 last and showed to us a copy of his letter to you of March 18. Under the circumstances, we are authorized to advise that Dr. Silver does not* desire to avail himself of the privilege of further appearing before the sub-committee. In so advising, we emphasize that Dr. Silver denies that there is any proper basis for charges of dismissal, and further and independently submits that there is no justification for the Board to direct the Administration of the University of Mississippi to prefer charges against him.

Your letter points out that the matter will be ended if no charges arise from the investigation. If it be otherwise, we would assume, academic due process and the circumstances considered, that any affirmative action will be deferred until Dr. Silver's present leave of absence has expired.

With kindest regards, we are

Yours very truly,
Teller, Biedenharn & Rogers

BY: (original signed: Landman Teller)
LT:la

---

*may at this point add the word "presently"

Faulkner and the Teaching of History
(1972)

*When the Southern Historical Association met in Jackson in
1948 to honor the Ole Miss centennial, I refused to put together
a talk on William Faulkner. While I had known him for more
than a decade, I had read little of his fiction. In 1972 I did read
for the same organization, this time meeting in Miami Beach, a
piece showing how Faulkner had influenced my life in the 1950s
and my teaching after I left Mississippi. The next year I was
asked back to Ole Miss to speak on the ODK-Mortar Board
forum. I thought it appropriate to use my Faulkner talk. From
the crowd that filled Fulton Chapel, I received a hearty reception.*

It is my guess that sixty hardback books, a hundred and fifty
dissertations, and some two thousand articles with appropriate cross references have been written to explain William Faulkner to the world. Not long
ago there was a symposium on "Faulkner and History" at the annual meeting of the South Central Modern Language Association, the three papers,
naturally, delivered by eminent professors of English. I would not estimate
how many doctors of literature have earned their bread and rank for the past
thirty years by kicking old Bill Faulkner around. Recently I have read a 583-
page Wisconsin dissertation on the reception by textbook writers and/or
historians in general of Faulkner's portrayal of the southern scene. Hence,
if anyone really wants to know how historians have received Faulkner, I
shall be glad to furnish bibliographic data where one can wallow in footnotes
and interpretation.

It is not my intention to say something about Faulkner as a source of
history nor about Faulkner's influence on history but about Faulkner's impact on one Jim Silver, the individual, not the amateur historian. I hope
there will be no footnotes and few quotations from anyone except Faulkner
himself.

First, I shall clear my meager conscience by suggesting that in evaluating
Faulkner historians have followed the election returns and the polls, the
Nobel Prize implications, their colleagues in English departments, and their
own personal whims. There is evidence that some text book writers have
read Faulkner. Among southerners the Mississippi author has been accepted as producing everything from the "privy school of literature" to the
most inspiring fiction of the twentieth century. [Which reminds me that in
my home state of Mississippi, historians with doctorates from Vanderbilt,

Duke, University of North Carolina, Chicago, and Harvard have played fast
and loose with that organization so loathed by Faulkner, the Citizens Council (one historian college president—Ph.D., Duke—proclaiming publicly
that the Kennedys brought on the 1962 Cuban crisis to get people's attention
away from their Ole Miss fiasco), while the most literate staff member of the
Mississippi Citizens Council earned his Ph.D. in English at Yale. It might be
worth investigation as to why such highly trained professionals have been
corrupted in Mississippi while the native Mississippi author without even a
high school diploma retained his integrity throughout life.] The textbook
longest in use in this country (Morison and Commager) was hostile to Faulkner in its 1930 edition (he took refuge in brutality and sadism) but by 1962
proclaimed Faulkner as "the historian of the transformation of the Old
South to the New." There was little attention paid by historians to Faulkner
before 1950 and most of that was negative. Later the number one historian
of the South (Woodward) wrote that Faulkner had "given history meaning
and value and significance as events never do merely because they happen.
These are things the historian also strives to do, and he should seek to do
them with the same fortitude and honesty." So much for judgment and
objectivity among the professionals.

I shall bore you only with those personal details I consider necessary to
my purpose. In the middle twenties I spent four somewhat fearful years at
the University of North Carolina where I quickly laid aside my thin veneer
of fundamentalism and indulged myself without enthusiasm in the conventional liberalism of the day, assuming that my kind of people would never
win political office. The depression brought me to Nashville among the
agrarians who were not only winning the Civil War but were restoring the
country's faith in the values of the Old South. I found little fault with
Phillips and Parrington and Freeman, and Owsley, who, lest we forget, had
already struck the cult of the Confederacy a lethal blow with his first book.
My interest was in the frontier, the New Deal, sharecropping, organized
labor in the South, poker, and eating regularly. In 1935 I got my degree, a
wife, and started teaching in one-crop Kansas, a splendid preparation for
Mississippi the next year.

In the middle of the depression we were a quarter of a century away from
James Meredith, exactly the same time between the incorporation of Yoknapatawpha and secession. My textbook was Odum's *Southern Regions*
and later Cash's *Mind of the South,* and I knew a man named Faulkner who
despised the inroads of industrialization and big government but who had
enough wit to laugh off the glories of the southern past as pictured by the
agrarians. I learned somewhere along the line that the most sensitive white
man was the Mississippian who grew up joyfully absorbing his heritage but
who somehow was able later to transcend the mythology in viewing the
enormity of injustice all around him.

In my first Ole Miss class was Faulkner's step-daughter, and my wife and I soon became intimate with the Faulkner family, later being the only non-relatives "invited" to the funeral of Miss Maud, Faulkner's mother. In those years I hardly saw Faulkner, Oxford's eccentric who was away from home much of the time and who, while always polite, was rarely sociable in his fierce determination to retain his privacy. My reading of Faulkner was desultory and uncomprehending.

From World War II until the desegregation decision in 1954 there was great optimism and excitement among those who sought to civilize Mississippi. The Ole Miss History Department grew from three to eleven and we were able to bring to the campus liberals and even radical labor leaders. The Board of Trustees seriously considered Bob Farley's suggestion that he seek out a couple of Negroes for the Law School. Frank Smith was elected to Congress. Along about the time of filming *Intruder in the Dust,* in Oxford, Faulkner and I began an interminable discussion of the race question reaching another crisis in Mississippi. His position was close to mine, that of a moderate who understood the inevitability of the future, one who rather desperately hoped to help his section prepare for what was on the way. Faulkner was greatly criticized for the comments in *Intruder* by Gavin Stevens, who was presumed to be Faulkner speaking. Although Faulkner often denied that he spoke through any of his characters, I am sure that Stevens's obsession with the South reforming itself was also that of Faulkner. My most persuasive evidence is that when I requested his permission to publish his remarks to the Southern Historical Association in 1955, he at first insisted that the pamphlet, *Three Views of the Segregation Decisions,* be paid for and distributed by "southern amateurs" instead of the Ford Foundation. It is a little amusing that when I asked where in Mississippi we would get the required $1500, he offered to seek it from his New York City publishers. Until that summer of 1954 Faulkner and I were in agreement that maybe the South could reform itself with little or no intrusion from the outside.

With the Nobel Prize William Faulkner became a public man. All of his twelve essays, thirteen of his fourteen speeches, and twenty-five of his thirty-one public letters were produced after 1950. He mellowed to the point of occasionally seeming to enjoy cocktail parties, which, of course, interfered with serious drinking. Always a man of responsibility he accepted what to him (at least at first) was the onerous chore of representing his country abroad, in Japan, Greece, Venezuela, etc. Unfortunately for his reputation, Faulkner was forced to make off-hand comments on everything under the sun, notwithstanding his unconcern for the questions of fools, his downright carelessness, and his compulsion to be witty or to shock his listener. So he got into trouble with such frivolous statements as "I am only a farmer who writes," and with the more serious allegation that under certain circumstances he would join white Mississippians in shooting down Negroes in the street (which subsequently, he denied). He continued to write letters to the editor as a Mississippi moderate. Faulkner was never an activist and never deserted what he considered his middle position. He was really speaking to Mississippi in a decade when only two or three lawyers in the state admitted publicly that sooner or later Mississippi would have to obey the Supreme Court; consequently, he was excoriated by the extremists of both sides. Many times Faulkner was just mistaken, as when he equated the Citizens Council and NAACP. My judgment is that Faulkner was primarily a responsible individualist (far removed from social Darwinism) who believed in Christian morality (but not Christian institutions), who thought the Negro wanted or should want equality *to,* not equality *per se,* who continued to believe that the South must expiate its past sins.

Along with Benjamin Mays, Faulkner spoke in 1955 at what may have been the most exciting session ever of the Southern Historical Association. On December 1, he wrote for me:

> We accept contumely and the risk of violence because we will not sit quietly by and see our native land, the South, not just Mississippi but all the South, wreck and ruin itself twice in less than a hundred years, over the Negro question.
>
> We speak now against the day when the Southern people who will resist to the last these inevitable changes in social relations, will, when they have been forced to accept what they at one time might have accepted with dignity and goodwill, will say, "Why didn't someone tell us this before? Tell us this in time?"

A handful of Mississippians held in Faulkner's home several meetings whose purpose was to contain the poison of the Citizens Council. We were completely ineffective, though we did publish one issue of the *Southern Reposure,* a modest satire on white supremacy, largely stolen from the sophomore "Nigble Papers." Both Faulkner and I believed, at least for a while, in the middle road of J. P. Coleman who became governor in 1956. We could not then see that in its massive resistance, Mississippi under Ross Barnett would be turned over to the Citizens Council. In his last couple of years Faulkner, having had his say, said little, but he emphatically did not, as his segregationist brother claimed, return to the family doctrine of white supremacy. To anyone who had read Faulkner's great novels, such a position would seem preposterous. The last time I saw him was on June 5, 1962, when he and Estelle walked to town to vote for Frank Smith (who was ousted from Congress because of his moderate position on race). I have often been asked what Faulkner would have said about the federal invasion of Mississippi in the Meredith crisis. I don't know. But I remember that Faulkner's nephew, a traditional conservative if there ever was one, a captain in the Mississippi Guard that President Kennedy nationalized, went to the rescue of the beleaguered marshals on the Ole Miss Campus and had his

arm broken for his pains. In the ten years since I have often wondered
whether the radicalization of the civil rights movement did not indeed bring
about its own collapse, as Faulkner in his last years seems to have known it
would.

My father died more than forty years ago. The family was noncom-
municative, especially when it came to the display of emotion. I really
learned about my father when I read and reread what he called his journal,
twelve hundred pages written over a period of thirty years. In the same way
I learned much of what I know about the real Faulkner by reading over and
over again, since his death, most of what he had written. In less than the last
decade I became a Faulkner addict. At times I have had the feeling that he
had been writing for me all along, even sometimes about my own problems
and values. But most of the time Faulkner, in his flashes of brilliance, was
able to illuminate for me my own obsessive inquiry into what made southerners act as they do.

Though Faulkner was never an activist, I consider him a reformer or even
a liberal crusader in the most cosmic sense. By that I mean that in his great
fiction he helped in a major way to clear away the debris of southern mythology. In his particular manner, Faulkner was a part of the non-Marxist egalitarian movement of the 1930s which in turn evolved from the explosion of
knowledge beginning perhaps with the new anthropology at the turn of the
century. This trend was essential to changes in values preceding, let us say,
the 1954 desegregation decision. Not that Faulkner considered himself a
reformer; it is just that he was such a close observer of past and present
reality that a serious reader must consider his fiction a challenge to old ways
of thinking. Essentially Faulkner was a great story teller, and I suppose the
reform impact of what he wrote impressed him no more than Hitler might
have considered his persecution of the Jews a component in the lessening of
racial prejudice in the United States. Certainly not many people read Faulkner during the depression or World War II, but in the last twenty years
Random House alone has published more than two million copies of his
Modern Library and paperback editions.

In 1958 Vann Woodward told us that there was only one way in which the
South is "immune from the disintegrating effect of nationalism and the
pressure for conformity," one way in which the South has not changed, and
that is in its history. Unquestionably, history has happened to southerners.
In both *The Sound and the Fury* and *Absalom, Absalom!* Quentin Compson—"his very body an empty hall echoing with sonorous defeated names;
he was not a being, an entity, he was a commonwealth. He was a barracks
filled with stubborn, back-looking ghosts . . ."—stands out as a southerner
created, overwhelmed, and crushed by his heritage. Quentin was "still too
young to deserve yet to be a ghost but nevertheless having to be one for all
that since he was born and bred in the deep South." It is almost as though

having been born in the South is the basic characteristic and problem of most of Faulkner's people, from Thomas Sutpen (whose mistake was in the acceptance of southern values) and all of his family, and John Sartoris to Ike McCaslin, Joe Christmas, Joanna Burden, and Gail Hightower. But this is not what I have in mind when I say that Faulkner has illuminated for me the South and its history in brilliant strokes. In the 1950s and until his death Faulkner without question, sustained me in what I suppose was my own slow radicalization. To cite one instance, for two months in the spring of 1962, he and Estelle came out to our house every Sunday evening, to watch his favorite television program, "Car 54, Where Are You?" Sometimes they stayed for "Bonanza"—and it was on these occasions that I was able to introduce to him many students who had come from Brandeis and Harvard and Notre Dame to see first hand what was going on down South. At the time I thought Faulkner talked with the utmost candor and sense. He castigated the Citizens Council, and as he had said earlier, accepted contumely and the risk of violence. It seems to me that Faulkner kept his balance in believing that the black man wanted and should demand only the elimination of the political, educational, and economic evils in the caste system— but I am doubtful that he ever seriously considered embracing social mixing in its most spectacular manifestation (which he had written about so eloquently)—that is miscegenation. "The Negro can be equal," he wrote, "without having to come in and sleep with you." I am sure, though, that if he had lived well into the 60s, he would have scorned violence, black nationalism, and above all the pandering of politicians like Wallace and Nixon to the basest instincts of human nature.

In the past few years, I have used several of Faulkner's novels in an advanced class in the history of the South. My favorite, I think, is *Absalom, Absalom!* because it requires considerable discipline but will entrap the student in its mystery if he applies himself. After the Civil War Henry Sutpen kills his half-brother and brings down their father's design for dynasty. Four people try their hands at explaining the family's tragedy; before he gets half way through the reader discovers that he is the fifth historical detective. With 80 percent of the novel quotation and with additional evidence and surmise forthcoming as though by chance, *Absalom, Absalom!* is marvelously like those historical riddles whose solution is bewildering because of a lack of all the parts. It requires a delicate and determined effort in historical criticism. As Quentin's father knew, the documents don't always explain: "We have a few old mouth-to-mouth tales; we exhume from old trunks and boxes and drawers letters without salutation or signature, in which men and women who once lived and breathed are now only initials or nicknames but of some incomprehensible affection which sounds to us like Sanskrit or Choctaw; we see dimly people, the people in whose living blood and seed we ourselves lay dormant and waiting, in this shadowy attentuation of time possessing now heroic proportions, performing their acts of simple passion and simple violence, impervious to time and inexplicable— yes Judith, Bon, Henry, Sutpen; all of them. They are there, yet something is missing, they are like a chemical formula exhumed along with the letters from that forgotten chest, carefully, the paper old and faded and falling to pieces, the writing faded, almost indecipherable, yet meaningful, familiar in shape and sense, the name and presence of volatile and sentient forces; you bring them together in the proportions called for, but nothing happens; you re-read tedious and intent, poring, making sure that you have forgotten nothing, made no miscalculations; you bring them together again and again nothing happens; just the words, the symbols, the shapes themselves, shadowy inscrutable and serene, against the turgid background of a horrible and bloody mischancing of human affairs." Another thesis down the drain.

Absalom, Absalom! is a story of American and southern values, of miscegenation and aristocracy. According to Jason Compson's interpretation of the views of Goodhue Coldfield, "the South would realize that it was now paying the price for having erected its economic edifice not on the rock of stern morality but on the shifting sands of opportunism and moral brigandage." Faulkner may be saying here that for a man to join the aristocracy in twenty-five years requires a considerable degree of Snopesism along the way. Surely Thomas Sutpen had most of the characteristics which Faulkner admired in John Sartoris; both might well have achieved great eminence in any other part of the country. *"Given the occasion and the need, this man can and will do anything."* One of the things Sutpen was willing to do was to enter the stable ring in deadly combat with the most powerful of his slaves, "perhaps for entertainment but perhaps as a matter of sheer deadly forethought toward the retention of supremacy, domination. . . ." When I first read this I wondered whether Faulkner was aware that during his own childhood a rough and tough mountaineer had come down from eastern Kentucky to boss a lumber camp in the county west of Lafayette, and that he maintained order in a region where there was no other law by means of a standing offer to fight any man, black or white, who dared oppose him. The son of this brawler presided over the trial of the murderers of Emmett Till, and his granddaughters made their debut in Jackson.

Absalom, Absalom! is a powerful novel which does no violence to the history of the South. No wonder that Shreve McCannon could shout: "Jesus, the South is fine, isn't it. It's better than the theatre, isn't it. It's better than Ben Hur, isn't it. No wonder you have to come away now and then, isn't it." Nor that when Shreve asked Quentin, "Why do you hate the South?" the answer came quickly, *"I don't hate it,"* "I don't hate it." "I don't hate it,* he thought, panting in the cold air, the iron New England dark; I don't. I don't! I don't hate it! I don't hate it!"* Neither did Faulkner.

To me *Light in August* is another bit of evidence that the biology of race has ever been subordinated to the sociology of race in the South. It is part of

Faulkner's genius that he never lets you know, he never even lets Joe Christmas know whether he has a trace of Negro blood. Yet the community which shapes so fiercely the destinies of its members, proceeds inexorably toward the doom of Christmas once it has made the perhaps erroneous assumption that he is the product of biracial parentage. The community, in fact, invents the Negro and establishes his characteristics. The town of Jefferson exhibits terrible aspects of fundamentalist fanaticism, embryonic fascism, Puritan morality, grotesque law enforcement and the fantastic ability of good women to ferret out sin.

But it is Faulkner's realization that even the most confirmed abolitionist may be racist that intrigues me. Joanna Burden's father sees the black as a race "doomed and cursed to be forever and ever a part of the white man's doom and curse for its sins." She could never escape from the curse, get away from under the shadow. She could not even die. "You must struggle, rise. But in order to rise, you must raise the shadow with you. *But you can never lift it to your level.*" In the early 1930s Joanna understands, "I see that now." Joanna understood this aspect of racism long before I did.

For a moment, muse with the unfrocked minister, Gail Hightower:

Sitting in the dark window he seems to see them. *Now they are gathering, entering the door. They are nearly all there now.* And then he begins to say, "Now. Now," leaning a little forward; and then, as though it had waited for his signal, the music begins. The organ strains come rich and resonant through the summer night, blended sonorous, with that quality of abjectness and sublimation, as if freed voices themselves were assuming the shapes and attitudes of crucifixions, ecstatic, solemn, and profound in gathering volume. Yet even the music has still a quality stern and implacable, pleading, asking, for not love, not life, forbidding it to others, demanding in sonorous tones death as though death were the boon, like all Protestant music. It was as though they who accepted it and raised voices to praise it within praise, having been made what they were by that which the music praised and symbolized, they took revenge upon that which made them so by means of the praise itself. Listening, he seems to hear within it the apotheosis of his own history, his own environed blood; that people from which he sprang and among whom he lives who can never take either pleasure or catastrophe or escape from either, without brawling over it. Pleasure, ecstasy, they cannot seem to bear: their escape from it is in violence, in drinking and in fighting and in praying; catastrophe too, the violence identical and apparently inescapable. And so why should not their religion drive them to crucifixion of themselves and one another? he thinks. It seems to him that he can hear with the music the declaration and dedication of that which they know on the morrow they will have to do.

Although I think of *As I Lay Dying* and *The Hamlet* as incisive pictures of southern rural white mentality, I have found myself using over and over two of Faulkner's "race" novels, *Go Down, Moses* and *Intruder in the Dust* (the latter because of the fine movie made from it), simply because to me race *is* the central theme of southern history.

The first part of *Go Down, Moses* may be the only hilarious account of the capture of a runaway slave in existence—complete with horses and dogs and romance but no ice. The reader of "Was" will never again be quite the same in his estimate of the pretensions of Mississippi aristocracy. In "Pantaloon in Black" there is a remarkable picture of the distorted mind of a southern sheriff who finds it impossible to understand the grief of one of Faulkner's most unforgettable Negro characters. I have talked with and observed Mississippi sheriffs and other police officers individually and en masse (in the Meredith situation) to the point that I believe Faulkner's many representations of the law are credible to a very high degree.

In *Go Down, Moses,* two events stand out sharply in my mind. One is the separation the caste system imposes on two seven-year old boys, one black and one white. Roth Edmonds "entered his heritage. He ate its bitter fruit,"—that was the "day the old curse of his fathers, the old haughty ancestral pride based not on any value but an accident of geography, stemmed not from courage and honor but from wrong and shame, descended to him." The other moment comes when Ike McCaslin, recipient of the perfect education in the woods at the hands of Sam Fathers, is confronted by Roth Edmonds' black mistress (and cousin) and can suggest nothing more than that she go north and marry a black man. ". . . the instant when, without moving at all, she blazed silently down at him." "Old man," she said, "have you lived so long and forgotten so much that you don't remember anything you ever knew or felt or even heard about love?" In the presence of inter-racial love (and possible marriage) Ike McCaslin, and I think William Faulkner, was helpless.

In general William Faulkner writes not of war and politics, and his violence is off stage. He says little about Reconstruction and like Cash he's apt to accept the older traditional values. Faulkner makes numerous errors. He is often inconsistent with himself. He writes in episodic fashion, telling you exactly what he pleases about his fabulous Yoknapatawpha. Which is of course precisely what historians do when they become famous enough to collect their essays into hardback volumes. By himself Faulkner would never quite do as a historian, but for flashes of insight and for an all round understanding of the South and Mississippi and Lafayette County, the examples which come to my mind are most likely to be from Faulkner.

Faulkner uses local history (he copies sizable chunks of the 1938 W. P. A. history of Mississippi into *Requiem for a Nun*) and folklore and real and imaginary folks and mixes them all up. The best example of this is his own autobiography, entitled "Mississippi" (*Holiday,* 1954) which includes people with such outlandish names as Hogganbeck, Snopes, Sartoris, Pemberton, Compson, Bilbo, McCaslin, Vardaman, Forrest, and Murrell. He doesn't let the facts interfere with his story. Yet there is no real clash between *Slavery in Mississippi* published in 1933 and *Absalom, Absalom!* in print two years later, written by two gentlemen residing within a mile of each other.

Along with Beard and Turner and Phillips, I could have and should have been reading Faulkner. And forty years afterward I would have discovered that the novelist had worn at least as well as the historians.

And living in the South, I might have known that "Loving all of it even while he had to hate some of it because he knows now that you don't love because; you love despite; not for the virtues, but despite the faults." Those of us gathered in the Faulkner home in 1955 had also to agree with him that "one has to hate it a little more than one did twenty years ago."

But then Faulkner also said, "the writer doesn't judge people; he has compassion for all people or he wouldn't be much of a writer." "He's got to take the truth and set it on fire so that people will remember it. That's his responsibility." At whatever sacrifice. "If a writer has to rob his mother he will not hesitate; an 'Ode to a Grecian Urn' is worth any number of old ladies."

Perhaps above all I like to think, as a direct result of reading Faulkner, of history as pursuit. For the good hunter there is no finality. The game is "not only to pursue but to overtake and then have the compassion not to destroy, to catch, to touch, and then to let go because then tomorrow you can pursue again." I wish I had written those words about hunting, about history, or about life.

William Alexander Percy:
The Aristocrat and the Anthropologist
(Address to the Southern Historical Association, 1975)

Some months before Pearl Harbor I wrote to an already legendary figure in Mississippi requesting that he speak at the state university in a fledgling forum program. His secretary replied that William Alexander Percy was pleased with the invitation but was too frail at the moment to come. In January 1942 he was dead.

Except for a snide remark from the Ole Miss Chancellor that Percy had never earned his keep, all I heard before and after the publication of *Lanterns on the Levee* was that Will Percy was an authentic southern aristocrat, a saint on earth, "the flower of civilization—the enlightened provincial." Though I never met him, I knew him intimately through our mutual friend, David Lewis Cohn, who described Percy as "wise, warm, whimsical, humorous, spontaneously generous in act and deed," possessing "an antique beauty suggestive of the Greece he loved and the poet that he was." According to Cohn, Percy "suffered fools, comforted the distressed, and caused iris to grow where iris had never grown before," *but* was "the loneliest man I have ever known . . . otherworldly, essentially austere, given to gaunt convictions . . . neither spiritually nor intellectually did Percy belong to the times in which he lived." Just as fulsome with praise was Hodding Carter, whose brilliant journalistic career in Greenville was promoted by Cohn and Percy. In fact, Will Percy seems to have charmed people of all persuasions, including liberals Virginius Dabney, Jonathan Daniels, Ralph McGill, Hortense Powdermaker, and even W. J. Cash who considered him "an excellent and admirable man," urbane, sensitive, candid, wise, witty and kind, in fact "a surviving authentic Southern aristocrat."

Percy's four volumes of relatively unacclaimed poetry were assailed (by Willard Thorp) because their author spoke "to those who stopped reading poetry in 1915," and (by a young man who was in the process of failing as a poet, William Faulkner) because Percy failed to see "the dark of modernity

216

which threatens the bright simplicity and the colorful romantic pageantry of the middle ages with which eyes are full." The poetry touches neither the old South nor the new but dwells on ancient Greece and thirteenth century Europe. Through it run themes of stoicism, the failure of large-scale reform, and skepticism. Percy glorifies the golden age of Frederick II when historically Frederick's bastard "son of light," Enzio, was "capable of hanging a hundred political enemies at a time." Abhorrence of twentieth century materialism left Percy with nothing to dissipate his gloom. What was left?— beauty (in nature), nobility, nostalgia, the sound of words. Accepting life as it is, with all of its injustices and contradictions, Percy was more concerned with "benevolence and religious brotherhood than social justice."

Will Percy was astonished and pleased by the popular and critical praise poured upon *Lanterns on the Levee. Time* saw *Lanterns* as "a sensitive Southern aristocrat's assertion of Stoic faith in the face of a world grown totally vulgar. . . ." The *New Republic* called the volume a "very creditable swan song," Alfred J. Nock thought *Lanterns* was "wholly free from the neurasthenic drivel which affects so many of the current sentimental outpourings about the Old South," and, not unexpectedly, the *Sewanee Review* loyally called it "not a biography; it is a gospel." On the other hand Clifton Fadiman thought Percy had made no airtight case for "the feudal regime whose tradition he inherited," while the *Nation* considered the book "pretty hollow nonsense," implying the possibility that the South was indeed the nation's primary economic problem "because it is first of all the nation's intellectual problem No. 1." James Orrick in the *Virginia Quarterly Review* considered Percy "so baldly reactionary, arrogant, and irrational that it is staggering," and Ulysses Lee in *Opportunity* called *Lanterns* as unbelievable as any Faulkner novel, yet "corroborating all that Faulkner has to say," that is, the upper class, pushed to the wall, drives scions of the past "into a mental as well as economic fog where a pleasant but vicious neuroticism supplants rationality." Most of this applause and displeasure said as much about the reviewer as the reviewed.

Walker Percy has stated that *Lanterns on the Levee* was written from the "ancient posture of Southern apologetics." We may easily forget how many volumes sustaining that posture and usually published in New York City were written by Mississippians of solemn integrity in the years before the Great Depression. Since Henry Hughes's defense of warranteeism (1854), there have been at least a dozen scholars, historians, educators, and churchmen (H. S. Fulkerson (1887), Charles Otken (1894), Dunbar Rowland (1902), Charles B. Galloway (1904), Alfred H. Stone (1908), Thomas Pearce Bailey (1914), Theodore DuBose Bratton (1922), and A. H. Shannon (1930) who have presented the proslavery argument in more or less modern dress. Will Percy added nothing to the century-old assumption that blacks were innately inferior, utterly content, and could best be taken care of by white southerners. The most that can be said for Percy in 1941 was that he wrote beautifully, as a gentleman, in contrast to the apologists who came after him, Senator Bilbo (1947) and Judge Brady (1955). At least Percy was the last of the saints.

So Will Percy accepted his heritage and, unlike Cash and Faulkner, glorified it. He failed to challenge the history which school children today recognize as mythology. At best he wrote class history, history by divine right, if you will. He concluded, "I have witnessed a disintegration of the moral cohesion of the South which had given it its strength and its sons their singleness of purpose and simplicity." And "it never crossed my mind I wasn't right."

It may be fruitful to glance at history as seen through Percy's eyes. Slavery being unprofitable in Virginia, "slave holders began to look for cheap fertile lands farther west that could feed the many black mouths dependent on them." His Delta, "as the whole south," consisted of only three groups: slave holders, poor whites, Negroes.

After the Civil War the aristocrats bore the brunt of the holy fight against scalawagery and Negro domination. Their leadership, a natural outgrowth of superior intellect, training, character, and opportunity, was assumed as a burden. Grandfather William Alexander Percy's life's work, the restoration of white supremacy, the elimination of "one glorious orgy of graft, lawlessness, and terrorism," required "courage, tact, intelligence, patience," as well as "vote-buying, the stuffing of ballot boxes, chicanery, intimidation."

Born in 1885, Percy sat at the feet of his heroes, men who loved Cleveland and hated Bryan and populism. These boyhood giants were turned out of Greenville politics in 1896, but it was the defeat in 1911 of his father LeRoy Percy in the "most vicious and sordid campaign . . . since reconstruction days," that brought to an end the "period in which great men represented our people." Three decades later, Will Percy wrote those famous words about the crowds his father tried to persuade: "They were the sort of people that lynch Negroes, that mistake hoodlumism for wit and cunning for intelligence, that attend revivals and fight and fornicate in the bushes afterwards. They were undiluted Anglo-Saxons. They were the sovereign voters. It was so horrible it seemed unreal." "Thus at twenty-seven I was inured to defeat! I have never since expected victory."

Senator Percy's views were about the same. He saw his fight with Vardaman as "a life and death struggle between decent law abiding progressive citizenship and blatant demagoguery, sacrificing the welfare of the state and the peaceful relationship existing between the races in order to prejudice and poison the minds of ignorant people." He thought Bilbo's election (as lieutenant governor) was fortunate for the state: "The more nauseous the dose the sooner will vomiting relieve the patient."

Later historians have seen things more dispassionately. William F. Holmes has concluded that the Levee Board turnover of 1896 simply meant that LeRoy Percy's law firm (which had received $30,000 in fees and/or salaries from the Board) was replaced by other representatives of the lawyer-planter-merchant class. Charges of inferior character were absurd. Will Percy had "helped to perpetuate a mystical view of Bourbon leaders."

In his classic *Revolt of the Rednecks,* Albert D. Kirwan saw most whites as cooperating to overthrow Reconstruction; however, "from 1876 to 1925 the central thread for Mississippi politics is a struggle between economic classes interspersed with the personal struggles of ambitious men." The dominance of the rich planters was finally broken. Aristocratic leadership had indulged in racial demagoguery; its white solidarity slogans "were nothing but appeals to prejudice and passion." On occasion the threat of Negro domination "was painted in such lurid colors that even the most illiterate might read." The Redeemers recognized no social responsibility other than the negative one of preventing "negro domination."

LeRoy Percy had been an attorney for banks, railroads, utilities; Vardaman demanded corporate regulation. Business men and planting lawyers endorsed Percy; small farmers and laborers backed Vardaman. The gentleman from the Delta was indeed courageous, even to shouting "cattle" at some of the sovereign voters. An "inept campaigner," Percy was a "sitting duck," an easy target who had little rapport with the Mississippi masses. In any case the lot of the black man remained unchanged. "No one thought of him except to hold him down. No one sought to improve him. Whether race baiters like Vardaman were in power, or whether 'respectable' politicians governed, he fared the same—no better, no worse."

A number of critics have pleaded that *Lanterns on the Levee* not be approached with a sociological measuring stick. As Walker Percy sees it, the tenant problem is gone anyway: "The displaced sharecroppers moved to Northern cities and the liberals moved out." Maybe so, but Will Percy's defense of sharecropping as a part of the plantation system illustrates his larger philosophy regarding the obligations of the superior caste.

Though he confessed to an ineptness at farming, in 1929 Percy inherited the three thousand acre Trail Lake plantation and for nine years operated it on a golden-rule basis. Fortunately for us, a young graduate student of Rupert B. Vance (who had written in 1932 that "ugly rumors of occasional peonage and the whipping of runaway tenants still come out of the Delta") conducted an intensive survey of Trail Lake which generally vindicated what Percy later had to say of his own operation. He *did* encourage home production of food, *did* foster education, *did* make honest settlements, and *did* work hard to improve health conditions of his all black tenantry. "Our plantation system," wrote Percy, "seems to me to offer as humane, self-respecting, and cheerful a method of earning a living as human beings are likely to devise." Having lost $100,000 in his first two years as landlord (just before the New Deal), he was surprised to learn that because of the bad name of sharecropping, "we were infamous and didn't even know it." His profit-sharing arrangement, he admitted cheerfully, offered "an unusual opportunity to rob without detection or punishment. . . . The white planter may charge an exorbitant rate of interest, he may allow the sharecropper less than the market price received for his cotton, he may cheat him in a thousand different ways, and the Negro's redress is merely theoretical."

David Cohn, a more trustworthy student of the Delta than Percy, acquainted with the works of Powdermaker, Dollard, Myrdal, Cash, and the North Carolina sociologists, agreed that logically sharecropping seemed to allow the tenant maximum opportunity. The Delta, he wrote, however, "remains a society almost feudal . . . a rich field for exploitation," with an "antique process of thinking, by spiritual refugees from the Civil War." He thought the planters would fight vigorously for an agricultural system that was "doomed to go." By 1948 paternalism had indeed gone and sharecropping was on its way to oblivion.

The 1930s and 1940s were the most productive years of sociological research regarding the agricultural South. As early as 1931, Edwin R. Embree had written that where the plantation system "flourishes, ignorance, prejudice, and cruelty are the rule, not the exception. The arrangement has behind it the weight of tradition, tainted by fear and hate. The white owners know no other order. The Negro tenant is poor, illiterate, and intimidated. There are few better landlords to whom he could transfer his allegiance if he tried." Gunnar Myrdal suggested in summary, "The plantation system fails flagrantly to meet the standards of social and economic efficiency and justice."

John Dollard understood the constant migration of sharecroppers, regardless of their treatment, a phenomenon that mystified Alf Stone and Will Percy. It was, Dollard said, the black's only weapon of protest. Hortense Powdermaker estimated that 20 percent of plantation housing was good, and that 25 percent to 30 percent of the Delta sharecroppers got an honest settlement. *Deep South,* the two-year investigation of Adams County by four Harvard anthropologists, published in the same year as *Lanterns,* provided the most exhaustive survey and condemnation of the plantation economy. White planters engaged in thievery with impunity while professing "a strong sense of responsibility for the welfare of these colored tenants. . . ." Blacks were handled as children, with whimsy, absolutism, caprice. On the plantation caste was almost "perfect" and "there is relatively little terrorization of the lower caste. In fine, where caste is most fully extended, there is little need for violence, because the colored people are thoroughly subordinated economically, occupationally, and socially." With his vested interest, the planter "sought to maintain a stable, hard-working and properly subordinate group of tenants."

Since then a great physical, chemical, mechanical, and political revolution has changed the face of the Delta. But, according to Tony Dunbar, the "great stretch of history" has left in the 1970s thousands of men and women with average incomes of $200 a year from plantation work, social security, and welfare. Though half of the remaining tenants do no work, there is no drive to evict nor to help them. Kindness has been replaced by callousness, the greatest "indignity in being excluded from . . . making decisions affecting their [own] lives." Plantation life, he concludes, *was* at least secure if terrible.

It is acknowledged that free-enterprise agriculture in the years from the Civil War to World War II simply could not compete in the new corporate monopolistic society. It is just as true that southern plantation life brought to its workers ignorance, misery, debasement, and hopelessness.

When *Lanterns on the Levee* was published, Will Percy indicated no sympathy with the egalitarian impulses of the New Deal period, nor of course could he have been aware of the revolutionary changes in racial values the next thirty years would bring. It is only fair to judge him by the wisdom of his time.

In *Lanterns,* Percy exclaims:

I am usually in a condition of amazed exultation over the excellent state of race relations in the South. It is incredible that two races, centuries apart in emotional and mental discipline, alien in physical characteristics, doomed by war and the Constitution to a single, not a dual way of life, and to an impractical and unpracticed theory of equality which deludes and embitters, heckled and misguided by pious fools from the North and impious fools from the South—it is incredible, I insist, that two such dissimilar races should live side by side with so little friction, in such comparative peace and amity. The result is due solely to good manners.

Just now we are happy that the brother in black is still the tiller of the soil, the hewer of our wood, our servants, troubadours, and criminals. His manners offset his inefficiency, his vices have the charm of amiable weaknesses, he is a pain and a grief to live with, a solace and a delight.

Apparently there is something peculiarly Negroid in the Negro's attitude toward the aptitude for crimes of violence. He seems to have resisted, except on the surface, our ethics and to have rejected our standards. Murder, thieving, lying, violence—I sometimes suspect the Negro doesn't regard these as crimes or sins, or even as regrettable occurrences. He commits them casually, with no apparent feeling of guilt. The American Negro is interested neither in the past nor in the future this side of heaven. He neither remembers nor plans.

Percy writes, too, of the Negro's "charm, his humor, his patience, his exquisite sensibilities, his kindness to his own poor, his devotion and sweetness to all children, black and white, his poetry of feeling and expression, his unique tactual medieval faith, his songs more filled with humility than Schubert's or Brahms's—I want with all my heart to help him. But helping him is well nigh impossible because. . . no Negro trusts unreservedly any white . . . no Negro trusts unreservedly any Negro." Percy's advice to the essentially pathetic black man: ". . . learn to be a white man morally and intellectually." For all mankind he spoke of the need for tolerance, pride, pity, justice, fearlessness, but felt "the pathos of a stronger race carrying on its shoulders a weaker race and from the burden losing its own strength!"

Small wonder that Charles C. Munz saw this as Percy's message: "Struggle on, Black Brother, be obedient, tip your hat to your betters, and in a thousand years or so maybe you will be as good and as smart as I am now." Or that Jonathan Daniels could write, "I had the feeling that Percy loved Negroes as another gentleman might love dogs." As a matter of fact, the leading light of the Citizens Council told me exactly that in 1963: we should treat blacks in kindly fashion—as we did our dogs.

It has been said that Will Percy believed in the education of Negroes, but I have found nothing in *Lanterns* other than high praise for the ideas on Negro education expressed by his father in the *Outlook* for 1907. According to the elder Percy, Negroes should be educated by Mississippians; otherwise money to do it would come in from the outside, which outsiders would control. "I deny," he wrote, "that rudimentary education makes a negro a more inefficient farmer." If illiterate the Negro becomes the slave of every white, for he has no master's protection. If the educated Negro leaves, he takes the race problem with him, in which case, he can be replaced with Europeans, who will help solve problems. "This the Negro will never do." Negro education was thus necessary to preserve the character and integrity of whites. That is, "education, simple and practical." LeRoy Percy always opposed anything that would cause panic among the blacks, and both father and son believed it a primary obligation "to educate whites not to prey on the Negro."

Will Percy correctly surmised that most American whites, North as well as South, felt the same way about Negroes. It may be said that in 1941 he was not much more than a decade away from the conventional wisdom of anti-Negro thought which, according to I. A. Newby, reached its zenith in the years 1900–1930. American "scientists of the highest academic standing . . . helped lay the groundwork and provided the framework within which a new 'science of race' matured." Disfranchisement, segregation, and discrimination grew from the idea of Negro inferiority, sponsored by such luminaries as Woodrow Wilson, Howard W. Odum, John R. Commons, William A. Dunning, Glenn Frank, Ellen Churchill Semple, E. A. Ross, Henry Fairfield Osborn, G. Stanley Hall, Albert Bushnell Hart, H. L. Mencken, John W. Burgess, Herbert Baxter Adams, Moses Coit Tyler, James Ford Rhodes, and Walter L. Fleming. Have we forgotten that scientists called for a "benevolent segregation" which is exactly what the "good" southern whites thought they had achieved in the racial compromise of the 1920s?

George Washington Cable thought blacks were inferior and social equality "a fool's dream." At least the historians were not as Negrophobic as the sociologists, the psychologists, and the eugenicists. Blacks, lacking in intelligence and willpower, imperceptive, incoherent in thinking, preferring an environment of immorality, ignorance, and poverty, were thought by one scientist to copulate "solely for the gratification of the passion—for the erotic pleasure it affords them." When it came to racial theory a great many of the academic scientists supported Social Darwinism as late as the beginning of the Depression.

Fortunately for us, race relations in the Mississippi plantation country were examined in the 1930s by eminent social scientists. Their conclusions have stood the test of time.

First I would like to return to David Cohn whose two books *(God Shakes Creation* and *Where I Was Born and Raised)* dealing with the Delta preceded and followed *Lanterns* by five and seven year intervals. Cohn was a native of Greenville, an intimate of Percy's, graduate of Virginia and Yale, journalist, lawyer, world traveler, and man of letters. He was not alien to the world of scholarship; among other accomplishments, he published ten books and more than sixty articles in the *Atlantic Monthly* over a twenty-five-year period. He wrote about his own people with a rare discretion and, I believe, with considerably more discrimination than Percy. In many ways Cohn's picture of the Delta Negro coincided with that of Percy. Cohn was not revolted by the "earthy animalism" of Delta blacks whose sex life he knew was "not embroidered with the roses and rapture of romantic love," and he understood the place of religion as "the asylum to which they retreat." His "Last Stand of Noblesse Oblige" must have originated in long talks with Percy. But he did not rationalize white behavior. Whites were responsible for black housing, and indirectly at least for black disease, crime, juvenile delinquency, and lowered efficiency. "White man's stories . . . are almost invariably lewd, lecherous, and mephitic as well as dreary." The plight of the blacks could be ameliorated: the Negro should get political rights, complete protection in person and property, equal justice, a fair share of tax moneys for education, health and public services. Included was "the right to earn a living," with pay according to worth, not color. In time, he thought, "the plantation will approach the conditions of a factory." But Cohn saw no solution to the race problem, little chance to obliterate segregation, and no hope from federal intrusion.

Hortense Powdermaker talked with Cohn and Percy and other whites but mainly with black people. Negroes wanted equal treatment, she wrote, but were in no position to demand it. They were kept in place through fear and their hostility *was* redirected toward each other. (Cohn: "A Negro *must not* raise his hand against a white man.") Most quarters were uninhabitable according to modern hygienic standards. Religion was "a social ritual well adapted to become an outlet for individual emotionalism." It might have surprised Percy to find that perhaps 5 percent of Delta upper class blacks had a stable family life based on the same puritanical standards that he endorsed.

Yale's John Dollard, spoken of scornfully by Percy as a three months Delta "oracle," agreed with Powdermaker about the in-turning of Negro aggression. Will Percy may have launched his sarcasm because Dollard concluded that whites had real affection only for "old-timey" blacks, that Negro manners (subservient behavior) were *demanded* by the whites, that the caste system "would relegate the Negro *forever* to an inferior position in that society." Caste gave to the whites enormous economic, sexual, and prestige gains. The Negro had no rights; whatever small gains he made were through the white man's benevolence. He was denied a personality. Dollard struck close again to Percy when he wrote of the white "ancestral routine," implying that white children were indoctrinated with a "sentimentalized version of southern life and history."

The most thorough and in many ways the best (though not the most readable) of the anthropological examinations of rural Mississippi concerned the Natchez region. In age, wealth, and historical influence, Adams County might have pronounced the Delta a Johnny-come-lately. In any case, the conclusions of the Harvard scientists were valid for both. In 1941 whites generally believed, according to *Deep South,* that blacks were "biologically more primitive, mentally inferior, emotionally undeveloped. The whole environment presents the black man as insensitive to pain, incapable of learning, and animal-like in behavior. It is assumed that he will work only under compulsion or immediate need, that in his irresponsibility he fails to anticipate the future and so remains dependent on the white man . . . the Negro lacks respect for property, does not possess the white man's concept of morality, allows his passions free run, and is therefore childlike with no chance to become a mature adult." Will Percy couldn't have said it better.

But *Deep South* had more to say. The Negro adapted to the mandates of caste when faced with violence (whipping being the most effective persuader). Threats by white landlords were universal. Court cases were decided according to the white man's concept of black behavior. Instead of "a pleasant society where justice has prevailed among a happy people," *Deep South* found potential terror. The properly deferential Negro was the good Negro. Whites often spoke "with wistful approbation of the politeness and 'good manners' of the country Negroes." Of such manners the authors concluded the Negro "must observe them whole heartedly and with no apparent reservation." The acquiescent black man "may achieve a high degree of security in his relations to the whites." Intimidation brought about economic, caste, and legal subordination. Physical violence "has been used consistently by both landlords and the police to teach the Negro child and adult to submit to their lower-caste position and to accept their helplessness to oppose the white system which exploited, segregated, and disfranchised them." Still, the Negro "hated his place and role in southern society." *Deep South* and *Lanterns on the Levee* have much in common as to the facts if not in their interpretation.

Like many southerners, Will Percy felt the urge to take a military part in World War I. He did see combat in the trenches, considering it "a great privilege . . . to go forth with the heroes." At one time he was an instructor of Negro officers, but he never forgot his southern heritage. "I was not going to permit them to be familiar," he wrote. They "tried me out once by inviting me to mess with them, but when that failed, our relations became cordial and natural."

In the early 1920s, Will Percy stood foursquare with his father (feared by the Klan "more than any other man in the South") in a courageous and successful stand against hooded terrorism. On one occasion he felt compelled to tell the local Cyclops, ". . . if anything happens to my Father or to any of our friends you will be killed."

The account of the 1927 Mississippi flood in *Lanterns on the Levee* tells us a great deal about William Alexander Percy as historian and white supremist, but still more about him as a man. He was appointed by the mayor of Greenville as chairman of the Flood Relief Committee. The whites were evacuated, the Negroes should have been but were put into encampments on the levee. LeRoy Percy "knew that the dispersal of our labor was a longer evil to the Delta than a flood." In any case the father tricked the son and Delta labor was saved. "Of course," wrote Will Percy, "none of us was influenced by what the Negroes themselves wanted: they had no capacity to plan for their own welfare; planning for them was another of our burdens." Percy considered it "unfortunate that Delta Negroes could read Negro newspapers during the flood," a northern press incidentally which villified Percy and which local blacks studied with some passion.

A Negro was killed by a policeman. "The next day my trusted Negro informant told me the Negroes had worked themselves into a state of wild excitement and resentment." The black community held Percy responsible for the killing. So he called a meeting and a church filled with surly black men. Percy was the only white present. "I could feel their excitement and hate mount to frenzy." The story he tells is incredible:

"A good Negro," he told the blacks, "has been killed by a white policeman. Every white man in town regrets this from his heart and is ashamed. . . . I look into your faces and see anger and hatred. You think I am the murderer. The murderer should be punished. . . . For months we Delta people have been suffering together. . . . God struck us all to our knees. He spared no one. He sent his terrible waters over us and He found none of us worthy to be His friend as Noah was. . . . For four months I have struggled and worried and gone without sleep in order to help you Negroes. . . . During all this time you did nothing, nothing for yourselves or for us. The Red Cross asked you to unload the food it was giving you, the food without which you would have starved. And you refused. Because of your sinful, shameful laziness . . . one of your race has been killed. You sit before me sour and full of hatred as if you had a right . . . to judge anybody. . . . I am not the murderer. That foolish young policeman is not the murderer. The murderer is you! Your hands are dripping with blood. Look into each others' faces and see the shame and the fear God has set on them. Down on your knees, murderers, and beg God not to punish you as you deserve."

"They went down on their knees and we prayed." Twelve lines later: "I sailed for Japan."

In *The Shadow of Slavery,* Pete Daniel tells a different story of the flood. He writes that the Red Cross and the Department of Commerce quashed black efforts to publicize conditions in the Delta. Black laborers were held in bondage. Governor Dennis Murphree warned of a "serious result which can be brought about if refugees are allowed to be taken from the refugee camps for selfish interests." Dr. Sidney Dillon Redmond claimed that "planters held labor at the point of a gun for fear they would get away and not return." Perry Howard said that blacks were being held "in a state of peonage." One refugee testified, "They made us work on the levees down in the delta, up to the last minute, tellin' us the levee wasn't going to break and then when it did break, we didn't have time to do nuthin' but save our families." The Negro Flood Commission (suggested by Robert Moton and appointed by Herbert Hoover) which visited all the flood area found the camps at Baton Rouge and Natchez good but the one at Greenville bad. Walter White said all were slave labor camps. In the *Nation* he insisted, "the most significant injustice is in the denial to Negroes of the right to free movement and of the privilege of selling their services to the highest bidder." That fall the Red Cross appropriated $100,000 for materials to rebuild cabins in the Delta at $150 each. President Moton asserted that when blacks tried to run away from the plantations, those caught "were whipped and at times threatened with death if they left the plantations again." The *Crisis* commented on the "dismal picture of the flood refugees as well as the Red Cross and the National Guard."

What happens to a black man during a great flood? I suggest as an antidote to *Lanterns* that one read Richard Wright's "Down by the Riverside," one of the short stories in *Uncle Tom's Children.*

Wright once told a Memphian he was from Jackson, Mississippi. "You act mighty bright to be from there," was the response. It is highly questionable that Wright could have achieved success in Jackson, or Memphis either. He wrote of the power and ferocity of the white world, the brutalities of a savage Christianity, of the "*emotional deprivation* [existing] in this land where Negroes are traditionally regarded as possessing, as a gift of nature, a superabundant fund of laughter, song, joy, and rhythm."

In 1940 Richard Wright saw his father for the first time in twenty-five years, "standing alone upon the red clay of a Mississippi plantation, a share-cropper, clad in ragged overalls, holding a muddy hoe in his gnarled, veined hands."

When I tried to talk to him I realized that, though ties of blood made us kin, though I could see a shadow of my face in his face, though there was an echo of my voice in his voice, we were forever strangers, speaking a different language, living on vastly different planes of reality. That day when I visited him on the plantation—he was standing against the sky, smiling toothlessly, his hair whitened, his body bent, his eyes glazed with dim recollection, his fearsome aspect of twenty-five years ago gone forever from him—I was overwhelmed to realize that he could never understand me or the scalding experiences that had swept me beyond his life and into an area of living that he could never know. I stood before him, poised, my mind aching as it embraced the simple nakedness of his life, feeling how completely his soul was imprisoned by the slow flow of the seasons, by wind and rain and sun, how fastened were his memories to a crude and raw past, how chained were his actions and emotions to the direct, animalistic impulses of his withering body. . . .

From the white landowners above him there had not been handed to him a chance to learn the meaning of loyalty, of sentiment, of tradition. Joy was as unknown to him as despair. As a creature of the earth, he endured, hearty, whole, seemingly indestructible, with no regrets and no hopes. He asked easy, drawling questions about me, his other son, his wife, and he laughed, amused when I informed him of their destinies.

Ralph Ellison might as well have been reviewing *Lanterns on the Levee* as *Black Boy* when he wrote that the southern community "renders the fulfillment of [black] human destiny impossible." In the South, he contended, the Negro is in "relative safety as long as the impulse toward individuality is suppressed." The black defense mechanism is "to protect the Negro from whirling away from the undifferentiated mass of his people into the unknown, symbolized in its most abstract form by insanity, and most concretely by lynching; and to protect himself from those unknown forces *within himself* which might urge him to reach out for that social and human equality which the white man says he cannot have. Rather than throw himself against the charged wires of his prison, he annihilated the impulses within him."

Southern whites, continued Ellison, "deny the Negro's humanity and feel no cause to measure his actions against civilized norms; or they protect themselves from their guilt in the Negro's condition . . . by attributing to him a super-human capacity for love, kindliness and forgiveness."

Will Percy was frank to admit that blacks did not trust him. One of his most revealing anecdotes has to do with a conversation with his chauffeur following a trip to Trail Lake on settlement day:

> The Negroes filled the store and overflowed onto the porch, milling and confabulating. As we drove up, one of them asked: "Whose car is dat?" Another answered: "Dat's *us* car." I thought it curious they didn't recognize my car, but dismissed the suspicion and dwelt on the thought of how sweet it was to have the relation between landlord and tenant so close and affectionate that to them my car was their car. Warm inside I passed through the crowd, glowing and bowing, the Lord of the manor among his faithful retainers. As we drove off I said: "Did you hear what that man said?"
>
> Ford assented, but grumpily.
>
> "It was funny," I continued.
>
> "Funnier than you think," observed Ford sardonically.
>
> I didn't understand and said so.
>
> Ford elucidated, "He meant that's the car *you* bought with *us* money. They all knew what he meant, but you didn't and they knew you didn't. They wuz laughing to theyselves."
>
> A few days later the managers confirmed this version of the phrase and laughed. I laughed too, but not inside.

William Alexander Percy "looked squarely at the reality of the dying world of the Old South." He wrote of "this time of doom. A tarnish has fallen over the bright world; dishonor and corruption triumph, my own strong people are turned lotus-eaters; defeat is here again, the last, the most abhorrent." He reflected sadly on the rise of the masses ("the herd is on the march"), on "that momentum commonly mistaken for progress," on the insolence of organized labor as well as organized capital. He felt that "Honor and honesty, compassion and truth are good even if they kill you," and whatever little hope there was for the future depended not on "national leaders so much as men of good-will in each of the little towns in America."

"I suppose the Southern aristocrat is dead," mused Will Percy. *Lanterns on the Levee* is his nostalgic description of faded and imagined glories.

In 1941 when *Lanterns on the Levee* was published, I was still open to conviction as to its contents. But as I grew more knowledgeable about the closed society, particularly in the 1950s, I underwent an accelerating radicalization. Today I have great empathy with William Alexander Percy for his possession of qualities associated with the image of the old (and the new) South: grace, manners, hospitality, virtue, sympathy, tolerance, love of family and the romantic life. Even more appealing to me are his ultimate courage, his loneliness ("I have never walked with God . . . there was no place to go when I was tired."), his honesty and integrity, his Aurelian stoicism (man is defeated "but attains victory . . . by virtue of the battle nobly fought."), his cynicism ("the world I know is crashing to bits"), and his capacity to live in another century, another world. Of course it is also true that I have been particularly delighted since 1941 with the civil rights movement and the further deterioration of Percy's "American Puritanism."

But since this assignment came to me months ago I have read *Lanterns* at least five times and I have even learned to like Percy's poetry. I have mulled over many of the books and articles as well as my own experience associated with Mississippi and the South. Here are some resultant thoughts:

1. There is a deep current of southern violence in Percy who decries violence among the common whites. He accuses the Negro of committing murder as little boys fight, but we see him sitting down with his uncle calmly deciding to kill a political opponent before breakfast. Percy abhors mob violence but he stands with a gun ready to kill to prevent a crowd from throwing eggs at his father. He threatens to murder a local KKK leader. These acts may have been necessary, even laudable, but they do show disregard for law and a tendency to take personal action that Percy so dislikes in others.

2. Percy wrote that man must live by myths. Anne Moody wrote that man had to grow up and face reality.

3. I can see no real difference in the basic assumptions regarding the Negro as between Will Percy and Ross Barnett.

4. I have wondered how many Negroes of education and sensitivity Will Percy communicated with at length. It took me a very long time to realize that Mississippi society demanded that I have no meaningful relationship with blacks except on a master-servant level.

5. How many Will Percys were lost on the battlefields of World War I? How many Richard Wrights were lost in the cotton fields of Mississippi?

6. Will Percy should not be tested (and praised) against the standards of the ignorant, the poor whites who lynched blacks and joined the Klan. He should be tested against the highest ethical standards of the most civilized people on earth. There is no great virtue in being hated by poor whites or even newly rich planters for being a "nigger lover," or a "flaming liberal." *Lanterns on the Levee* should not be looked at from the vantage point of 1975, but from the time of implied prophecy in *A Preface to Pleasantry*.

7. Will Percy obviously had an affinity with the five poets of *I'll Take My Stand*. He grasped the substance of Frank Owsley's essay, "The Irrepressible Conflict," but remained oblivious to the Owsley studies of the southern yeomen.

8. Many times did I ask David Cohn whether the much publicized tolerance toward Jews, Italians, Chinese, Syrians, and Irish in Greenville might not have stemmed from guilt about intolerance toward blacks. I cannot remember ever getting an answer.

9. *Lanterns on the Levee* is today significant for people of all classes and beliefs not because the book tells it like it was but because it sets the scene as many white Southerners saw it. What you see is not what you get!

10. By 1941 the formerly poor whites had gained considerable economic and political clout in the Delta, while the blacks were still in their place. So they could be loved, humored, or chastized as the occasion demanded.

11. Will Percy asks for sympathy for whites living habitually as superiors among inferiors without seeming to understand that black inferiority was imposed by the suffering whites. The Negro really has been the invention of the white man.

12. As a child Will Percy listened to heroic tales of the immediate past and sat at the feet of private tutors; his undergraduate education was taken at a college dominated by Confederate veterans and their widows; his fragile body mandated a life in a dream world of imagination, poetry, mythology, and mysticism. No wonder that he outdid Houdini as an escape artist.

13. When I first went to Ole Miss there were a half dozen faculty members and their wives who had been around a long time. To me they were intellectual but poor aristocrats who lived within a monolithic racist society partly by doing "good works" (as Percy did) but they did not necessarily defend that society.

Index